This textbook provides an excellent and timely contribution to the field of cross-cultural management. It skilfully exposes the limitations of conventional cultural frameworks, which have dominated much contemporary thinking about international business and offers the reader an alternative way of addressing culture in the multicultural workplace. It is a must-read!

Dr. Maria Dasli, *Lecturer, The University of Edinburgh, Scotland, UK.*

For a long time, I have been hoping for someone to take up the challenge of applying the cultural theory pioneered by Dame Mary Douglas to the study of corporations – realizing that, sometimes, 'more tears are shed over answered prayers than over unanswered ones'. In this book, my wishes are more than fulfilled. In it, Taran Patel highlights the limits to previous understandings of the roles that culture plays in companies and the ways in which cross-cultural management ought to be undertaken. She also shows how the Douglas' framework surpasses these limits, and offers a theoretically sophisticated and eminently practical approach to cross-cultural management. Now I have new hope: that this excellent book will launch many graduate theses and practical applications.

Marco Verweij, *Professor, Jacobs University, Germany.*

This is a very complete and inspiring book: it not only gives a very elaborated overview of the well known cross-cultural models (Hofstede, Schwartz and others); it also critically reviews these models, and offers an interesting alternative model for qualitative analysis of cultural differences.

Joost Bücker, *Senior Lecturer, Radboud University Nijmegen,*
The Netherlands.

Cross-Cultural Management

The internationalization of business via the process of globalization has brought issues of culture to the forefront of management thinking. The resulting study of 'cross-cultural management' has had the effect of treating culture as a proxy for nationality and an assumption that culture within a nation, society or company is homogenous. This assumption however falls short when one tries to make sense of the new breed of international managers who have travelled and worked in cultures other than their own, acquired new cultures and adapted to the continuous structural changes in their organizations. The dynamic context within which business is carried out today demands a new way of looking at cultural preferences and resulting behaviours.

This textbook begins by providing an overview of the existing conventional culture paradigms, which focus on the national, societal and/or corporate levels of culture in the context of business (both domestic and international). It also challenges some of the limitations of these paradigms. Further, it exposes the criteria that any cultural approach would need to meet if it were to claim to be a credible theory/approach to culture and offers a possible alternative to the conventional culture frameworks.

Students studying from this textbook will benefit from a variety of conceptual tools that can be used to make sense in a variety of business contexts. Additionally, features such as real-world examples and stories will bring to life some of the concepts presented in the book. As such, this text will be core reading for students of cross-cultural management and essential reading for all those studying or researching international business.

Taran Patel is an Associate Professor of Cross-Cultural Management, Organizational Behavior, and Human Resource Management in the People, Organization, and Society Department at Grenoble Ecole de Management, France.

Cross-Cultural Management
A transactional approach

Taran Patel

Routledge
Taylor & Francis Group

LONDON AND NEW YORK

First published 2014
by Routledge
2 Park Square, Milton Park, Abingdon, Oxon OX14 4RN

and by Routledge
711 Third Avenue, New York, NY 10017

Routledge is an imprint of the Taylor & Francis Group, an informa business

© 2014 Taran Patel

British Library Cataloguing in Publication Data
A catalogue record for this book is available from the British Library

Library of Congress Cataloging in Publication Data
Patel, Taran.
  Cross-cultural management : towards alternative tools for cultural sensemaking / Taran Patel.
    p. cm
  1. Management–Cross-cultural studies. 2. Culture. I. Title.
  HD30.19.P37 2014
  658.3008–dc23
            2013016474

ISBN: 978-0-415-50166-8 (hbk)
ISBN: 978-0-415-50167-5 (pbk)
ISBN: 978-1-315-88750-0 (ebk)

Typeset in Times New Roman
by Taylor & Francis Books

MIX
Paper from
responsible sources
FSC
www.fsc.org   FSC® C013604

Printed and bound by CPI Group (UK) Ltd, Croydon, CR0 4YY

I dedicate this book to my husband, Chirag, to my sister, Poonam, and to all the friends who have supported us in our journey over the past 20 years. Some of these friends are no longer with us, but their unquestioning love and total faith will forever inspire us. From these friends, we have learnt the lessons of humility, resilience and love.

Contents

Illustrations

Preface

The audience of this book

This book is intended as a textbook for modules on cross-cultural management and/or intercultural communication. Ideally, the book targets masters-level students in business schools and has been written in a way to encourage critical thinking as opposed to offering simplistic ways of applying existing cultural frameworks. Through this book, we hope to give business students – or future managers – an understanding of the multitude of frameworks available to them for cultural sense-making in the different contexts they will encounter in their managerial careers. It is not our objective to direct students towards one specific approach or framework of culture. Instead, the book encourages readers to make their own informed decisions regarding the validity and usefulness of different approaches and frameworks. However, it is inevitable that some personal preferences, biases and convictions will have infiltrated the writing and will have influenced this discussion and critique of different frameworks.

Structure of this book

This book is composed of four parts: Part I: Overview: Culture and its impact on business; Part II: Introducing and critiquing conventional frameworks of culture; Part III: Alternative cultural paradigms and their comparison to conventional cultural paradigms; and Part IV: Applications of the Douglasian Cultural Framework to resolve a variety of business problems and conclusions. Part I is composed of two introductory chapters. Part II includes four chapters. Part III is divided into three chapters. Finally, Part IV consists of two chapters.

The book begins with a general introduction to the term 'culture' and then moves on to elaborate on the role of culture in businesses. It offers an overview of the commonly cited frameworks of culture, but, more importantly, it encourages the reader to shed a critical eye on these commonly accepted frameworks. It compels the reader to ask these questions: Can I only make sense of the variety of cultures around me by categorizing people into static groups based on their geo-ethnic identities? Is it valid to make sense of people's behaviours by categorizing them as 'French', 'Indian', 'German' or 'American'? What other ways are there to make sense of people and their behaviours? In addition to the commonly cited national and corporate culture frameworks, we offer the reader an alternative way of addressing culture – the transactional culture approach. In so doing, we propagate a more dynamic way of addressing cultures. Additionally, we also illustrate the transactional culture approach through the discussion of the Douglasian Cultural Framework (referred to hereafter as DCF) and demonstrate how past studies have applied it to make sense of inter-firm, intra-firm and firm–community interactions. The last chapter of the book summarizes the key points from all the previous chapters and offers business students an insight into future developments in this field.

The sources

This book relies on varied sources. It draws extensively on previously published material, notably from academic journals. For instance, Chapter 2 is almost entirely derived from research papers published in academic journals, and the last section of this book (i.e. Part IV) relies on published empirical research conducted by various colleagues and my own past empirical work. In addition to research papers from academic journals, I also base my arguments on various books on culture published over the last three decades by business scholars. Many of the anecdotes cited in this book come from past and ongoing research in the domain.

Taran Patel
April 2013

Acknowledgments

I sincerely thank my mentor, Dr Steve Rayner (Institute of Science, Civilization, and Society, University of Oxford), who first introduced me to cultural studies. Steve always encouraged me to 'look beneath the surface' and to attempt to answer the 'why' and 'how' questions in lieu of simply focusing on the 'what' questions. One can never qualify or quantify the tacit knowledge that one gets from one's teachers. One can only recognize their generosity and thank them for it. I also thank my colleagues and mentors Gerald Mars, Mike Thompson, Perri 6 and Marco Verweij, who have taught me so much over the years through formal and informal interactions and discussions.

The initial idea of this book emerged while I was still a PhD student and painfully realized during the course of my field study that understanding culture and making sense of human behaviour is a lot more complicated than simply categorizing people based on their national origin and/or their corporate affiliations. The idea gained strength while I was doing postdoctoral research with Steve Rayner in 2008. The need to write a book that offers not only an overview of different cultural frameworks but also a critical perspective on the same while furnishing alternative ways for cultural sense-making became even more pressing when I started teaching courses on intercultural communication and cross-cultural management to bachelors and masters students in business schools. I continued to draw inspiration from students as they challenged existing paradigms, knowingly or unknowingly, in search of solutions to the cultural challenges they encountered every day. Their questions prompted me to dig deeper for answers in past and contemporary literature. I believe I have gained almost as much as, if not more than my students have through these interactions. These discussions were most influential in crystallizing in my mind the need for a book on culture and business that goes beyond the commonly cited national and organizational level frameworks of culture. I thank each and every one of my students who have inspired me with their questions over the years and have shared with me their doubts and challenges emerging from varied cultural experiences.

A sincere word of thanks is also due to Alexander Krause and Terry Clague from Routledge who were patient and supportive throughout the time I was working on this project. Finally, I am deeply indebted to Maureen Walsh for reading and commenting on various versions of this manuscript and for painstakingly helping me improve my work.

About the author

Professor Taran Patel is an Associate Professor in the People, Organization, and Society Department of Grenoble Ecole de Management in Grenoble, France. She holds a PhD from the Open University at Milton Keynes, UK, an MBA, and a bachelor's degree in pharmacy. Dr Steve Rayner from the University of Oxford externally supervised her work for her PhD, which she completed in 2006. She also received the prize for the Best Thesis in the Corporate Governance category by the European Foundation for Management Development (EFMD) for her PhD.

Taran has spent the last decade teaching in business schools in France and has also taught in Finland, India, the UK and Spain. She has published articles in many peer-reviewed academic journals, including the *Journal of Business Ethics*, *European Management Review*, *Business and Society*, *Management Decision*, *European Journal of Training and Development*, *Human Resource Development International*, *European Accounting Review*, and more. In addition to intercultural management, Taran also conducts research in the areas of business ethics, corporate social responsibility and learning across cultures. Many companies in France and in India have invited her to consult with them, and she has been a speaker at the United Nations during the World Diversity Summit. In April 2013, Taran (with Professor Robert G Hamlin, Professor Carlos Ruiz, and Ms Sandra Whitford) received an award for 'Research Excellence' from the President of India, Dr Pranab Mukherjee.

List of acronyms

AC	Affective Commitment
CT	Cultural Theory
CVF	Competing Values Framework
DCF	Douglasian Cultural Framework
DJ	Distributive Justice
ECM	European Common Market
EJV	Equity Joint Venture
FDI	Foreign Direct Investment
GLOBE	Global Leadership and Organizational Behaviour Effectiveness
HC	High Context
IJ	Interactional Justice
IJV	International Joint Ventures
IMF	International Monetary Fund
ISA	International Strategic Alliances
IWOS	International Wholly Owned Subsidiaries
LC	Low Context
M&A	Mergers and Acquisitions
MNC	Multinational Corporations
NC	Normative Commitment
OC	Organizational Commitment
OFOR	Organizational Frame of Reference
OJ	Organizational Justice
OPEC	Organization of Petroleum Exporting Countries
PC	Psychological Contract
PD	Power Distance
PJ	Procedural Justice
R&D	Research and Development
VSM	Value Survey Module

Part I

Overview: Culture and its impact on business

1 Culture: A complex construct of many layers

'And take upon the mystery of things, as if we were God's spies.'

Shakespeare, *King Lear* (i.i.6)

What you will learn in this chapter:

- the varied definitions of culture;
- the ongoing debates with regards to culture and its nature;
- the various alternatives to the term 'culture';
- the varied epistemological stances towards the understanding of culture.

Introduction

Although cultural understanding has become crucial in this age of globalization, culture is by no means a new topic of interest for practitioners and scholars alike. In fact, accounts of cultural differences in the workplace have been traced to the writings of early Greek scholars such as Herodotus (Gelfand, Erez and Aycan 2007) who noted differences in work behaviour in the Persian Empire (Herodotus *et al.* 2003). Literature describing trading practices along the Silk Road, which stretched from Rome to Syria in the West, to China in the East, and to Egypt and Iran in the Middle East dating from the second century BC (Elisseeff 2000), also describes disparate habits. Therefore, references to culture and culturally different work practices are not new. However, in recent times, the ease and scope of cross-cultural interactions have led to an exponential increase in the interest in cross-cultural studies. While we acknowledge that significant advances have been made towards better understanding of culture and its impact on businesses in past decades, we also believe that we are no closer to a conceptual consensus regarding culture than our predecessors. Despite being the focus of numerous studies in recent decades, both in business studies and in anthropology, culture remains both an elusive and a grossly misunderstood term. Therefore, this chapter begins by reviewing the many definitions of culture that one finds in the literature of both business and anthropology.

Varied definitions of culture and the resulting intellectual debate

Culture is a term that business literature defines in diverse ways. In this section, we cite a few definitions that we find most relevant for subsequent discussions in this book. Louis (1981: 246) defined culture as 'a shared system of values, norms and symbols. The term culture conveys an entire image, an integrated set of dimensions/characteristics and the whole beyond the parts'. Gelfand *et al.* (2007) explained that culture has been defined as the human-made part of the environment (Herskovits 1955), including both objective and subjective elements (Triandis 1972); as a set of reinforcements (Skinner 1981); as a shared meaning system (Shweder and LeVine 1984); and as unstated standard operating procedures or ways of doing things (Triandis 1994). For Hall and Hall (1990: 3), culture 'can be likened to a giant extraordinarily complex, subtle computer. ... its programs guide the actions and responses of human beings in every walk of life'. For Hofstede (1980), culture is 'the collective programming of the mind which distinguishes the member of one human group from another' (Hofstede 1980: 25). This definition implies that members of a social group, say a company or a nation, have similar 'programming' governing their minds; hence, they may be expected to behave in similar ways. There is, therefore, an assumption of cultural homogeneity within and cultural heterogeneity between social groups as well as the assumption that culture represents a stable core. The past view was that culture was a 'weight of habits and beliefs that is passed on unchanged from generation to generation' (Schwarz and Thompson 1990: 2). Much before Hofstede (1980), Kroeber and Kluckhohn (1952) identified no fewer than 156 definitions of culture. One of these, suggested by Adler and Doktor (1986: 181) was that:

> Culture consist of patterns, explicit and implicit of and for behaviour acquired and transmitted by symbols constituting the distinctive achieve-ment of human groups, including their embodiment in artifacts; the essential core of culture consists of traditional (i.e. historically derived and selected) ideas and especially their attached values; culture systems may, on the one hand, be considered as products of action, on the other, as conditioning elements of further action.

Scholars have taken issue with one or more elements of this definition. The discussion in the following subsection addresses some of these points of contention

Contention 1: Is culture shared?

While most scholars have agreed that culture is shared, is adaptive, has been adaptive at some point in the past and is transmitted across time and generations (Triandis 1994), others remind us that culture is not always 'shared'. Joanne Martin has offered a particularly eloquent and convincing argument on this point. She has explained that 'No matter how you "slice it" culture still cannot be defined only as that which is shared. The idea that culture is that which is shared is a Lazarus of a theory: It just will not die' (Martin 2002: 155). She countered this viewpoint by arguing that culture can also be defined as an incompletely shared system. Martin (2002) offered Meyerson's (1991) conceptualization of culture to support her argument:

> Members do not agree upon clear boundaries, cannot identify shared solutions, and do not reconcile contradictory beliefs and multiple identities. Yet these members contend they belong to a culture. They share a common orientation and overarching purpose, face similar problems, and have comparable experiences. However, these shared orientations and purposes accommodate different beliefs and incommensurable technologies, these problems imply different solutions, and these experiences have multiple meanings ... Thus, for at least some cultures, to dismiss the ambiguities in favor of strictly what is clear and shared is to exclude some of the most central aspects of members' cultural experience and to ignore the essence of their cultural community.
>
> (Meyerson 1991: 131–32)

In the same way, Tsui *et al.* (2007) have argued that, while culture is commonly acknowledged as a group level construct, a group construct can be global, shared or configural. Citing the earlier work of Klein and Kozlowski (2000), Tsui *et al.* (2007) have explained that a global property is one that is objective, easily observable and independent of the perception of individual group members, such as the GDP or the population of a country. A shared property, on the other hand, originates in the common experiences, perceptions or behaviours of the members of a group, and it represents a consensual aspect of culture. Finally, a configural property resides in the variations in individual characteristics within a group; these configural properties emerge from characteristics of individual group members, but they are not expected to be consensual, as in the differences among the individual value systems within the same country. Tsui *et al.* (2007) have reminded culture scholars that, although culture has often been explored as a global and consensual property of a group, its configural nature has often been neglected. While culture might involve some shared and global characteristics, the members of the cultural group might not necessarily share several aspects of it.

Contention 2: Is culture unique and homogenous within a geographic entity?

While some scholars question the 'shared' nature of culture, others object to the idea of culture within a geographic entity being homogenous and unique. Again, Joanne Martin has led the argument, saying,

Cultural members may believe their organization's culture is unique, but often what is believed to be unique to a particular context is found elsewhere as well (Martin 1992a: 111), a contradiction labeled the 'uniqueness paradox' (Martin *et al.* 1983). For example, when people tell stories that illustrate 'what makes this place special,' these anecdotes share the characteristics of seven common story types found in most organizations.

(Martin 2002: 63)

Rosalie Tung has also offered similar arguments challenging the uniqueness and homogeneity of culture within social entities. Tung (2008) offered a variety of arguments challenging the idea of cultural homogeneity within a country. In particular, she used the example of Canada, with its two official languages, to point out the cultural diversity that exists between the French-speaking and English-speaking parts of the country. These Canadian Anglophone and Francophone populations are further believed to be distinct from the 'Allophones' who speak languages other than English or French. Tung (2008) has pointed out that, in countries such as Canada, intra-national differences can be far more significant and influential than cross-national differences. In other words, there might be more similarities between Anglophones in Canada and their American neighbours than between Anglophone and Francophone Canadians. Tung (2008) has offered the following explanations behind increasing diversity within nations such as Canada: (1) reduced immigration and emigration barriers for people (Johnston 1991) and (2) the increasingly boundary-less nature of the workforce (Tung 1998, Stahl, Miller and Tung 2002). Jean-Claude Usunier has also offered similar arguments. Usunier (1998) noted a variety of reasons why assuming cultural homogeneity within a nation would be misleading:

- some countries are deeply multicultural, such as India with its highly diversified ethnic, religious and linguistic groups;
- some nation-states are explicitly multicultural. Switzerland, for example, places a strong emphasis on the defence of local particularism in the political system;
- colonization and decolonization have resulted in borders that are sometimes straight lines on a map with little respect for cultural realities; for African countries, 'ethnic culture' matters, whereas 'national culture' is in many cases meaningless.

Contention 3: Is culture stable or is it dynamic?

As seen so far, many scholars have objected to the commonly accepted conceptualization of culture as a shared property of a group. Other scholars have challenged the assumption of cultural homogeneity and uniqueness within cultural entities (whether these are organizations or nations). Yet others object to the idea that culture represents a stable traditional 'essential core' or that it represents some kind of 'distinctive achievement'. Supporting the stable conceptualization of culture, Hoecklin (1993) has defined culture as a set of values with which an individual grows up. She has added that it is a combination of the personal values and morals as well as the society's influence on individuals in their growing years. Hence, it is the shared way groups of people understand and interpret the world. She concluded that culture influences the ways in which a person perceives and reacts to certain situations. In such definitions (see also Schein 1985), there is the underlying assumption that culture is static. However, several scholars (Levitt 1983, Ohmae 1985, O'Reilly 1991) have questioned this 'permanent nature' of culture.

Prominent among researchers who have opposed the static conceptualization of culture are transactional culture scholars (see Kapferer 1976) who have considered culture as emerging through the process of interaction. They have believed that cultural rules have a dynamic quality, capable of producing transformations in meaning and changing or redirecting behaviour along new paths (see Chapter 7 for detailed discussions). Similarly, proponents of the Douglasian Cultural Framework (e.g. Douglas 1978, 1982, 1996, Gross and Rayner 1985, Wildavsky 1987, Thompson 1992, 1996) not only have questioned the 'permanent nature' of culture, but they also have demonstrated that members of one cultural group can easily become members of another (see Chapter 8 for detailed discussions). In fact, people could be members of many different cultural groups depending on the situation in which they find themselves (Rayner 1995).

Mary Douglas, the creator of the Douglasian Cultural Framework, defined cultures as the frameworks of accountability. Culture, argued Douglas (1996), is the way people live together. Raising the issue of culture means addressing questions of solidarity; securing solidarity (that is living together in an organized way) implies the use of force and 'heavy tactics of persuasion'. According to Thompson and Wildavsky (1986), who are proponents of the Douglasian Cultural Framework, a culture sustains a particular arrangement of social relationships, and the conjunction stimulates and is stimulated by other contradictory conjunctions. This means that cultures constantly evolve and are generated from, and supported by, differences from other cultures. Thompson and Wildavsky (1986) believed that cultures are not countries nor customs nor myths nor races nor ethnicities. Cultures are ways of life. The dimensions of social life build them, and they are continually put to the acid test of social viability. This viewpoint indicates that cultures evolve and are not 'permanent' after all.

Similarly, Gross and Rayner (1985: 3) have contended that culture 'is the common way that a community of persons makes sense of the world'. Cultures are 'general regulatory mechanisms of human behaviour': they represent 'a set of plans, instructions and rules or less purposively, a means of social accounting'. Cultures control the behaviour of individuals by recourse to shared values and ideas. However, culture also has a cognitive dimension in that it creates meaning. Schwarz and Thompson (1990) have gone as far as to maintain that 'knowing ... presupposes culture'. Scholars adhering to this school of thought suggest that culture does not necessarily have to coincide with the (socially constructed) fault lines drawn by ethnicity or nationality. Rather, culture is a structural phenomenon; it describes those ideational and institutional structures that enable social cooperation.

Other scholars have tendered other ways of looking at culture. Marvin Harris (1968: 16) proposed that 'culture comes down to behaviour patterns associated with particular groups of people, that is, to "customs" or to a people's "way of life"'. Spradley (1979) believed that behaviour patterns, customs and a people's way of life could all be defined, interpreted and described from more than one perspective. Culture, as defined by Spradley (1979), refers to the acquired knowledge that people use to interpret experience and generate social behaviour, and he suggested that we may see this interpretive aspect more clearly if we think of culture as a cognitive map. He explained that, in the recurrent activities that make up everyday life, we refer to this map, which serves as a guide for our behaviour in a specific context and for interpreting our experience, but it does not compel us to follow a particular course. Although our cultures may not include a detailed map for all occasions, they do provide principles for interpreting and responding to them (Spradley 1979). A few years before Spradley provided us with this metaphor for culture, Frake (1977) had provided another metaphor for culture by likening it to map-making. In comparison to Spradley's (1979) somewhat 'static' metaphor of maps, Frake found that culture is more 'dynamic' and is not simply a cognitive map that people acquire, in whole or in part, and then learn to read. People are not just map readers; they are mapmakers. They are cast out into the imperfectly charted, continually shifting seas of everyday life. Mapping these seas out is a constant process, resulting not in an individual cognitive map but in a whole chart case of rough, improvised and continually revised sketch maps. Culture does not provide a cognitive map; instead, it provides a set of principles for map-making and navigation. Although Frake (1977) has suggested different cultures are like different schools of navigation designed to cope with different terrains and seas, he does not explain how these schools of navigation come about or how they are re-created over time.

The aforementioned scholars have proposed a dynamic perspective to culture; they subscribe to the idea that culture is refreshed each morning and concerned primarily with everyday experiences rather than some kind of historically distinctive achievement (Douglas 1970, Thompson and Wildavsky 1986, Wildavsky 1987, Thompson 1996, Thompson 2008). On the extreme end of this dynamic conceptualization of culture are scholars such as Baudrillard (1988), for whom culture represented a 'network of floating signifiers that offers momentary seduction rather than the ability to store and transmit meaning' (Poster 1988: 3). Many scholars supporting the dynamic conceptualization of culture have adopted a critical approach to culture and have suggested that one should drop the use of the term 'culture' altogether (due to its underlying implication of a shared, stable and homogenous set of characteristics) and adopt alternative terms that allow for a more dynamic conceptualization of culture. For instance, Mats Alvesson (1987: 13) has recommended using terms like 'ideologies' or 'organizational frames of reference' in lieu of the term 'culture'. The following section offers some suggested alternatives to replace the term 'culture'.

Alternative nomenclatures for the term 'culture'

Many scholars adopting a critical approach to culture prefer to drop the use of the term 'culture' altogether and use other terms to escape the static implication accompanying the expression and to allow for a more dynamic and evolving tone. Mats Alvesson (1987) has agreed with this and has offered two alternatives to the term 'culture': 'ideologies' and 'organizational frames of reference'. For Alvesson, ideologies are a set of beliefs about the social world and its operation, and they focus on what values and ideals are worth striving for (Alvesson 1987: 25–26). This implies that ideologies are a system of values that may change or evolve with circumstances and contrasts with the conventional conceptualization of culture, which presents it as static and unchanging. Geertz (1973: 231) also evoked the concept of ideologies, which he defined as 'the justificatory (dimension of culture) – it refers to that part of culture which is actively concerned with the establishment and defence of patterns of belief and value … it seeks to motivate action'. Alvesson (1987) explained that replacing 'culture' with 'ideologies' offers some advantages. First, unlike the static concept of culture, the concept of ideologies offers the possibility of mutually contradictory and conflicting viewpoints coexisting within the same entity and within the same person when faced with varying scenarios. It is quite possible to imagine several competing, complementary or similar ideologies cohabiting within an individual, an organization and even a nation. The concept of ideology also opens up the possibility of relating organizational dynamics with larger influences from the societal and/or national levels. Finally, ideology is more clearly defined than culture. Ideology consists of a selection from the cultural and symbolic world that is easier to identify and less difficult to address than culture, which has over time become a term that encompasses everything and yet is capable of explaining very little (Child and Tayeb 1983).

Alvesson (1987: 29–30) also proffered another term – 'Organizational Frame of Reference' (OFOR) – as a replacement to 'culture'. OFOR describes how an organization processes information – what type of information it relies on, how it makes sense of information and what its primary criteria for checking reality are. While, in Alvesson's understanding, organizational frames of references apply to the organizational level of sense-making, we do not see any reason why the same frames could not be applied to the higher national or societal levels. Additionally, organizational frames of reference are tangible and allow for the coexistence of varied and different ways of information processing within the unit under consideration. Alvesson's organizational frames of reference remind one of Max Boisot's (2000) more recent concept of information cultures or I-Spaces (see Chapter 6 for details). Both Alvesson and Boisot have challenged the more static understanding of people's behaviours by promoting the idea that people process information in organizations in dynamic and pluralistic ways, which obviously influences their behaviours.

Thompson *et al.* (1990) have suggested the term 'cognitive schemas' in lieu of culture. Cognitive schemas are tacit theories people hold about the world, which enable them to make sense of an otherwise bewildering array of information. These schemas help people figure out what they prefer by interpreting new events in terms of old knowledge.

We have identified three alternative terms suggested in literature to replace the term 'culture': 'ideology', 'organizational frame of reference', and 'cognitive schemas'. While many scholars of organization studies conceptualize culture as dynamic and evolving (Westley and Jaeger 1985), other scholars have chosen to continue using the term 'culture', which might be because the historical legacy of the word 'culture' is difficult to undermine. Although these other terms allow for more dynamicity than the traditional concept of culture, scholars have continued to find objections to them. For instance, consider the term 'ideology'. While the concept of 'ideology' allows for changing thoughts and actions, it has political connotations – people holding an ideology vigorously attempt to realize the ideals that the ideology propounds (Westley and Jaeger 1985, Filby and Willmott 1986). This political connotation acts as a deterrent in adopting the term 'ideology' in lieu of 'culture', which is a more neutral term.

Like many other scholars, we support the dynamic conceptualization of culture; yet, like some of them, we continue to use the term 'culture' in writing this book. This choice is guided by the following reason: while each of the three terms – 'ideology', 'cognitive schemas', 'organizational frame of reference' – suggested in this subsection as alternatives to the term culture support the dynamic conceptualization of culture, they also emphasize a focus on the cognitive process of cultural sense-making. For us, culture is both a cognitive and a sociological process. We believe that cultural preferences are not disembodied ideas; they are embedded in social relations (Thompson *et al.* 1990). Hence, using terms that undermine the 'social' aspect of culture does not do justice to our conceptualization of culture. Therefore, for this book, we continue to use the term 'culture' and to clarify the differences between our conceptualization and those of other scholars.

Various epistemological stances guiding culture studies

The continuing debate regarding whether culture is static and stable or whether it is dynamic is in part a function of the wide variety of epistemological stances that past scholars have adopted in their work. Schultz and Hatch

(1996) provided a very useful overview of the functional, interpretivist and postmodernistic stances guiding past culture studies. They explained that functional scholars prefer to focus on the so-called static characteristics of culture. Functionalist analysis, therefore, makes it possible to compare various cultures and to show differences and similarities among them (see the work of Schein 1992). Hofstede's (1980) comparison of over 72 national cultures in three regions has followed the functionalist standpoint. Similarly, consider Denison's (1990) study, which has also followed the functionalist tradition, and in which the author has compared a number of cases to explore the relationship between culture and effectiveness. In order to make such comparisons, researchers 'freeze' culture by representing its characteristics in a static way. Although some functionalist researchers acknowledge group development and learning stages, Schultz and Hatch (1996) explained that this development follows predictable and deterministic step-by-step phases (see Schein 1992). Thus, functionalist analysis results in a static model linking elements of organizational culture together, even when the focus is on transformation through the cultural stages of development.

On the other hand, interpretivists focus on the ongoing processes of sense-making and meaning creation (Schultz and Hatch 1996). Interpretive researchers look at the interrelated cyclic processes of interpretation, sense-making, understanding and action, and, thereby, they seek to understand the construction of culture (Weick 1979, Smircich and Morgan 1982, Czamiawska-Joerges 1992, Hatch 1993). They rarely explore the ruptures, discontinuity and fragmentation of sense-making (cf. Clifford and Marcus 1986). The results of most interpretive analyses are case studies or organizational ethnographies that are at best static representations of dynamic processes (Clifford 1986).

Finally, the works of Baudrillard, Lyotard and Derrida (Martin 2002) exemplify the postmodernistic tradition in culture studies. Postmodernism focuses 'on the processual as opposed to structural character of human institutions' (Cooper and Burrell 1988: 100 as cited by Schultz and Hatch 1996). Postmodernist scholars 'show how theoretical rhetoric hides its own weaknesses as it attempts to claim an inviolable place from which objective truth can be espoused' (Martin 2002: 76). Examples of cultural scholars adhering to postmodernism include Linstead (1991) who examined how advertisements reflected cultural assumptions about consumers. Instead of searching for the origin of things, postmodernist scholars prefer to focus on 'disparity, difference and indeterminacy' (Cooper and Burrell 1988: 101). Baudrillard's work on the temporary and fragile character of organizational life in consumer society is also an illustration of the postmodernist tradition. Baudrillard explained that a 'network of floating signifiers' that offer momentary seduction rather than the ability to store and transmit meaning (Poster 1988: 3) now replaces any fixed meaning.

Although we appreciate the distinctive contribution that scholars adhering to each epistemological standpoint make to the understanding of culture, we wonder whether the field of culture studies itself is losing something in the process. Is it not possible that there are areas or topics of study that require a crossing over of epistemological approaches? Is it not possible that these areas or topics of study are being neglected just because they just 'don't fit' with the main epistemological standpoints? Surely, each epistemological standpoint has its strengths and weaknesses. While treating culture as a 'network of floating signifiers', as Baudrillard suggested in the postmodernist tradition, offers the advantage of making sense of a cultural occurrence within its unique context, it also has one disadvantage: it renders cultural comparisons impossible. If each culture is a 'network of floating signifiers', this implies that each cultural context is unique, thereby making it impossible to compare one cultural context with another. We wonder whether there are cultural frameworks capable of bridging at least some of the gaps between different epistemological standpoints. Could we have a cultural framework that focuses on the processual character of human institutions (like postmodernist scholars) but does not treat culture as being absolutely volatile and chaotic (as Baudrillard suggests)? While maintaining the dynamicity of culture, such a framework would also be capable of offering a valid system of comparisons between them. In simpler words, we call for cultural frameworks that are capable of explaining both the conformity and deviations in human behaviour. Identifying and exposing such frameworks is one of the aspirations of this book.

Culture and its significance in an era of globalization

Irrespective of the different epistemological stances, the various definitions and nomenclatures and the ensuing debates that have emerged in extant studies on culture, it can be safely deduced from the previous discussion that there is significantly increasing interest on the topic, both among practitioners and business scholars. Increasing globalization explains this trend in part. Martin (2002) has pointed out that, in Western industrialized societies, inter-organizational alliances, international markets and multinational corporate structures are very common. Air travel and information technology have also facilitated crossing international boundaries. Cross-border ventures have encouraged international managers and scholars to question the impact of culture on how business is conducted across nations. International alliances, such as the European Common Market (ECM), the Organization of Petroleum Exporting Countries (OPEC) and the International Monetary Fund (IMF), have increased cooperation between nations and have blurred national boundaries (Martin 2002, Tung 2008). Increasing globalization has also led to a shift in what a business organization means and to a questioning of what the role of the manager is within such organizations. Boisot and Cohen (2000) have drawn attention to a sudden proliferation of inter-organizational ventures and the resulting generation of an ecological perspective on business organizations and the growing interest in complex systems. They added that the view of an organization as an entity of tightly knit objects no longer holds true. There has been a shift towards defining organizations as a loosely coupled system of interactions. Along with this shift, the role of the manager has evolved as well. No longer regarded as only responsible for controlling production, managers have become active agents who juggle multiple roles and interact with multiple other agents within networks. Therefore, we contend that a cultural understanding of the interactions that the manager has with these different agents is crucial. Our past research indicates that, while managers in international strategic alliances often lay blame on culture for their failures, they rarely, if ever, use it as an explanation behind their successes (Patel 2007a). If practitioners continue to treat culture like this, then it will always remain the 'uncaused cause' or the explanation of 'the last resort' (Thompson 1996). In other words, people will continue to evoke culture when all other economic, political and organizational explanations have failed (Schwarz and Thompson 1990); yet, they will be incapable of explaining culture itself. Using culture in such a superficial way is not only dissatisfactory but also reductive. We hope to redress this wrong by offering alternative ways of conceptualizing and operationalizing culture.

What knowledge gap does this book address?

In this book, we expose different cultural frameworks, including some that treat culture as static at a variety of levels, such as societal, national, corporate, professional and occupational. We refer to these static cultural frameworks as 'conventional frameworks of culture'. Additionally, we examine cultural frameworks that treat culture as dynamic. We do not aim to direct students of culture in one specific direction or towards a particular cultural framework and/or approach. Our only intent is to offer a comprehensive and extensive overview of the various ways of making sense of culture so that students may make informed choices about cultural interactions in personal, social and professional domains.

Past literature on culture, specifically from business studies, has focused excessively on national cultures and differences between these national cultures. It is believed that these differences influence business practices across countries, and those managers who aspire to succeed should adapt their business practices in light of these differences. 'What works here does not work elsewhere' has been the guiding principle of globalizing businesses. International managers receive advice to adapt their managerial styles, training programmes, performance evaluation methods, etc. to 'fit in' with the new countries where they are doing business. Although we agree that every country has certain demographic, social and environmental conditions that make it distinct from other countries, focusing excessively on differences between national cultures may be delimiting as an approach and may lead to undermining possibilities of exploring similarities between cultures. The scholars who have studied these differences have posed questions and found responses in line with their 'difference-oriented' lens (Ofori-Dankwa and Ricks 2000: 173), which may

inadvertently lead to preserving 'the symbolic production of a sense of difference' (Ailon-Souday and Kunda 2003: 1090). In contrast, we support the
viewpoint that there might be just as many similarities between people from
different countries as there are between people from the same country. Conversely, there might be just as many differences between people from the same
country (based on other factors such as educational level, level of exposure,
age, etc.) as there are between people from different countries. Nonetheless,
past literature on culture, at least in the field of international business, continues to focus largely on the differences between nations/countries. In this
book, we attempt to address this weakness.

Furthermore, past research on international business centres mostly on the
role of culture in inter-firm relationships in the international context. For
example, a major part of the past literature addresses the role of culture in the
creation of international business collaborations (such as international strategic
alliances, mergers and acquisitions, international wholly owned subsidiaries,
equity joint ventures and other forms of inter-firm relations) (Anderson and
Gatignon 1986), trust generation in such entities (Parkhe 1998), their success
or failure (e.g. Spekman and Lynn 2000), and on many such related topics.
There is comparatively less focus on the role of culture in domestic firms and
in the contexts of intra-firm and firm–community relationships. This is
because, in focusing on cross-national ventures, scholars have inadvertently
assumed that cultural differences are encountered only when one crosses
national boundaries. In contrast, we direct our attention not only on the role
of culture in cross-national business ventures but also on intra-firm dynamics
and firm–community interactions. In so doing, we hope that this book
provides a more complete understanding of culture and cultural interactions
to business students.

Structure and layout of this book

We have divided this book into four main parts. Part I is comprised of two
chapters. In Chapter 1, an overview of culture is presented, with its various
definitions, the diverse epistemological standpoints used by culture scholars
and the resulting debates. In Chapter 2, we offer a review of past literature
regarding different aspects of organizational life and of international business
that are believed to be influenced by culture. This chapter relies almost
entirely on recently published academic literature. In Part II of the book,
which is comprised of four chapters, we offer an overview of the different
theoretical frameworks of culture from past literature, and we expose the
reasons behind the popularity of some of these frameworks with practitioners
and scholars. Chapter 3 elaborates on conventional theories of national/
regional/societal culture that are the most popular in Western management
literature, although anthropologists and business researchers in other parts of
the world have not embraced these theories. Chapter 4 provides a comparison
between the predominant cultural frameworks addressing culture at the

national/regional/societal levels discussed in Chapter 3. After analysing these different approaches, Chapter 4 also expounds upon the recent advancements and developments that have occurred in this area of research. Chapters 5 and 6 provide an overview of different frameworks of corporate culture. In these chapters, we address two major approaches to corporate culture. The first approach treats corporate culture as static and homogenous within an organization, and the second regards corporate culture as emerging through daily, ongoing interactions among employees. Each chapter ends with a critique of the respective approaches to corporate culture. After analysing the conventional frameworks of culture (i.e. national/societal/regional and corporate culture frameworks) in Chapters 3 through 6, we move on to alternative tools for cultural sense-making in Part III of this book. In Chapter 7, we introduce the transactional culture approach and trace the history of this approach in anthropology literature with a particular focus on the work of Fredrik Barth, the famous social anthropologist. The chapter ends by citing the advantages that the transactional culture approach offers over the more conventional frameworks of culture discussed in Part II of this book. Also listed are some of the challenges that the transactional culture approach has not been able to overcome. Chapter 8 provides an example of the transactional culture approach, the Douglasian Cultural Framework (referred to hereafter as DCF), which is consistent with Fredrik Barth's transactional approach but overcomes some of the weaknesses of the latter. In Chapter 9, DCF is compared with the conventional frameworks of culture discussed in Chapters 3 through 6 of this book. Also explained is how DCF overcomes the limitations of conventional frameworks of culture. However, like all other frameworks, DCF also has certain limitations, which are also exposed. Part IV of this book is composed of two chapters. In Chapter 10, we offer examples of three managerial scenarios, where the use of conventional frameworks of culture offers superficial and somewhat reductive insights; then examples of studies in which each of the three managerial scenarios has been explored using DCF. The outcomes of these studies are compared with those conducted using conventional frameworks of culture, to show how DCF-based studies offer richer and more usable insights. Chapter 11, which is the concluding chapter of the present volume, summarizes key points from the previous 10 chapters. Additionally, it offers directions for future cross-cultural studies, and concludes by emphasizing the key knowledge contributions of this book.

Concluding remarks

This opening chapter has introduced the many definitions of the term culture and has attempted to expose its various conceptualizations. In order to facilitate the thought process for the reader, we have structured the initial part of these discussions around three key questions: (1) Is culture shared? (2) Is culture unique and homogenous within a geographic entity? (3) Is culture stable or is it dynamic? In the attempt to answer each question, we have exposed the different viewpoints surrounding each of these contentions. We have also offered an overview of alternative terms that may be used in lieu of the term 'culture'. Many scholars have called for culture scholars to completely abandon the use of the term 'culture' due to its historical legacy as a stable unchanging core within a specific geo-ethnic entity. Finally, we have linked the varied viewpoints discussed in this chapter with a broader understanding of the varied epistemological stances that scholars have taken in past cultural studies. In conclusion, we hope that through this chapter we have engaged students' interest in the topic of culture and its role in business. After reading this chapter, we hope that the reader realizes that there are many definitions and conceptualizations of culture. In subsequent chapters, the reader will also discover that there are many ways of operationalizing culture. The objectives behind exposing these varied conceptualizations and operationalizations of culture are to expose the reader to the range of cultural sense-making tools available and to uncover the strengths and weaknesses of each tool so that the reader may be able to choose the best tool for the exercise undertaken.

2 The impact of culture on businesses

For too long, we have focused on our differences – in our politics and backgrounds, in our race and beliefs – rather than cherishing the unity and pride
that binds us together.

Bob Riley

Ask the right questions if you're going to find the right answers.

Vanessa Redgrave

What you will learn in this chapter:

- the impact of culture on various aspects of organizational life;
- the impact of culture on various aspects of international business
  collaborations;
- the contradiction between perspectives: focus on differences versus
  focus on similarities.

Introduction

As mentioned in Chapter 1 of this book, while culture has been the focus of
much reflection and writing since ancient times, research on culture has virtually
exploded in recent decades. Increased focus on globalization during this time
can partially explain this. Culture is believed to influence many different
aspects of organizational life and international business. This chapter examines
the impact of culture on business and assesses whether culture scholars have
been asking the right questions in terms of understanding culture's impact.
An overview of past literature suggests that most culture scholars have been
focusing on cultural differences, mostly between nations, in order to make
sense of the impact of culture on business. Others, like us, argue that focusing
on differences does not take us far, especially when these are considered
detrimental to the relationship. Asking questions focused on unearthing
differences will only lead to reinforcing the perception of differences. On the

other hand, focusing on similarities between entities and people gives us something to build on and thereby helps us create synergistic relations. In this chapter, we present arguments from both sides, from proponents of the difference-oriented perspective and from their critics, and urge culture scholars to ask 'the right questions', not simply the ones oriented towards unearthing differences.

Gelfand, Erez and Aycan (2007) have offered an excellent overview of past literature related to the impact of culture on different aspects of organizational behaviour. While discussing the impact that culture has on all the aspects of organizational life is beyond the scope of this book, in this chapter, we offer some examples of micro-organizational and meso-organizational phenomena, which are influenced by culture. We ground this part of our discussions in the summary of past literature furnished by Gelfand *et al.* (2007) and offer the opposite viewpoint proffered by other scholars. We then go on to discuss the impact of culture on specific aspects of international business collaborations (for instance, trust-building among partners in international business collaborations, perceived performance of alliances, the success or failure of international strategic alliances, etc.). Before we begin this discussion, we will reiterate two points:

- Past literature on the impact of culture on organizational outcomes (at least the ones we cite in this chapter) takes a very functionalist approach to culture. It largely treats culture as being static and quantifiable. In other words, scholars who support this viewpoint 'freeze' culture at a point in time and use this to compare one nation against another (see discussion of the functionalist epistemological stance in Chapter 1). Thus, many of the studies summarized in this chapter focus on culture at the national level, which they term 'national culture'. National culture, however, is not a concept that all scholars agree upon, as readers will discover in subsequent chapters of this book.
- We do not always agree with what past literature has to say about the impact of culture on business. When this is the case, we provide our own arguments to counter the viewpoint of past scholars. Nevertheless, discussing these diverse viewpoints is required in order to offer the reader a more complete understanding of the debate around the topic.

Since much of our discussion in subsequent sections relies on the use of one specific cultural framework provided by Geert Hofstede, the well-known organizational psychologist and cultural scholar, briefly introducing this framework first is appropriate. Chapter 3 will discuss Hofstede's national culture framework in much more detail.

Brief introduction to Geert Hofstede's framework of national cultures

Hofstede (1980) explored the differences in thinking and social action that exist between members of several nations.[1] According to Hofstede (1980), the four main dimensions on which national cultures differ are power distance, uncertainty avoidance, individualism and masculinity. These four dimensions describe the collective programming of the mind, which distinguishes members of one national group from those of another (Hofstede 1994). This collective programming affects how people organize as both leaders and followers using written and unwritten rules. Table 2.1 defines the four dimensions offered by Hofstede.

Having introduced the basic premise of Hofstede's work, we now revert to the main objective of this chapter, i.e. to present a review of past literature regarding the impact of culture on varied aspects of organizational life and of international business.

Culture's impact on various micro- and meso-organizational phenomena

In this section, we illustrate the impact of culture on various micro- and meso-organizational phenomena, and we rely on the prior work of Gelfand *et al.* (2007) in which they summarized the findings of past research on the topic. Gelfand *et al.* (2007) agreed with some of the findings of past scholars, but they have disagreed with others (see the subsection on culture and negotiations). In the latter case, we offer alternative viewpoints and arguments from these and other scholars. While Gelfand *et al.* (2007) provided an exhaustive review of past literature on the impact of culture on various aspects of organizational behaviour (conflict resolution, team work, organizational commitment, psychological contract, organizational justice, and many more), in the present chapter, we only offer illustrations of three micro-organizational (i.e. personal

Table 2.1 The four cultural dimensions proposed by Geert Hofstede

High- versus low-power distance	'Power Distance is the extent to which inequality is seen by the people of a country as an irreducible fact of life' (Hofstede 1984: 19).
Masculinity versus femininity	'Masculinity/Femininity concerns the extent of emphasis on work goals (earnings, advancement) and assertiveness, as opposed to personal goals (friendly atmosphere, getting along with the boss and others) and nurturance' (Hofstede 1984: 19).
Individualism versus collectivism	'Individualism is a concern for yourself as an individual as opposed to concern for the priorities and rules of the group to which you belong' (Hofstede 1984: 19).
Uncertainty avoidance versus risk-taking	'Uncertainty avoidance is the lack of tolerance for ambiguity and the need for formal rules. This dimension measures the extent to which people in a society feel threatened by and try to avoid ambiguous situations' (Hofstede 1984: 20).

Source: Hofstede (1984)

motives, rewards and feedback) and three meso-organizational (i.e. job-satisfaction, learning, negotiations) phenomena. Since our discussion on the topic is not exhaustive, we invite readers to refer to the work of Gelfand *et al.* (2007) for a more complete understanding of the topic (see additional reading section for full reference).

Culture's impact on micro-organizational phenomena

Culture and personal motives

In past literature, culture has been related to personal motivation and drive. In particular, Hofstede's cultural dimension 'individuality versus collectivism' has been cited as influencing people's motivations. For instance, Gelfand *et al.* (2007) explained, that according to many scholars, although motives such as self-efficacy, need for achievement and intrinsic needs for competence are universal (Erez and Earley 1993, Bandura 2002), the specific factors that drive such motives vary across cultures. While personal feedback influences members of individualistic cultures, group feedback influences those of collectivistic cultures (Earley and Erez 1993). Similarly, while the need for control seems to be universal, members of individualistic cultures give importance to personal control, and members of collectivistic cultures give importance to collective control (Yamaguchi *et al.* 2005). Some scholars (see Sagie *et al.* 1996) have claimed that achievement motivation is stronger in individualistic rather than in collectivistic cultures. Gelfand *et al.* (2007) have argued that the meaning of 'achievement' could vary across cultures. For instance, in individualistic cultures, achievement could mean getting a sought-after position accompanied by an increment in salary; while, in collectivistic cultures, achievement could mean getting social recognition. Differences may also exist in terms of what intrinsically motivates members of different cultures. According to Iyengar and Lepper (1999), while Anglo-Americans are intrinsically motivated when they can make their own choices, Asian-Americans are intrinsically motivated when a trusted superior makes the choice for them. It is also argued that members of individualistic cultures find exploration, curiosity and variety to be more intrinsically motivating than do members of cultures that value conformity (Kim and Drolet 2003).

While attempts at understanding individual motivation through cultural dimensions such as individuality versus collectivism may help to shed some light on human behaviour, we believe that other factors could also influence individual motivation. Consider the following real-life example:

> One of our colleagues had a terminally ill child. The health condition of the child required constant medical attention, which was possible only in a specialized medical facility. Any delay in the treatment of the child's condition could seriously compromise his health. This preoccupation influenced many of the choices that the colleague in question made at

work. For instance, he avoided travelling for international conferences requiring him to be away from home for long. He gave up opportunities of promotion simply because these required him to be more mobile and spend more time on professional activities than his personal circumstances allowed. He always sought professional stability in order to ensure stability for his family, and, in particular, the healthcare that his child needed on a daily basis.

It goes without saying that attempting to explain the scenario presented in the previous account solely from the perspective of the individuality versus collectivism argument presented earlier would be a futile exercise. The motivation of our colleague to retain a stable and less challenging job had more to do with his personal situation – the health problem of his child – than with the level of individualism versus collectivism inherent in his Canadian national culture. While Hofstede has classified Canada as individualistic, the day-to-day behaviour of this colleague does not coincide with this broad expectation. In all fairness, Hofstede did not intend his generalizations to be used to explain individual-level behaviour either. Nevertheless, this has not deterred subsequent scholars, such as those cited earlier in this subsection, from doing exactly that. Drawing inferences about lower levels from higher-level data is a common error in culture studies. In fact, relationships identified at one level of analysis may be stronger or weaker at a different level, or may even be in the reverse direction (Ostroff 1993, Klein and Kozlowski 2000, McSweeney 2009). In the same way, drawing inferences about higher levels from individual-level data is erroneous and is termed as the 'atomistic fallacy' (Tsui *et al.* 2007: 466). Therefore, our challenge is to make sense of people's behaviours in the workplace using instruments other than broad generalizations at the national (or other) level(s) offered by Hofstede and other scholars.

Consider another example of how people's motivations change over time as they pass through different stages of their lives. While a challenging job and a hefty salary may motivate a young graduate of 24 years, a mother of two in her early thirties may find working from home and having days off more motivating than financial rewards. A well-accomplished senior executive may be more motivated to mentor younger executives by sharing knowledge and experiences with them, compared to running the day-to-day operations in a department/unit. Therefore, we argue that people's motivations may be more a function of their environment or circumstances rather than their national cultures. We also argue that individual motivation changes with time and situation, and it is therefore not a pre-determined outcome of static national cultures.

Culture and feedback

Gelfand *et al.* (2007) explained that past scholars find both giving and receiving feedback varies across cultures. Citing the works of Earley (1986,

1989), De Luque and Sommer (2000) explained that feedback and evaluation techniques that work in the United States do not necessarily work across other cultures. Morrison *et al.* (2004) showed that American newcomers seek more feedback than individuals from Hong Kong – a difference that the authors relate to differences in assertiveness and power distance across these two cultures. Culture is also believed to influence the perception of positive and negative feedback by different collaborators. Positive feedback is universally perceived to be of higher quality than negative feedback, and even more so in collectivistic cultures (e.g. Van de Vliert *et al.* 2004). Japanese employees seem to have a stronger emotional reaction to negative feedback than to positive feedback (Kurman *et al.* 2003), and they are more responsive to feedback than their American counterparts are (Brockner and Chen 1996, Heine *et al.* 2001, Kitayama *et al.* 1997). Van de Vliert *et al.* (2004) showed that individual performance induces positive evaluations from individualist cultures, but group performance induces positive evaluations from collectivists. Matsumoto (2004) has explained that Japanese managers provide implicit and informal feedback – a behaviour that provokes frustration among their American colleagues.

While we find many studies propagating such broad generalizations between cultural dimensions and practices regarding both giving and receiving feedback, we do not find an abundance of literature contesting such generalizations. Nevertheless, it might be worthwhile to scratch the surface of some of these generalizations. First, if we accept the basic premise of Hofstede's cultural frameworks (1980) that countries can be classified into categories, such as individualistic versus collectivistic countries, and that those cultures are homogenous within nations – then would it not be natural to assume that individual performance would induce more positive evaluations from individualist cultures and group performance would induce positive evaluations from collectivists? The relationship between a country's category and the expectations of its members' behaviour is a tautological one. Once a country is classified as individualistic, is it not natural to assume that its members have a preference for individual performance appraisals and vice versa? In light of the current literature relating cultural dimensions and feedback practices and preferences, we were compelled to raise other questions such as: Would there not be factors other than culture (such as level of commitment, personality characteristics, sector or industry of activity) that influence people's expectations of and reactions to feedback? Our review of past literature revealed that, indeed, there is much evidence supporting a correlation between personality characteristics and expectations of/reactions to feedback (Bell and Arthur, Jr. 2008, Kluger and DeNisi 1996, Ilgen *et al.* 1979). We also believe that the level of expertise and the sector of activity also influence the kind of feedback people would appreciate. Consider knowledge-intensive sectors or high-tech and innovative sectors where people are often brought together to work in teams. While each of these individuals is an expert in their domain, they still acknowledge the importance of working in teams. In these circles, it is commonly acknowledged that no individual can be an expert in every domain, and, therefore, individual interest lies in collaborating with others who have complementary skills. In such cases, individual feedback often incorporates (as it should) the individual's contributions to the team. In this context, even the most individualistic team members will consciously prioritize and contribute to the output of the team. Additionally, in such a context, the manager will need to include contributions to the group project within the individual feedback. This inspires us to ask another question: To what extent do variables like personality characteristics, level of expertise, sector of activity, etc. moderate the impact of culture on feedback? While our review of extant literature has currently failed to provide an answer to this question, we encourage students of culture to bear in mind the possibility of other variables moderating the impact of culture on feedback.

Culture and rewards

Once again, we call upon the review of past literature on the impact of culture on rewards by Gelfand *et al.* (2007). One belief is that cultural values shape both the kinds of rewards that employees seek and the way cultures implement the reward system (Erez and Earley 1993). Studies have shown (see Corney and Richards 2005, King and Bu 2005) that students from developing countries like Chile and China find higher salaries and bonuses to be the most preferred rewards, while American students prefer promotions and interesting assignments. Gelfand *et al.* (2007) observed that both cultural and economic factors might explain these findings. Citing the work of Adigun (1997), Gelfand *et al.* (2007) explained that, although money is a motivator, members of both developing and developed countries value work for reasons beyond money. Past literature also has shown that, at a macro level, different cultures support different dominant reward systems. For instance, while U.S. firms, in line with their individualistic values, prefer performance-based reward systems, Japanese firms favor seniority-based pay systems, which is consistent with their respect for seniority (Brown and Reich 1997). Tosi and Greckhamer (2004) have found that CEO pay is related to power distance; they have explained that the higher the power distance, the greater the pay differential between CEOs and other senior managers in companies.

We agree with some of the findings of scholars cited in the previous paragraph. For example, we agree with Gelfand *et al.* (2007) who observed that, in addition to cultural factors, economic factors explain the kinds of rewards people prefer. As countries become economically stronger, people start feeling financially secure and, therefore, their preferences shift from financial rewards (such as a higher salary) to non-monetary rewards that affect their quality of life and give them a better work–life balance. We also agree with the finding of Gelfand *et al.* (2007) that people across developing and developed countries value work for reasons beyond money. This argument suggests that perhaps all human beings irrespective of national culture look for outcomes other than money (e.g. salary, bonus, etc.) from their jobs. For some people, the workplace offers a sense of belonging to an organization or a professional community; for others, the workplace represents a sense of accomplishment or pride (in being a member of a certain organization), and, for still others, the job presents a means of self-exploration and self-actualization. Since such needs (social belonging, social recognition or pride, and self-actualization) are universal, we agree with the argument that people, irrespective of their national cultures, may look to meet these needs (in addition to their monetary needs) in the workplace.

However, we also disagree with some of the findings from past studies cited in the first paragraph of this subsection. As an example, Tosi and Greckhamer (2004) have claimed that the higher the power distance, the greater the pay differential between CEOs and other senior managers in companies. Following this argument, and in light of the fact that the U.S. has been categorized as being low on power distance (Hofstede 1980), one would expect a lower salary differential between American CEOs and other senior managers. However, it is common knowledge that American CEOs rank among the highest paid in the world. As Liberman (2011) has noted, Philippe Dauman, the CEO of Viacom, earned $84.5 million in 2010. In fact, in the past three decades, the salaries of CEOs have increased by 30 to 60 times the salary of the top 5 per cent of employees in the U.S. (Liberman 2011). Therefore, we find that drawing sweeping generalizations between power distance and salary differential or, more broadly, between scores on certain cultural dimensions and reward systems may be a bit simplistic.

Finally, intra-national differences also exist regarding differential rewards. Gelfand *et al.* (2007) have exposed differences in rewards-related preferences of Chinese employees. While Chinese employees who emphasize vertical collectivism prefer differential rewards, those employees who emphasize horizontal collectivism (Chen *et al.* 1997) resist them. This difference in preference is explained in part by the ongoing market changes occurring in China in the twenty-first century. This implies that, although Hofstede (1980) has categorized China as being highly collectivistic, there are nonetheless differences in how this collectivism plays out in the workplace and how this influences Chinese employees' attitudes towards differential rewards. This example draws our attention towards the intra-national differences in culture that Rosalie Tung (2008) has talked about (see Chapter 1 of this book) and compels us to question the merit of using national culture dimensions to draw broad generalizations of people's cultures and their perceptions of rewards systems in the workplace.

Culture's impact on meso-organizational phenomena

Culture and job satisfaction

As Gelfand *et al.* (2007) reported, it is a common belief that culture influences job and pay satisfaction (Diener *et al.* 2003). Past research reveals that, while the meaning of job satisfaction is equivalent across countries, the equivalence in its meaning decreases with increasing cultural distance (Liu *et al.* 2004). While a warm and congenial work environment produces higher job satisfaction among members of collectivistic cultures, it does not have the same impact on members of individualist cultures (Hui and Yee 1999). Similarly, Huang and Van de Vliert (2004) showed that, while job level is related to job satisfaction in individualistic cultures, this is not the case in collectivistic cultures.

Many of the studies cited in the previous paragraph follow a functionalist epistemological standpoint. That is, these scholars (Liu *et al.* 2004, Hui and Yee 1999, and others) have conceptualized culture as being static. They have proposed that those countries that share similar scores related to different culture dimensions (see Hofstede 1980) have a smaller cultural distance between them, and those countries that have a wider difference between their scores on these cultural dimensions have a greater cultural distance between them. As discussed in Chapter 1, scholars taking an interpretive or post-modernist viewpoint would object to such static conceptualizations of culture. For them culture is a process – it is a moving film and not a static photograph; therefore, measuring culture or cultural distance would be neither a meaningful nor an appealing exercise for them. Besides, many scholars offer variables other than culture to explain perceptions of job satisfaction. Piccolo *et al.* (2005) and Spector *et al.* (2002) have explained that personality characteristics, such as positive self-concepts and internal locus of control, influence how people perceive job satisfaction. One may also argue that people derive job satisfaction from different job characteristics at different stages of their professional trajectory. During a conversation with a highly reputed academic colleague, I heard,

> I've spent the last 25 years of my life publishing in top-ranked journals of international repute. I've been invited to speak to varied audiences across business schools in many different countries. I've taught groups of students across a variety of programmes and have received much recognition both as a professor and as a scholar. Now, I look forward to travelling back to […] [his country of origin] and sharing with younger scholars there what I have learnt in all these years. Going back to […] [his country of origin], observing the growth and development occurring there, nurturing promising young talent there is what motivates me. The potential is endless … and that is what motivates me now.
>
> (personal communication, June 2010)

As read in the previous excerpt, people draw job satisfaction from different sources at different stages of their career paths. Satisfaction is a moving target – just as the individual achieves one dream, a new one takes its place. Hence, relying solely and excessively on (national) culture to explain an individual's perception of job satisfaction would be a flawed exercise.

Culture and negotiations

Extant literature has cited many national cultural dimensions, such as individualism versus collectivism and low- versus high-power distance, as influencing on various aspects of the negotiation process. Some believe that culture affects negotiators' frames or cognitive representations of conflicts. For instance, Gelfand *et al.* (2002) found that Americans perceive conflicts to be more about winning and violations to individual rights, whereas the Japanese perceive the same conflicts to be about compromise and violations to duties. Negotiators' biases also differ between Western and non-Western cultures. While U.S. negotiators are prone to competitive judgement biases, such as fixed pie biases (Gelfand and Christakopolou 1999) and self-serving biases (Gelfand *et al.* 2002, Wade-Benzoni *et al.* 2002), in non-Western cultures, negotiators are more influenced by relational concerns. Culture is also believed to influence the types of negotiation strategies (Adair and Brett 2005), persuasion tactics (Gelfand and Dyer 2000) and preferred concession patterns (Hendon *et al.* 2003) observed during the negotiation process. Finally, negotiators from different national cultures may find satisfaction with different kinds of outcomes. While maximizing economic gains satisfy U.S. negotiators, East Asian negotiators are satisfied when they use integrative tactics and achieve equalization of outcomes (Tinsley and Pillutla 1998, Ma *et al.* 2002).

While many scholars cited in the previous paragraph have offered differences in national culture as a way of making sense of differences in negotiation tactics, strategies, styles, etc., others have disagreed with this practice. We see this in Gelfand *et al.* (2011) who complained that past research on culture and negotiation seems to have completely overlooked 'cultural dynamics' or the conditions in which cultural impact is amplified, reduced or reversed. They clarified that negotiations always occur in a specific context, never in a vacuum. Hence, attempting to explain negotiation practices solely in light of differences in national culture without considering the impact of situational variables is fairly delimiting. In their own work, Gelfand and her colleagues (see Gelfand and Cai 2004, Morris and Gelfand 2004) have exposed how the impact of culture on negotiation practices is modified by factors such as situational context and/or individual personalities. Cultural tendencies in negotiations become amplified in conditions of high accountability (Gelfand and Realo 1999), high need for closure (Morris and Fu 2001), and high ambiguity (Morris and Gelfand 2004). Therefore, Gelfand and her collaborating authors called for moving away from a static to a more dynamic understanding of how culture affects negotiation practices. They warned that the static perspective on culture and negotiation leads to the propagation of cultural stereotypes and provides no real tools to help managers navigate the cultural differences they may encounter while negotiating in the workplace.

Research by Warden and Chen (2009) also showed that culture is not monolithic and plays out differently when negotiators face different circumstances. Their study employed the example of Chinese negotiators, whose negotiating styles tend to differ significantly from their Western counterparts, and revealed that Chinese negotiators demonstrate increased cultural accommodation when they perceive the counterpart's culture as more 'distant'. Additionally, they do not use the same negotiation strategies when they negotiate with their Chinese counterparts as they do with foreigners. To conclude, we support the call by Gelfand *et al.* (2011) for culture scholars to adopt a more dynamic approach towards understanding the impact of culture on negotiation.

Culture and learning

Gelfand *et al.* (2007) explained that culture might influence learning and performance orientation. In past studies, national culture (Herbig and Dunphy 1998) and even corporate culture (Tellis *et al.* 2009) have been evoked to explain learning and innovations. In previous subsections, we have identified two schools of thought: the first takes a static and functionalist approach to culture, and the second treats culture as dynamic. These two schools understandably lead to different findings in terms of culture's impact on learning. As an illustration of the functionalist and static approach to culture, Li (2002) explained that Confucian teachings emphasize the need to perfect oneself. Under the influence of the Confucian philosophy in the Chinese culture, learning appears more fundamental than achievement. Li (2002) also observed that, while learning and performance orientation are highly correlated for students from Hong Kong, this is not the case with American students. In contrast, other scholars have shown that contextual and/or situational variables, not simply the respective national cultures, influence inter-firm learning (as in the case of international alliances). For instance, Emden *et al.* (2005) argued that learning from experiences is a key factor enhancing the alliance performance, and that two cultural aspects influence learning from experience: organizational commitment to the alliance relationship and learning orientation. In this case, the dimensions of culture they evoked are more context-specific in nature rather than those related to national culture. Other scholars have taken a dynamic perspective in understanding the impact of culture on learning and innovation. Taking a transactional approach to culture, Patel and Patel (2008) have shown that people regularly shift from one culture to another, and, as members of each culture, people learn differently at different stages of the innovation process. These researchers also charted out the learning pathway for sustained innovation success in companies. They shifted the focus away from creating a culture of learning and innovation (as functional scholars would have suggested) to nurturing different learning cultures at different stages of the innovation process to facilitate sustained innovation success in firms (which, as seen in Chapter 1 of this book, is more in line with the interpretive and postmodernist epistemological standpoint).

Having presented an overview of the micro- and meso-organizational phenomena influenced by culture, we now move on to discussing the impact of culture on various aspects of international business collaborations.

Culture's impact on various aspects of international business ventures

In the previous section of this chapter, we elaborated on culture's influence on some aspects of organizational behaviour. We have not yet explicitly focused on how culture affects relations between firms, which may become even more complicated with firms grounded in different national and corporate cultures. Therefore, in the next section of this chapter, we focus on the impact of culture on varied aspects of international business relations. First, we will focus on the possible impact culture may have on the very creation of international business ventures, and then we will explore how culture may influence trust-building, and finally, the success or failure of international business collaborations.

Culture and the creation of international business ventures

Patel (2007b) has explained that culture is a commonly cited factor that influences many aspects of companies' international business ventures. Companies can conduct their business abroad in many ways. These include licensing, subcontracting, franchising, marketing, manufacturing, research and development (R&D) and exploration agreements, the creation of joint ventures, or resorting to mergers, acquisitions and/or foreign direct investment (FDI). Culture may have an influence on the kind of international business collaboration that potential partners choose to create. Brahy (2006) wrote that culture is a key factor that companies need to consider before they finalize their Merger and Acquisition (M&A) deals. Weber, Shenkar and Raveh (1996) have shown that, if the merging/acquiring parties are familiar with each other's environments and if the acquiring or acquired organization conducts the operations in their countries, there is an assurance of a high level of post-M&A integration. In reference to Foreign Direct Investment (FDI), Anderson and Gatignon (1986) explained that a high 'cultural distance' might cause potential foreign investors to avoid direct ownership due to high information costs and the difficulty in transferring management techniques and values. However, this will not happen if the business methods of the foreign parent are perceived as providing a substantial advantage to the host country. In the same line of thought, Shane (1991) has shown that one specific cultural dimension – 'individualism versus collectivism' – significantly influences decisions regarding whether companies would opt for FDI or for simply exporting its products. Barkema and Vermeulen (1997) have shown that a difference in scores on uncertainty avoidance and long-term orientation (cf. Hofstede 1980, 1991) between potential partners decreases the likelihood that the firms in question will enter a foreign country through an International

Joint Venture (IJV) rather than through an International Wholly Owned Subsidiary (IWOS). To conclude, past literature seems to indicate that culture does have a role to play in firms' decisions regarding how they wish to set up their international business ventures, but the impact of culture does not stop after the creation of the international venture. If anything, and as discussed in the next subsection, once the venture becomes active, the challenge of managing these cultural differences becomes even more accentuated.

Culture and trust-building in international business relations

The propensity to trust is the extent to which people have a general belief in the goodness of human nature (Tanghe *et al.* 2010). In addition to the influence of a variety of factors, the propensity to trust is considered a culturally learned attitude. Many scholars have linked cultural dissimilarities with potential difficulties in generating and sustaining trust in international business collaborations (e.g. Fukuyama 1995, Putnam 2000). Shane (1992) found that U.S. multinational corporations (MNCs) are less likely to establish foreign affiliates in countries with different trust levels from the U.S. Following the same line of thought, Zaheer and Zaheer (2006) explained that when firms from different countries collaborate with one another, they bring their different levels of general trust and their different understanding as to how trust plays out in a business relationship. In the same way, other scholars suggest that building trust is a time-consuming exercise and that it is easier for alliance partners to trust one another when they have similar value systems grounded in similar national culture (see Doney *et al.* 1998). Parkhe (1998) also referred to intercultural differences as an impediment to creating trust. However, unlike his predecessors, Parkhe looked at the relationship between national culture dimensions and trust-building in a more critical way. He observed that, in contradiction to Hofstede's (1980) classification of the U.S. as being low on uncertainty avoidance and Japan as being high on uncertainty avoidance, Americans have a lower tolerance for ambiguity, which stems from their desire to 'seek mastery of a situation'. He explained that this lower tolerance for ambiguity makes American managers unable to go as far as the Japanese managers in their willingness to build trust in the face of unpredictable, inconsistent and ambivalent behaviour. Parkhe's (1998) study draws attention to three important points. First, his findings contradicted Hofstede's categorization of the U.S. as being low on uncertainty avoidance. Second, his study showed that relating one culture dimension to a specific human behaviour without incorporating the impact of other cultural dimensions might be erroneous. In the case of his study, it is the American managers' desire to 'seek mastery of a situation' (masculinity) that leads them to become less tolerant towards uncertainty, which subsequently leads to the inability to generate and maintain trust with Japanese counterparts. This point also leads to the third, and important, insight that people do not always behave in accordance with their national cultural profiles. In fact, more often than not, situational or circumstantial variables influence them. Therefore, treating people as passive recipients of culture and viewing their behaviours as a predetermined template of their national culture is erroneous (Ailon-Souday and Kunda 2009).

Trust-building is particularly problematic in cases of international mergers and acquisitions (IM&A), and this becomes a crucial challenge, particularly, for the top managers of acquired firms. As we know, the motivation and commitment that the senior managers display has a major influence on the motivation of other employees (Kitching 1967, Sales and Mirvis 1984) because they play a very important role in transmitting values and corporate culture signals (Schein 1985). However, in an IM&A scenario, the differences between the national and corporate cultures of the two parties become highlighted. In such scenarios, others perceive senior managers as champions of the national culture they represent, and this may be posited against the national culture of the other party in the merger/acquisition (Weber, Shenkar and Raveh 1996). Furthermore, the nature of the 'acquisition' relationship itself reduces the autonomy of the acquired top executives. This loss of autonomy creates stress and negative emotions (feeling of being threatened or distrustful of others) among the top managers of the acquired company, which eventually affects the collaboration and its outcome (Weber, Shenkar and Raveh 1996).

Culture and the success/failure of international business collaborations

Culture is also believed to influence the success or failure of international business collaborations. In fact, the stream of literature related to this thought has received considerable attention from business scholars (e.g. Spekman and Lynn 2000). According to Meschi (1997), careful access to, and control of, cultural differences are necessary in order for cross-border alliances to succeed. Li, Lam and Qian (2001) have also studied culture as a success factor and culture's implications on alliance performance. Woodcock and Geringer (1991) and Shenkar and Zeira (1992) highlighted that differences in the cultural backgrounds of partners are commonly believed to be problematic in IJVs. Barkema and Vermeulen (1997) went a step further and showed that some differences in national culture are more disruptive than other differences. For example, differences in uncertainty avoidance and long-term orientation (cf. Hofstede 1980, 1991) have a negative impact on IJV survival. While some scholars have related the success or failure of inter-firm alliances to national culture, others have attempted to link their success or failure with corporate culture. Haspelasgh and Jemison (1991) and Nahavandi and Malekzadeh (1998) have shown that differences between two organizational cultures affect the outcome of a merger. Differences in organizational cultures have also been associated with lower commitment and cooperation of acquired employees (Sales and Mirvis 1984, Buono *et al.* 1985 as quoted by Veiga, Lubatkin, Calori and Very 2000), diminished relative standing and increased turnover among acquired executives (Hambrick and Cannella 1993, Lubatkin *et al.* 1998) and lower financial success (Datta 1991, Chatterjee *et al.* 1992 as quoted by Veiga,

Lubatkin, Calori and Very 2000). Broadly speaking, many investigators (from the functionalist epistemological school) have agreed that culture clashes are likely to be more pronounced in cross-national mergers than in domestic ones since such mergers bring together not only two firms that may have different organizational cultures but also two firms whose organizational cultures are rooted in different national cultures (Schneider 1988 and Very *et al.* 1993 as quoted by Veiga, Lubatkin, Calori and Very 2000).

Studies cited so far in this subsection have clearly adopted a functional and deterministic approach to culture – both at the national and corporate levels. In contrast, other scholars have gone beyond the broad generalizations at the national level and have attempted to understand how new cultures might be generated through international collaborations. Consider the work of Rodriguez (2005) who has suggested that, in order to ensure stability and good performance in international strategic alliances, it is important to understand how leaders in that alliance experience culture. Using the example of American-Mexican alliances, the author confirmed that, in addition to national culture, the top management team culture and managers' personalities also shape the intercultural fit through predominant managerial styles. Rodriguez (2005) addressed culture at three different levels: national, group and individual. He revealed that American and Mexican managers construct their own social reality with rules and norms bounded primarily by existing organizational culture in the alliance. If social realities can be created, then this compels us to rethink the static conceptualization of culture inherent in most national and corporate culture literature. Rodriguez (2005) explained that, in the American-Mexican alliances that he studied, managerial styles from both companies converged into a 'third culture' – a participative and consultative one. This 'third culture' brought together the task innovation and emotional concern of American managers and the task support and social focus of Mexican managers. Thus, Rodriguez's (2005) study has illustrated a somewhat dynamic conceptualization of culture in which the amalgamation of key characteristics of the two parent cultures creates a new culture. While the innovator style of American managers supports the dynamics of change for the culture to advance, the adapter style of Mexican managers builds stability and order and maintains group cohesion and cooperation. Hence, Rodriguez concluded that achieving an intercultural fit in an alliance could occur by designing an organizational culture that incorporates the partners' cognitive diversity into the relationship. We agree with the viewpoint that contradictory cultures in an alliance are not necessarily problematic. In fact, they may be complementary to one another and thereby contribute to the durability and success of the alliance. We also agree with Rodriguez (2005) that intercultural differences, if understood correctly, can be a source for a unique interdependence between alliance partners. However, whether or not using national cultural dimensions is the best way of conceptualizing cultures and the differences between them is a completely different question – one that we will address in subsequent chapters of this book.

Concluding remarks

In this chapter, we have summarized two main streams of literature. The first explores the impact of culture on various micro- (motives, feedback and rewards) and meso-level (job-satisfaction, learning and negotiations) organizational phenomena. The second stream of literature summarized in this chapter covers aspects of international business collaborations (trust-building, modes of collaboration, and success and failure of collaborations) that culture may influence. There are many other aspects of organizational life (such as teamwork, team dynamics, organizational commitment, psychological contract, and many others, see Gelfand *et al.* 2007 for full details) and of international business collaborations (such as role ambiguity of CEOs, nature of contractual agreement between partners, and many others, see Shenkar and Zeira 1992, Woodcock and Geringer 1991) that culture may impact, and which are not discussed in the present chapter. Notwithstanding, we believe we have given readers a satisfactory overview of past literature on the impact of culture on various aspects of business.

We find that most scholars relating culture to aspects of organizational life and to aspects of international business collaborations have tended to focus on national cultural differences. More precisely, these studies have been inclined to focus on certain key dimensions of national cultural differences, such as individualism versus collectivism and high- versus low-power distance. Some studies have linked aspects of domestic and international business to corporate culture. Nevertheless, most past studies treat culture as static – they choose to 'freeze' culture either at the national or at the corporate levels. We believe that such static approaches offer certain advantages. They offer an unchanging picture of culture, thereby facilitating cultural comparisons across nations and companies. This implies that culture is controllable – that managers can regulate culture and can bring about a desired change in it. It is for this reason that such static models of culture find popularity with many practitioners and researchers. The idea of a controllable culture, which can be manipulated in a desired direction, inspires both interest and hope among managers. However, as we have already hinted in this chapter, such static frameworks of culture also have many drawbacks. Subsequent chapters of this book (Chapters 3, 4, 5 and 9) will discuss in detail these static frameworks of culture, referred to as conventional frameworks of culture, and their strengths and weaknesses.

To conclude, we believe that scholars, practitioners and students of culture have focused on differences between cultures for too long. It may well be time to move away from the excessive focus on cultural differences and move towards cultural similarities, seeking how these similarities will make for better collaboration in both the business and the social spheres of life. If we continue to focus on differences, differences are what we will find. Therefore, if scholars are looking for ways to 'build bridges' between different cultures, they need to ask different kinds of questions and use different kinds of cultural frameworks, as opposed to scholars who adhere to the categorical, deterministic and static conceptualization of culture. Those interested in this alternative way of addressing culture may find this present volume to be of help. In particular, Part III of this book (Chapters 7, 8 and 9) offers an in-depth discussion of some alternative frameworks that treat culture as dynamic and evolving with context and time.

Note

1 It should be noted that, unlike McSweeney (2009), Hofstede did not make a distinction between nations and countries (see detailed discussion in Chapter 3 of this book).

Additional reading

M. Gelfand, M. Erez and Z. Aycan (2007) 'Cross-cultural organizational behavior', *Annual Review of Psychology* 58: 479–514.

Part II

Introducing and critiquing conventional frameworks of culture

3 Introducing and critiquing national, societal and regional culture frameworks

> It makes sense that whatever the topic is, it's more compelling if you can provide the audience with a range of perspectives, and you can cross disciplines.
>
> Bernice Johnson Reagon

What you will learn in this chapter:

- Geert Hofstede's framework of national culture;
- Edward Hall's framework of contexts and time;
- Fons Trompenaars and Charles Hampden-Turner's framework of societal culture;
- the GLOBE study on leadership effectiveness across cultures;
- Shalom Schwartz's cultural orientations framework and values theory;
- a critique of all the aforementioned frameworks.

Introduction

This chapter provides readers with a variety of perspectives, approaches and frameworks for addressing culture across different levels. The theoretical frameworks discussed in this chapter conceptualize culture as a set of distinctive characteristics at the national, societal and/or regional group levels. Prominent among the national culture approach is the work of Geert Hofstede (1980), which we have briefly introduced in Chapter 2 of this book. This framework has received extensive critical attention from many scholars (e.g. Levitt 1983, Ohmae 1985, Singh 1990, O'Reilly 1991, Yeh and Lawrence 1995, McSweeney 2002, 2009). We begin Chapter 3 by elaborating on Hofstede's framework and by critiquing it in the context of international business studies. In this chapter, we also elaborate upon societal culture frameworks, including those offered by Trompenaars and Hampden-Turner (1997) and the Global Leadership and Organizational Behaviour Effectiveness (GLOBE) (2002) study, and regional culture frameworks, such as the work of Shalom Schwartz (2004, 2006). After explaining each framework, we offer some of its strengths and weaknesses. The purpose behind exploring these varied frameworks of culture, which we broadly refer to as conventional frameworks of culture in subsequent sections of this book, is to see whether they help make cultural sense in the diverse business scenarios in which managers often find themselves.

Hofstede's national culture framework

As introduced briefly in Chapter 2, Hofstede (1980) initially had offered four, and subsequently five, cultural dimensions upon which nations can be distinguished from one another. At the outset, Hofstede did not make a distinction between nations, nation-states and countries as other scholars (see McSweeney 2009) have done, and, although Hofstede has acknowledged that several intricate variations exist within countries that may be indiscernible to an outsider, his focus was largely on identifying the commonly shared attribute within clearly defined national boundaries. Therefore, Hofstede's framework inadvertently led culture to be equated with nation, and to the terms 'international' and 'inter-cultural' being used interchangeably. Hofstede (1984) supported the premise that the importance of cultural influences on businesses cannot be underestimated. He explained that the differing interpretations that cultures give to their environment are important influences on interactions between people working and managing across national boundaries. At the centre of cultural patterns is a general system of transferable core values, which are broad preferences for one state of affairs over others. He added that corporate value systems evolve from national value systems. A company's founder and dominant elite determine the prevalent value system, which in turn influences internal communication, integration, cooperation, negotiation, etc.

Hofstede (1980) explored the differences in thinking and social action that exist between members of several nations, collecting over 116,000 questionnaires in 20 different languages between 1967 and 1973. Initially, Hofstede (1980) identified four main dimensions on which country cultures differ from one another: power distance, uncertainty avoidance, individualism and masculinity. These four dimensions describe the collective programming of the mind and distinguish members of one national group from those of another (Hofstede 1994). Using written and unwritten rules, this collective programming affects how people organize as both leaders and followers. Table 3.1 offers the definitions of Hofstede's four dimensions.

By way of illustrating the scores attributed by Hofstede to different countries, we offer a comparative table between France, India, the U.K. and the U.S.A. (see Table 3.2). This table does not compare the selected countries on the fifth dimension (Confucian Dynamism or long-term orientation) as the scores for this dimension are not yet available for all countries included in the original study. Hofstede's five cultural dimensions are generated from very different underlying criteria and do not emerge from a common basis. In other words, there are no binding principles that limit the proliferation of new categories.

Table 3.1 The four cultural dimensions proposed by Geert Hofstede

High- versus low-power distance	'Power Distance is the extent to which inequality is seen by the people of a country as an irreducible fact of life' (Hofstede 1984: 19).
Masculinity versus femininity	'Masculinity/Femininity concerns the extent of emphasis on work goals (earnings, advancement) and assertiveness, as opposed to personal goals (friendly atmosphere, getting along with the boss and others) and nurturance' (Hofstede 1984: 19).
Individualism versus collectivism	'Individualism is a concern for yourself as an individual as opposed to concern for the priorities and rules of the group to which you belong' (Hofstede 1984: 19).
Uncertainty avoidance versus risk-taking	'Uncertainty avoidance is the lack of tolerance for ambiguity and the need for formal rules. This dimension measures the extent to which people in a society feel threatened by and try to avoid ambiguous situations' (Hofstede 1984: 20).

Source: Hofstede (1984)

Table 3.2 Comparison of France, India, the U.K. and the U.S.A. using Hofstede's four dimensions of national culture

Cultural dimension	France: Score out of 100	India: Score out of 100	U.K.: Score out of 100	U.S.A.: Score out of 100
Power Distance Index (PDI)	68	77	35	40
Individuality Index (IDV)	71	48	89	91
Uncertainty Avoidance Index (UAI)	86	40	35	46
Masculinity Index (MAS)	43	56	66	62

Source: Hofstede (1980: 77, 122, 158, 189)

Therefore, one may anticipate the generation of additional dimensions in the future.

As Alkailani, Azzam and Athamneh (2012) have pointed out, Hofstede's studies (1980, 1991, 1997) have been replicated to explore a variety of topics – information technology (Harvey 1997), economic dynamics and institutional stability (Tang and Koveos 2008), work-related values (Kirkman, Lowe and Gibson 2006), international marketing (Soares, Farhangmehr and Shoham 2007), transformational leadership (Ergeneli, Gohar and Temirbekova 2007), and 'cross-vergence' and cultural tendencies (Kelley, MacNab and Worthley 2006). Hofstede's national cultural framework is considered by many as the most reliable framework of national culture (Hambrick and Brandon 1988, Gong *et al.* 2007). In particular, this framework enjoys immense popularity with those taking marketing decisions (Holden 1999). Despite this popularity, we, like many other scholars, believe that this framework has some serious weaknesses that limit its use and applicability. Some of these weaknesses are discussed in the next subsection.

A critique of Hofstede's national culture framework

As is commonly known, Hofstede conducted his study across international branches of IBM. Since his study explored one company, he assumed that it had a common corporate culture, and he attributed any differences observed in how business was conducted in these various branches to the national cultural differences of the employees. Hofstede (1980) has explained that, in his study, the scores on the four dimensions were calculated based on answers to three questions each for power distance and uncertainty avoidance, and on factor scores derived from answers on 14 work goals for individualism and masculinity. For each question and in each country, mean scores were calculated for IBM employees in seven different occupations at two points in time. The average of those 7 x 2 occupations means became the country score for the question. Therefore, the country scores were based on identifying central tendencies in the responses collected in each country. Although the scoring method has been well documented, it is still difficult to understand how managers in their day-to-day interactions with fellow employees may use these scores or central tendencies. This is particularly true in complex environments such as those found in international strategic alliances, which are often the result of the mergers, acquisitions and takeovers of several different entities from divergent parts of the world. It is also difficult to see how Hofstede's scores or central tendencies can be used for making sense of the day-to-day behavioural patterns of people from different backgrounds when they are brought together in a complex, competitive and sometimes, conflicting working environment. Besides, we believe that it is simplistic to reduce individual differences to mean central scores. Doing this gives us easy-to-remember broad generalizations, which might facilitate a broad understanding of cultural differences, but they do not help to understand individual variations and behavioural dynamics in complex realities.

A by-product of Hofstede's (1980) research was an instrument called the Values Survey Module (VSM), which he recommended as a tool for future cross-cultural comparisons (Singh 1990). Using the VSM, Singh (1990) carried out a closer examination of the four cultural dimensions in India. This replication study revealed that, considering the effective range of scales, Indian managers' scores were low on all four dimensions and that the cultural scores tended to vary selectively with age, education, nature of job and economic sector. The scores that Singh (1990) obtained on the four cultural dimensions for India deviated considerably from the scores that Hofstede had originally attributed. In particular, there were significant variations in Power Distance Index (PDI) scores among different groups of respondents in India, and these variations were related to the preferred and perceived style of the superior. In the case of uncertainty avoidance, variations in scores were related to stress at

work and employment stability, in individualism to the importance of cooperative colleagues and desirable area of living, in masculinity to cooperative
colleagues and opportunities for earning and advancement. Finally, Singh's
(1990) results showed that the four cultural dimensions have varying degrees
of stability. In the same way, Bosland (1985a) conducted a replication of
Hofstede's study in China using the VSM. He found significant differences
among Chinese respondents concerning the four cultural dimensions, which
he attributed to factors other than national culture: level of education, mean
age, occupational level and the organizational subculture. Proponents of
Hofstede's national culture framework may contest the findings of Bosland
(1985a) and Singh (1990) by arguing that Hofstede's instrument was not
designed for intra-national comparisons, and it would be particularly inappropriate to use it for culturally plural countries like India (and China) (Singh
1990). Nevertheless, the findings of both Bosland (1985a) and Singh (1990)
emphasized the need to focus on intra-national variations and suggested that
cultural variations within countries are at least as great as between countries.

A key assumption of Hofstede's work (1980, 1991) is that values – the core of
national culture – are stable constructs and have been present in people from
different nations for a long period of time (also Schein 1985). The research
resulting in Hofstede's four dimensions took place over three decades ago.
Since then, many scholars have challenged the idea of stable cultures. Consider
the work of Lockhart (1997) who showed that culture, far from being static, is
constantly changing as adherents continually forge, break apart and rene-
gotiate (cultural) alliances. On the same lines, Thompson and Ellis (1997)
argued that just because culture is 'deep' does not automatically mean that it
is stable. They compared culture to tectonic plates – although buried deep
within the earth, they are by no means stable. Other experts endorsed the idea
that cultures are converging (e.g. Levitt 1983, Ohmae 1985, O'Reilly 1991).
They have explained that, due to economic development, technological
advances and ease of travel and interaction, cultural differences have given
way to cultural convergence (Harbison and Myers 1959). However, Hofstede
(1991) challenged this idea of cultural convergence and argued that, despite
globalization, national cultures continue to remain distinct because values
(the core of culture) remain unchanged. Any observed changes, he explained,
relate to convergences in so-called practices, superficial appearances of culture;
they do not necessarily signal a convergence in the values embedded in
national cultures. Thus, Hofstede maintained that differences between
national cultures are still relevant (Barkema and Vermeulen 1997). A third
group of scholars, including Rosalie Tung (2008), supported the idea of
'cross-vergence'. They explain that cross-vergence is an attempt to create a
balance between the two divergent schools of thought: one supporting the
convergence of cultures and the other contesting it. The work of Ralston *et al.*
(1993) evidenced the idea of cross-vergence, showing that, when managers
encounter new cultures, they choose to adopt some new values while also
maintaining some of their own values. Such emerging schools of thought have

cast a doubt on the explanatory power of Hofstede's dimensions in later periods (Adler and Doktor 1986).

Hofstede's framework has also been criticized for its methodology. Brendan McSweeney (2002) suggested that the very basis of the Hofstedian approach, i.e. the so-called 'national culture paradigm', is unconvincing. Using examples of different definitions provided by scholars like Wallerstein (1990), he explained that there is ambiguity on what the term 'nation' implies. This point will be discussed in detail in Chapter 4 of this book. The following presents some of the main methodological critiques that McSweeney (2002) offered regarding Hofstede's (1980) study:

- Hofstede (1980) claimed that, in his original study, he had collected over 116,000 questionnaires in 66 (subsequently 72) countries. However, a closer look revealed that the number of questionnaires collected in some countries was minuscule. Besides, although 66 countries were explored, the final report contained results for only 40 countries. This gives rise to a valid question: Why were the results of the other 26 countries not declared?
- When questioned about a small sample size in some countries, Hofstede (1980, 1984: 65) replied,

  > if a sample is really homogenous with regard to a criteria … then there is very little to gain in reliability over an absolute sample size of 50. I could therefore, have done my research over 40 (countries) x 50 (respondents per country) x 2 (survey rounds) – 4000 respondents in total – and obtained almost equal results.

- McSweeney (2002) found this response to be problematic. He asked, if the same logic were applied to a classroom setting and if a teacher attempted to draw conclusions regarding the intellectual level of an entire nation based on the academic performance of a few students from that country, would that be justified?
- McSweeney (2002) also criticized the broad generalizations that Hofstede drew at the corporate and occupational levels of culture. For instance, Hofstede explained that he focused only on the marketing and sales employees of IBM for his questionnaire because not only do these employees share a common 'organizational culture' (that of IBM), but they also share the same 'occupational culture'. Other scholars have taken issue with two aspects of this argument. First, they disagreed with the idea of 'one over-arching organizational culture'. (Chapters 5 and 6 of this book address this point in some detail.) Second, experts have disagreed that people of one profession or occupation have similar behavioural preferences. If this were the case, this would imply that, since 'laboratory clerks' in Germany and those in Bangladesh have the same 'occupational cultures', the only variable explaining their different behaviours is their national cultures – a claim that many social scientists would be quick to contest (McSweeney 2002).

- Many years after the original study, Hofstede (1991) acknowledged that his initial assumption of a unique and homogenous organizational culture was flawed. This realization logically raises questions about the validity of the findings of the previous study as one of its basic assumptions no longer holds (McSweeney 2002).
- McSweeney (2002) further commented that, in Hofstede's study, values and behaviours exist, as it were, in vacuum. Hofstede did not attempt to explain their creation, persistence, regeneration or change. In our understanding, Hofstede did not attempt to explain 'social change' since his work was guided by the assumption that national cultures are largely stable (Hofstede 1991). This inability to explain social change has been a source of dissatisfaction to social scientists and anthropologists alike for many decades (see Barth 1967).

In conclusion, while Hofstede's study has been a source of inspiration for many scholars and practitioners, it has many weaknesses that have attracted considerable criticism from other experts. Although researchers have used Hofstede's dimensions for calculating scores for in-country analysis (e.g. Singh 1990), as well as for comparing the cultures of different nations (e.g. Deshpande and Farley 1999), many questions can be raised about the validity of Hofstede's findings and their usefulness in understanding dynamic human behaviours both in international and domestic contexts. The most significant drawback of this framework lies in the practice of assigning mean values to countries on each of the four cultural dimensions, thereby categorizing people from different countries into different behavioural stereotypes with little or no attention paid to the potential fluctuations in people's behaviours. Although Hofstede (1984) acknowledged that there are several intricate intra-national variations, he chose to focus on cultural similarities within national boundaries, rather than the former. This limitation is also observed in the other national, societal and regional culture frameworks discussed in subsequent sections of this chapter.

Edward Hall's framework of context and time

Like Hofstede's framework discussed in the previous section, Edward T. Hall's work is also very commonly cited in international business literature, especially in cross-cultural communication studies (e.g. Driskill 1997, Cardon 2008). Hall has published a series of books (*Beyond Culture* [1977], *Hidden Differences: Studies in International Communication* [1985], *The Dance of Life* [1983], *Hidden Differences: Doing Business with the Japanese* [1987]) – all highlighting the role of cultural differences in international interactions. Edward Hall and Mildred Reed Hall (1990: 3) compared culture to 'a giant extraordinary complex, subtle computer. Its programs guide the actions and responses of human beings in every walk of life'. They defined context as 'the information that surrounds an event; it is inextricably bound up with the meaning of that event' (Hall and Hall 1990: 6). In his earlier work, Hall (1960) identified two kinds of cultural contexts that influence the way people communicate with one another: high context and low context. He defined them as the following:

> A high context (HC) communication or message is one in which most of the information is already in the person, while very little is in the coded, explicit, transmitted part of the message. A low context (LC) communication is just the opposite; i.e., the mass of information is rested in the explicit code. Twins who have grown up together can and do communicate more economically (HC) than two lawyers in a courtroom during a trail (LC), a mathematician programming a computer, two politicians drafting legislation, two administrators writing a regulation.
>
> (Hall 1977: 79)

In high context cultures, providing too much information is considered to be talking down to others, while, in low context cultures, this is a mark of being thorough.

In addition to context, Hall and Hall (1990) also cited time as a variable; its perception and experience vary across nations. While there are many kinds of time systems in the world, Hall and Hall (1990) explained that there are two systems that are most important for international business: monochronic and polychronic time; and past, present or future orientation. Monochronic and polychromic time systems are explained below:

> Monochronic time means paying attention to and doing only one thing at a time. Polychronic time means being involved with many things at once … In monochronic cultures, time is experienced and used in a linear way – comparable to a road extending from the past into the future. Monochronic time is divided quite naturally into segments; it is scheduled and compartmentalized, making it possible for a person to concentrate on one thing at a time. Polychronic time is characterized by the simultaneous occurrence of many things and by a great involvement with people. There is more emphasis on completing human transactions than on holding to schedules.
>
> (Hall and Hall 1990: 13–14)

Hall and Hall (1990) cited the U.S.A. Germany, Switzerland and the Scandinavian countries as examples of monochronic cultures. In contrast, Mediterranean and Latin countries are believed to fall into the polychronic category. They explained that 'interactions between monochronic and polychronic people can be stressful unless both parties know and can decode the meanings behind each other's language of time' (p. 21). They explained that, when members of different cultures interact with one another, there is the need for 'interfacing', which they illustrate through the following example:

It is impossible to interface an American appliance with a European outlet without an adaptor and a transformer. Not only are the voltages different, but the contacts on one are round, on the other thin and flat. [p. 26] ... The greater the cultural distance the more difficult the interface [p. 27].

As can be seen above, Hall and Hall (1990) believed that it is more difficult to succeed in a foreign country than at home due to the cultural distance between the two cultures. Hall and Hall (1990) also classified treatment of time as being past-, present- and future-oriented. They offered cultures in countries such as Iran, India and Far Eastern countries as being past-oriented. Urban U.S.A. is classified as present- and short-term future-oriented, and Latin American countries are classified as being both past- and present-oriented. Readers should note that our discussion of Hall's (1960) and Hall and Hall's (1990) framework is not exhaustive. In addition to time, these authors have also offered a deeper insight into how cultures differ in terms of their attitudes towards space, friendship, material goods and agreement (or lack thereof). Readers may refer to the additional reading suggested at the end of this chapter for a more complete understanding of the work of these scholars.

A critique of Hall's framework of context and time

While Hall's (1960) framework of high and low context, and Hall and Hall's (1990) framework of differences in perceptions of time have offered much to international business literature, we find them delimiting for a variety of reasons. First, and most evidently, we find that Hall and Hall (1990) (in *Understanding Cultural Differences: Germans, French and Americans*) focused excessively on categorizing countries into monochronic versus polychronic and as high versus low context, and, in the process, undermined the impact of situational variables on individual behaviour. We revert to Hall's (1977) earlier illustration of twins who have grown up together to make our point. Hall (1977) noted that twins who spend their childhood years together communicate much more economically (HC) than two lawyers arguing their case in a court of law (LC). The fact that the twins have spent several years in the same household and shared close physical proximity, coupled with family and emotional ties, brings them closer and affects the way they communicate with one another. The impact of this physical proximity and family ties creates a higher context of communication between them than between two lawyers who share a common profession and common educational background. What we deduce from this is that situations influence the way people communicate with one another, and some situational variables exercise a stronger influence on the context of communication than others do. It also follows that situational variables, and not just national culture, have an impact on the kind of context (high versus low) that develops between people. Continuing with the same example, it would be logical to assume that, when the twins grow up, move away from the family home, go to different universities and take up jobs in different cities, it is likely that their relationship (and the closeness they share with one another) will be slightly altered, even if this change is imperceptible to outsiders. When such individuals meet up again, they might find a subtle change in the way they communicate with one another. They will indeed share common jokes and stories from childhood, but they will not be effective in their communication if they make an assumption of a high (and shared) context on other more recent changes in their lives. A change in the level of physical proximity and frequency of their interactions will necessitate a change in the way they communicate with one another.

Let us now consider another scenario. Employee from a so-called low context culture may find themselves sharing common jokes and past references with those who have been their colleagues for several years. Over time, what might initially have been a low-context communication gives way to a much more contextually laden form of communication emanating from shared experiences. Consider, for example, a social gathering where two retired armed forces personnel are introduced to each other. While the initial communication between them may be formal and distant, they may soon find a lot to talk about, such as common experiences, war stories, missions, etc. The conversation might soon become one involving common jargon, references to common friends/contacts, events, jokes and so on. Civilians observing the interaction may find themselves to be on the periphery of the discussion and may describe the communication between the two ex-army personnel as high context. While the communication between the two retired army personnel began as a low-context communication, it soon develops into a high-context one due to commonality in their experiences. Thus, situational variables (such as common profession, time spent together, etc.) may influence the context of communication. Additionally, people may shift from high-context to low-context communication and vice versa depending on the situation. Therefore, categorizing nations on a whole as high context or low context might be overly simplistic.

Second, like other scholars who adopt a geo-ethnic conceptualization of culture, we find that Hall and Hall (1990) also focused excessively on cultural differences. As we have stated in Chapter 1 of this book, while focusing on cultural differences might help a novice to make sense of cultural experiences, researchers relying selectively and solely on a 'difference oriented lens' may inadvertently be contributing to the symbolic reinforcement of these cultural differences (Ofori-Dankwa and Ricks 2000). We find that Hall and Hall (1990) have committed the same error. They focused excessively on how 'Americans', 'the French' and 'the Germans' behave as cultural groups. This broad and somewhat stereotypical discussion reinforces the differences between these people and their supposed national cultures. It does not provide us tools for bridging the so-called cultural gap. For instance, Hall and Hall (1990: 124) stated that 'The French are too individualistic to be good team players'. Quoting an advertising executive, they stated, 'You must be very

French in France, very German in Germany, and very American in America' (p. 170). While we appreciate the authors' efforts to emphasize the need to adapt to local cultures, we are compelled to ask what they mean by 'become very French' (or very American for that matter). Indeed, there is no single and homogenous 'French culture' – France, like other countries, encompasses within it a wide variety of local and regional diversity. Therefore, we are compelled to ask whether it is feasible or even possible for individuals to become 'very French in France', 'very German in Germany' and 'very American in America'. Such excessive focus on national culture differences and reliance on broad generalizations lead to what Osland and Bird (2000) have referred to as 'sophisticated stereotypes'.

Fons Trompenaars and Charles Hampden-Turner's societal culture framework

Another cultural framework that business literature commonly cites is Fons Trompenaars and Charles Hampden-Turner's (1997) societal culture framework. In an earlier work entitled *The Seven Cultures of Capitalism: Values Systems for Creating Wealth in the United States, Britain, Japan, Germany, France, Sweden, and the Netherlands,* Trompenaars and Hampden-Turner (1993) explored seven cultures (equated with 'countries' as they appear in the title) using the framework of seven dilemmas. This framework of seven dilemmas can be considered as a precursor to the societal culture framework that these scholars subsequently proposed in 1997. Although Trompenaars and Hampden-Turner's (1997) framework referred to 'societal' rather than national cultures, the underlying conceptualization of culture within this framework remains very similar to that inherent in the work of Hofstede – both frameworks conceptualized culture as being homogenous and stable within geo-ethnic boundaries. Trompenaars and Hampden-Turner (1997) identified the cultural dimensions in Table 3.3 as distinguishing societies from one another.

Similar to the frameworks discussed earlier in this chapter, Trompenaars and Hampden-Turner's framework also has its strengths and weaknesses. These are discussed next.

A critique of Trompenaars and Hampden-Turner's societal culture framework

We begin this section with a quick review of the strengths and weaknesses of the dilemmas framework proposed initially by Trompenaars and Hampden-Turner (1993). Lowe (1996) explained that, while the dilemmas framework does not provide any significantly different or new information about cultural differences, it is nonetheless a useful tool for synthesizing existing knowledge on the topic. This, as he has explained and as we agree, is of use to those who have little or no exposure to a country in question. However, as Lowe (1996)

Table 3.3 Trompenaars and Hampden-Turner's seven cultural dimensions

Universalism versus Particularism	Universalistic societies believe that laws are written for everyone and must be respected by everyone at all times. In particularistic societies, the nature of a particular relationship takes precedence over the details of the situation. Some researchers have claimed that this dimension is a potential source of conflict in cross-border partnerships since mutual trust can be difficult to establish between partners from universalistic and particularistic cultures (Adler 1997, Child and Faulkner 1998).
Individualism versus Communitarianism	This dimension is the same as Hofstede's individualism versus collectivism dimension and refers to the degree of an individual's orientation towards themselves rather than towards common goals and objectives (Child and Faulkner 1998).
Affective versus Neutral	This dimension explains the degree to which a society allows its members to express their emotions. In a neutral culture, people control and subdue their feelings effectively, whereas, in affective cultures, people express their feelings openly.
Specific versus Diffuse	This dimension explains whether people engage others in specific areas of their life and personality or diffusely in multiple areas of their life and personality at the same time.
Achievement versus Ascription	In an achievement-oriented society, status is attributed to people based on their achievements; it reflects 'doing'. On the other hand, in an ascription-oriented society, status is ascribed based on age, class, education, gender, etc., and it reflects 'being'.
Sequential versus Synchronic perception of time	In a sequential culture, time is considered as a series of passing events. In contrast, according to the synchronic approach, the past, present and the future are interrelated.
Internal versus External locus of control	This last dimension addresses societal orientations towards nature. If society dictates that individuals can and should control nature by imposing their will upon it, then this reveals an internal locus of control. On the other hand, if society supports that individuals are part of nature and should follow its laws, directions and forces, then this indicates an external locus of control.

Source: Trompenaars and Hampden-Turner (1997)

rightly pointed out, culture scholars and academics would view such frameworks with a certain amount of scepticism since they emerge from responses sought to hypothetical questions with no specific context to frame the response. Lowe provided a pertinent example to bring home his argument. American managers, he explained, would be more focused on profitability (as Trompenaars and Hampden-Turner (1993) have explained) than their counterparts in other parts of the world would, but this could be for reasons other than culture. For instance, the financial infrastructure that demands that businesses emphasize dividend growth may be more influential in explaining American managers' focus on profitability than their culture per se. Second, although Trompenaars and Hampden-Turner's (1993) project boasted of an impressive database of 15,000 responses from mid-level managers, there was criticism for its methodological design. For instance, the questionnaire relied on a series of hypothetical questions and compelled respondents to make a forced choice between a restricted number of responses, thereby compelling them to choose one category or another (Lowe 1996). Such forced choice responses are subject to errors because they do not allow respondents any flexibility.

The cultural dimensions that Trompenaars and Hampden-Turner (1997) proposed in their subsequent study classified societies (just as Hofstede's framework classified nations) into dichotomous cultural types. For instance, according to this framework, a society is either neutral or affective, but it cannot be both. We wonder whether entire societies can be affective or neutral. Are 'societies' so homogeneous that they can be grouped under one category and be treated as one entity? Is it not true that people can often be very affective in one situation (e.g. with close friends and family) and relatively neutral in another (e.g. at work)? The same argument can be offered with regards to all the cultural dimensions proposed by these authors. As demonstrated by the studies carried out by Bosland (1985a) and Singh (1990), people from the same country often exhibit different behaviours from one another. Would not the same logic apply to societies or clusters of countries? Further, a recent study conducted by Tompkins, Galbraith and Tompkins (2010) questioned the categorizations of countries by Trompenaars and Hampden-Turner (1997). In particular, their study revealed that, contrary to Trompenaars and Hampden-Turner's (1997) finding, Turkish students tend to be more universalistic, and American students tend to be more particularistic. Further, as Tong (2009) revealed, the concept of universalism itself may be interpreted differently across Western and non-Western countries. For instance, the broad concept of universalism can be distinguished between religious and secular universalism. Further, in China, a distinction can be made in secular universalism between the 'universal validity of certain ideas' and 'the general extension of ideas'. Universalism, it would seem, is a much more complex construct than Trompenaars and Hampden-Turner (1997) allowed for.

While Trompenaars and Hampden-Turner (1997) offered broad generalizations at the societal levels, we find that there are too many exceptions to these societal behavioural stereotypes. While the societal culture dimensions might be interesting from the point of view of understanding broad tendencies across vast populations, they can explain neither the variations seen within people from the same societal group nor the similarities observed in people's behaviours across different societies. We are therefore compelled to ask ourselves: How can frameworks that focus solely on cultural differences be of use to managers who need to get people to collaborate despite their cultural differences?

Global Leadership and Organizational Behaviour Effectiveness (GLOBE) study

Another recent example of a framework that conceptualizes culture at the level of a geo-ethnic entity was offered by the GLOBE (Global Leadership and Organizational Behaviour Effectiveness) study. The GLOBE study explored the effectiveness of leadership behaviours across societies. Over 170 scholars from different countries contributed to this study and collected data from about 17,000 managers in 951 organizations. It covered a variety of sectors including the food processing, finance and telecommunications industries, among others, across 62 societies. GLOBE scholars defined societal culture as 'the shared motives, values, beliefs, identities, and interpretations or meanings of significant events that result from common experiences of members of collectives that are transmitted across generations' (House and Javidan 2004: 15). These scholars distinguished between cultural practices and cultural values, explaining that whether one should address cultural practices or cultural values would depend on the underlying research question. If the basic research question focuses on how society performs, then one should focus on cultural practices. However, if the research question is about how the society should perform, then one should focus on societal value dimensions (House, Quigley and de Luque 2010). GLOBE scholars identified nine cultural dimensions that they believed distinguish societies from one another. These nine dimensions and past frameworks that have influenced the generation of these dimensions are summarized in Table 3.4.

The central premise of the GLOBE study involved two basic propositions: (1) the characteristics that distinguish one society from another also influence organizational practices and (2) leaders enact attributes and behaviours that are considered to be the most accepted and expected in a particular society (House and Javidan 2004). House, Quigley and de Luque (2010) explained that, while the nine dimensions shed some light on cultures when considered separately, for a more complete picture the scores on practices and values should be considered together. In addition, the nine cultural dimensions are not orthogonal, but they correlate with one another. Following a rigorous analysis of the data collected from 62 societies on the 9 cultural dimensions, the GLOBE scholars identified 10 regional clusters that shared some cultural characteristics (Gupta and Hanges 2004). These ten regional clusters were considered 'a convenient way of summarizing intercultural similarities as well as intercultural differences' (Gupta and Hanges 2004: 178). The regional clusters offered by the GLOBE study and the countries included in each cluster are summarized in Table 3.5.

The GLOBE study has gained significant popularity since it was first published, and it led to the production of two comprehensive volumes (House *et al.*

Table 3.4 The nine societal culture dimensions proposed by GLOBE scholars

Cultural dimension proposed by GLOBE scholars	*Past frameworks that have influenced the emergence of GLOBE cultural dimension*
1. Uncertainty avoidance: the extent to which members of an organization or society try to avoid uncertainty by relying on social norms, rituals and bureaucratic practices.	This dimension is similar to Hofstede's (1980) uncertainty avoidance versus risk-taking dimension.
2. Power distance: the degree to which members of an organization or society agree with a power differential between people (i.e. people at higher levels of an organization or the government hold more power).	This dimension is similar to Hofstede's (1980) high- versus low-power distance dimension.
3. Collectivism I (Institutional collectivism): the degree to which organizations and societies reward collective distribution of resources and collective action.	In Hofstede's (1980) framework, these two dimensions are treated as one dimension, namely, individualism versus collectivism.
4. Collectivism II (In-group collectivism): the degree to which individuals express pride, loyalty and cohesiveness in their organizations or families.	
5. Gender egalitarianism: the extent to which a society minimizes differences and promotes equality between genders.	These two dimension draw on Hofstede's (1980) dimension of masculinity versus femininity.
6. Assertiveness: the degree to which individuals in organizations or societies are assertive, confrontational and aggressive in social relationships.	
7. Future orientation: the degree to which individuals in organizations or societies plan and invest in the future and the extent to which they are comfortable with delayed gratification.	This dimension is similar to the future-orientation component of Hofstede's fifth dimension – Confucian dynamism (Hofstede and Bond 1988).
8. Performance orientation: the extent to which an organization or society rewards members for performance improvement and excellence.	This dimension is influenced by McClelland's (1985) 'need for achievement'.
9. Humane orientation: the degree to which individuals in organizations or societies encourage their members to be fair, altruistic, friendly, generous, caring and kind to others.	This dimension is influenced by Kluckhohn and Strodtbeck's (1961) dimension 'human nature as good' versus 'human nature as bad', Putnam's (1993) work on civic society and McClelland's (1985) concept of the affiliative motive.

Source: House, Quigley and de Luque (2010)

Table 3.5 Country clusters offered by the GLOBE study

Regional cluster	Countries included in the cluster
Anglo	Australia, Canada, England, Ireland, New Zealand and South Africa (white sample)
Latin Europe	France, Israel, Italy, Portugal, Spain and Switzerland (French-speaking)
Nordic Europe	Denmark, Finland, Sweden
Germanic Europe	Austria, Germany (former East), Germany (former West), the Netherlands and Switzerland
Eastern Europe	Albania, Georgia, Greece, Hungary, Kazakhstan, Poland, Russia and Slovenia
Latin America	Argentina, Bolivia, Brazil, Colombia, Costa Rica, Ecuador, El Salvador, Guatemala, Mexico and Venezuela
Sub-Saharan Africa	Namibia, Nigeria, South Africa (black sample), Zambia, Zimbabwe
Middle East	Egypt, Kuwait, Morocco, Qatar and Turkey
Southern Asia	India, Indonesia, Iran, Malaysia, Philippines and Thailand
Confucian Asia	China, Hong Kong, Japan, Singapore, South Korea and Taiwan

Source: House, Quigley and de Luque (2010)

2004, Chhokar *et al.* 2007). Subsequent publications have included many book chapters and several journal articles (for example, Javidan and House 2001, House *et al.* 2004, House, Quigley and de Luque 2010). This growing popularity does not imply, however, that the study is without criticism; the following subsection summarizes some of these criticisms levelled against the GLOBE study.

A critique of the GLOBE study

Unlike Hofstede's (1980) framework, discussed earlier in this chapter, which defined culture at the level of nations, and Trompenaars and Hampden-Turner's (1997) framework that defined culture at the level of societies, the GLOBE study categorized clusters of nations into more or less homogenous regions. Despite this minor difference, at the core, all three frameworks use geo-ethnic parameters to define culture. It is therefore not surprising that the GLOBE framework shares some of the limitations of the other two frameworks. For example, one can raise the following question in the case of the GLOBE study: Is a member of a 'humane-oriented' region or society humane with everyone to the same extent at all times? Or does their behaviour depend on the persons they are interacting with and on situational variables? Furthermore, is it correct to categorize entire societies, regions or clusters of countries as 'humane-oriented' or otherwise? We believe that there are several differences in behaviours of people from within a social entity, and studies have demonstrated that there are just as many variations in people's behaviours within a nation as there are between people from different nations (see Singh 1990). Hence, it is logical to assume that such variations will also be observed within regional clusters. In fact, these variations may be multiplied many times over when addressed at the level of regional clusters, and, therefore, they cannot be ignored.

Shalom Schwartz's cultural orientations framework and values theory

In this section, we summarize Shalom Schwartz's cultural orientations framework and his values theory. In many ways, Schwartz's work indicates a shift from the other frameworks we have discussed so far in this chapter. Alan Gutterman (2010) offered a concise summary of Schwartz's cultural orientations framework. Gutterman (2010) explained that Schwartz (2004) conceptualized culture as a rich complex of meaning, beliefs, practices, symbols, norms and values. For Schwartz (2004), those values that could be identified as prevalent among the members of a society expressed the 'cultural ideals' of the society – all that was considered good and desirable by the members of the society. These ideals defined the central traits of societal culture that shape and justify individual and group beliefs, as well as actions and goals within the society. Further, Schwartz (2006) conceptualized cultural orientations as a set of problems that individuals in each culture are required to resolve. He suggested three main problems with which societies are universally challenged and corresponding cultural orientations that represent alternative methods for resolving these problems. These cultural orientations, which help distinguish one society from another, are summarized in Table 3.6.

Schwartz (2004) observed that, while the three cultural orientations are often described separately, they occur concomitantly in societies. For instance, Western European society has a preference for both egalitarianism and intellectual autonomy. Schwartz proposed that, rather than conceptualizing cultural orientations as mutually independent (which he claimed was Hofstede's approach), it would be more accurate to view them as an integrated system. This integrated system could be depicted as a circle in which compatible cultural orientations are adjacent to one another and incompatible orientations are at a distance from one another. This integrated system of cultural orientations is presented in Figure 3.1.

While analysing data collected for these cultural orientations across 67 national groups, Schwartz (2004) concluded that, with a few exceptions, the spatial mapping of the national groups revealed seven transnational cultural groupings: West European, East European, English-speaking, Latin American, South Asian, Confucian-influenced and sub-Saharan Africa. He noted that the transnational groups that emerged were composed of countries in close geographical proximity. He conceded that values, norms, practices and

Table 3.6 The three cultural dimensions proposed by Schwartz (2004)

Conservatism versus Autonomy	This dimension deals with the relation between the person and the group. To what extent are people autonomous versus embedded in their groups? Embeddedness (conservatism) appears when individuals identify with the group and find meaning through social relationships, through participating in the group's shared way of life and by striving towards common goals. The values that are cherished are social order, respect for tradition, security, obedience and wisdom. In contrast, autonomy refers to the situation where individuals are viewed as independent entities and they find meaning in their own uniqueness. Autonomy could be either intellectual or affective. In some respects, this dimension is similar to Hofstede's (1980) individualism versus collectivism dimension.
Hierarchy versus Egalitarianism	This dimension deals with the extent to which equality is valued by members of a society. In hierarchical societies, individuals and resources are organized hierarchically. People willingly comply with the roles assigned to them and to the obligations and rules attached to their roles. If they fail to comply with the rules, they are subject to sanctions. Conversely, in egalitarian societies, individuals are equal. They demonstrate commitment and cooperation and voluntarily concern themselves with everyone's welfare. The values cherished by egalitarian societies are: social justice, caring for weaker members, honesty, equality, sympathy, voluntary cooperation, etc. To some extent, this cultural dimension overlaps with Hofstede's (1980) high- versus low-power distance dimension.
Mastery versus Harmony	This last dimension deals with the extent to which members of the society seek to change their relationship with nature and the social world in order to advance personal interests. Mastery refers to a situation where individuals value succeeding and getting ahead through 'self-assertion'. They proactively seek to master the natural and social world to advance their personal interests. The values that are cherished are independence, ambition, hard work, drive and competence. In contrast, harmony refers to the situation where individuals are happy to fit into the natural and social world. They seek to protect and preserve it rather than change or exploit it. Important values are peace, unity with nature and protecting the environment. Again, this dimension reflects some similarity with Hofstede's (1980) masculinity–femininity dimension.

Source. Schwartz (2004)

institutions influenced people across national borders and that shared histories, religion and the level of development also had a role to play. He also noted that his findings were strikingly similar to those of Hofstede (Gutterman 2010). We find that, while Schwartz's cultural orientations framework shares some basic similarities with Hofstede's national culture framework, it also has several features that distinguish it from Hofstede's framework and other frameworks discussed in this chapter. These nuances of Schwartz's work will be

Figure 3.1 Schwartz's integrated system of cultural orientations
Source: Schwartz (2004)

discussed in the next subsection of this chapter. But before we get there, we would like to offer to our readers a summary of Schwartz's value theory.

A major part of Schwartz's (1992, 2005a, 2006) work has focused on the concept of values. While discussing Schwartz's values theory in full detail is beyond the scope of this chapter, we nonetheless summarize some of his key findings in this subsection. Based on the data collected in over 70 countries, Schwartz (2006) identified 10 motivationally distinct value orientations: self-determination, stimulation, hedonism, achievement, power, security, conformity, tradition, benevolence and universalism. Of these ten values, some values con-tradict one another (e.g. benevolence and power), whereas others are compatible (e.g. conformity and security). According to Schwartz (2006), these ten values are universal because they are grounded in basic human requirements. Nevertheless, there are individual differences in the significance people attach to different values. People's life circumstances allow them to pursue some values more easily than others. For example, wealthy people can pursue power values more easily. Life circumstances also impose constraints against pursuing certain values, such as when one is surrounded by people who value conformity, it is difficult to offer and defend an idea that might 'rock the boat'. Schwartz explained that usually people adapt their values to their circumstances, highlighting those values that can be readily attained and downplaying those values whose pursuit is blocked (Schwartz and Bardi

1997). People's age, education, gender, income and other characteristics affect their socialization, their learning experiences, the social roles they play, the expectations and sanctions they encounter, and the abilities they develop. Thus, differences in backgrounds determine differences in life circumstances to which people are exposed, and these, in turn, affect their value priorities.

Further, Schwartz (2006) also explained how values interact with one another. Pursuing one value has consequences: it conflicts with some values but is congruent with others. For instance, pursuing achievement may be congruent with pursuing power, but it may be in conflict with pursuing benevolence. People can and do pursue competing values, but they do so in different acts occurring in different spheres of their lives. Values form a continuum of related motivations. For instance, power and achievement form a continuum – they both focus on social superiority and esteem. Similarly, hedonism and stimulation form a continuum since they both focus on arousal. Therefore, Schwartz (2006) presented values and their motivational continuum in a circular manner. The closer any two values are in either direction around the circle, the more similar are their underlying motivations. This implies that the whole set of ten values relate to one another in an integrated manner. Finally, at the societal level, a high level of consensus can be observed regarding the hierarchical order of priorities. While benevolence, universalism and self-direction values are most important, power and stimulation are considered least important (Schwartz 2006). In the following subsection we offer a critique of Schwartz's cultural orientations framework and values theory.

A critique of Schwartz's cultural orientations framework and values theory

While, at first glance, it might seem that Schwartz's framework and his values theory do not offer much conceptual distinctiveness from the other frameworks discussed in this chapter, there are many subtle differences between Schwartz's conceptualization and operationalization of cultural orientations and those of other conventional culture scholars. The same can also be said of his understanding of values. First, Schwartz has acknowledged that, while describing each cultural orientation separately facilitates the task of exposing the framework, in reality, different cultural orientations are intricately linked with one another due to common underlying values. The circular model of cultural orientations offered by Schwartz (see Figure 3.1) allows us to treat these cultural orientations as integrated with one another rather than mutually independent. This offers a major conceptual advantage over other frameworks of culture discussed in earlier sections of this chapter. Schwartz's (2004) integrated system of cultural orientations implies that we can now accept the idea of mutually congruent, conflicting and sometimes, antagonistic cultural orientations coexisting within the same society. Indirectly, this raises questions about the assumption of cultural homogeneity within an entity (nation, society, region, etc.) that conventional culture scholars (Hofstede 1980, Trompenaars and Hampden-Turner 1997) have emphasized in their work. Second, Schwartz has cautioned against excessive reliance on transnational cultural groups. He noted that, while each transnational group is quite homogenous and distinctive, there are also considerable in-group variations. He suggested that 'whether regions can be used as a unit of analysis is therefore a matter of which orientations are of interest' (p. 32). He also calls for further studies in the degree of cultural homogeneity within each group and the extent to which this differs from one group to the next. In so doing, Schwartz has drawn our attention to the relative in-group cultural differences and potential inter-group cultural similarities. In other words, he has refrained from simplistic and deterministic categorizations of societies and presents them as complex and culturally diverse entities. We conclude that not only is Schwartz's cultural orientations framework a sounder framework of societal culture, but it is also one that urges culture scholars to focus on cultural diversity as much as cultural conformity.

Second, and regarding Schwartz's values theory, while most past research has examined empirical relations between a few target values and a particular background variable, attitude or behaviour (e.g. equality and civil rights in Rokeach 1973), Schwartz's values theory allows us to relate the full set of values to other variables in an organized, integrated manner (Schwartz 2006). The integrated structure of values makes it easier to theorize about relations of value priorities to other variables and also serves as a template, helping to identify 'deviations' from the expected pattern whenever they occur (Schwartz 2006). Deviations, as Schwartz (1996) has explained in his earlier work, are especially interesting because they draw our attention towards those conditions that either strengthen or weaken the relationship between a said variable and the value in question. In addition, it is important to note that Schwartz's conceptualization of values allows for a much more dynamic understanding of human behaviour. Consider his discussion of how individual situations and circumstances influence which values will be manifested in action and which will be undermined. We find this explanation of human behaviour to be far more convincing than the conceptualization of human behaviour as a passive embodiment of predetermined values dictated by one's national/regional/societal origin. To conclude, we find that Schwartz's cultural orientations framework and his values theory offer many nuances as compared to the other frameworks discussed in this chapter.

Concluding remarks

In this chapter, we have examined various cultural frameworks that address culture at the national, societal and/or regional levels. We have also offered a critique of these different frameworks. By and large, most of the frameworks discussed in this chapter adhere to the idea of a stable and homogenous culture at the level of a geo-ethnic entity. Nevertheless, we find many nuances in the work of Shalom Schwartz that have influenced our thinking and that we will revisit in Part III of this book. The objective behind exposing these different frameworks to students of culture is to equip them with a basic knowledge of how different experts have conceptualized and operationalized culture. We believe cultural frameworks are like any other tool – users need to know how and when to use them if they wish to be effective. In addition, one cannot effectively decide which tool is best for the 'task at hand' unless one knows what a tool can and cannot do, which tools one has in one's tool box and what the strengths and weaknesses of each tool are. In the following chapter, we provide a more profound critique of the different cultural frameworks discussed in this chapter and a more in-depth comparison of the same. More importantly, we present an overview of some of the recent advances in the field of national culture research that signal major progress in the field and offer much hope for a better understanding of culture in business studies.

Additional reading

P. Rosenzweig (1994) 'National Culture and Management', *Harvard Business School Note* no. 9-394-177 March 1994.

4 Comparing national, societal and regional frameworks of culture and exposing recent developments in the field

Criticism may not be agreeable, but it is necessary. It fulfils the same function as pain in the human body. It calls attention to an unhealthy state of things.

Winston Churchill

What you will learn in this chapter:

- the strengths and weaknesses of cultural frameworks introduced in Chapter 3;
- recent advances in the field of national/societal/regional frameworks of culture.

Introduction

In Chapter 3, we have presented different frameworks that address culture at the national, societal and/or regional levels. These include Hofstede's (1980) national culture framework, Hall's (1960) high- versus low-context framework, Hall and Hall's (1990) framework of different perceptions of time, Trompenaars and Hampden-Turner's (1997) societal culture framework, the GLOBE study's regional culture framework and, finally, Schwartz's (2004, 2006) cultural orientations framework and values theory. In that chapter, we also offered a preliminary review of the strengths and weaknesses of these frameworks. To recap, one of the biggest advantages of such frameworks is that they simplify the cultural discourse for both practitioners and researchers. By attributing human behaviour to national, societal and/or regional origin, they simplify the otherwise intricate and complex task of making sense of human behaviour. A manager following these frameworks is not required to decipher the behaviour of his colleagues in terms of values, needs or motivations and to interpret these behaviours in terms of the impact of temporary situational variables or more profound and long-lasting influences. Instead, the national, societal and/or regional category to which the individuals belong is used to explain and even predict their behaviour. Conversely, these frameworks have been criticized for generating and supporting stereotypes at the national, societal or regional levels (see Osland and Bird 2000) and for propagating the idea of geographically bounded cultural entities that are internally coherent, culturally homogenous and stable (Patel 2007a, 2007b). In Chapter 4, we analyse and present a more detailed comparison among the national, societal and regional frameworks of culture, which we now refer to as conventional frameworks of culture. We also review some of the advances made in this area of research since 2000. Interestingly, these works encourage culture scholars to move away from their static conceptualization of culture towards a more dynamic one.

Comparing national, societal and regional frameworks of culture

All the cultural frameworks discussed in Chapter 3 of this book have one common characteristic: they all emphasize broad cultural similarities within geographical entities and broad differences between them. Although many of these frameworks acknowledge cultural variations within geographic entities, their focus remains on identifying broad similarities within and broad differences between entities. One framework that stands apart among the different frameworks discussed in Chapter 3 is Shalom Schwartz's (2004, 2006) cultural orientations framework. Although Schwartz's cultural orientations framework does group nations into culturally similar transnational regions, he has cautioned us against excessive reliance on these transnational groupings. He has also explained that, while each transnational group is quite homogenous and distinctive, there are also considerable in-group variations. He has, therefore, called for further studies on the degree of cultural homogeneity within each group and the extent to which it differs from others. We believe that Schwartz's cultural orientations model is not only a sounder framework of culture but also offers a distinct advantage: it encourages culture scholars to focus on both cultural diversity and cultural conformity. A preliminary review of the conventional culture frameworks reveals some interesting insights.

First, Hofstede has offered five cultural dimensions by which countries distinguish themselves from one another, the GLOBE study has given us nine cultural dimensions of comparisons between country clusters and Trompenaars and Hampden-Turner have offered seven cultural dimensions to distinguish societal cultures. The implicit assumption in all these frameworks is that culture is common, homogenous and shared within these geographic parameters. This assumption leads to the generation of broad generalizations at the level of geographic entities. For instance, while Hofstede has offered broad generalizations at the level of countries (e.g. India is more collectivistic than France is), the GLOBE study promoted even broader generalizations at the level of country clusters (e.g. Latin American versus Eastern European cluster). According to the GLOBE study, citizens of a specific country share common behavioural preferences, but, more importantly, countries falling into the same cluster also share common cultural traits (e.g. a country falling into the

'Anglo' cluster shares more cultural similarities with other countries in the same cluster than with countries that fall into the 'South Asian' cluster). We are compelled to ask how managers working in the complex business scenario, domestic or international, may use the knowledge of these broad generalizations to guide their day-to-day interactions with colleagues. For instance, what purpose does it serve to inform a German manager that Chinese people have a collectivistic orientation (Hofstede 1980)? At best, this makes the German colleague behave in a collectivistic way with Chinese counterparts, who might then take this as their behavioural cue and adapt their own behaviour accordingly. In addition, for the German manager, preconditioned by a categorization of China as a collectivistic culture, any contradictory observation may lead to confusion and 'cultural shock'. When people interact with one another in dynamic contexts, such as international strategic alliances, they do not always behave in accordance with their national, societal or regional cultural profiles. In other words, people's behaviours do not always match the stereotypical categories that they are believed to represent. If managers were to enter the work setting with preconceived ideas concerning people from different nations, societies or clusters, they may find themselves ill-equipped to handle the dynamic reality of human behaviour.

Second, although there are underlying conceptual similarities between the different conventional culture frameworks, this does not imply that their findings concur. For instance, there are significant differences between the findings of Hofstede's (1980) study and the GLOBE study on several cultural dimensions (Koopman, Den Hartog, Konrad *et al.* 1999). Among scholars who subscribe to the finding of these studies, some, like Koopman and his colleagues (1999), have chosen not to undermine cultural differences in country clusters. For example, using data from the GLOBE study, Koopman *et al.* (1999) explored 21 European countries, identified at least 2 different cultures in the north-eastern and south-western parts of Europe, and simultaneously acknowledged that, in some cultural aspects, European countries are distinct from countries in other parts of the world. We find that the real difference between the viewpoints of different scholars is not so much about whether or not they recognize in-group differences (by and large, most scholars recognize a certain amount of in-group differences) but whether and to what extent they choose to emphasize them. While most proponents of conventional frameworks of culture choose to downplay in-group differences, other scholars such as Schwartz (2004 2006) and Koopman *et al.* (1999) have chosen not to.

As a final point, while GLOBE scholars (House *et al.* 1999) have started off by acknowledging that people behave differently in different social contexts (families, schools, work organizations, economic and legal systems and political solidarities), their final results do not reflect these contextual influences. In calculating the mean scores for different countries on the nine cultural dimensions, the context-specific cultural differences have been averaged out. If

GLOBE scholars had continued addressing the context-specific variations in people's behaviours, they would have identified a wide variety of situational variables that influence whether or not certain cultural values will be manifested in a certain context. This is the context-specific nature of culture, which is exactly what many culture scholars are now attempting to understand (see section entitled 'Recent advances in national culture frameworks: A shift from a static to a dynamic conceptualization of culture' for examples).

Next, we offer an in-depth critique of the conventional frameworks of culture.

Critiquing national, societal and regional frameworks of culture

In order to give better orientation to our in-depth critique of the conventional frameworks of culture, we structure our discussion around six points of reflection:

Reflection point 1: Have the conventional frameworks of culture satisfactorily conceptualized and operationalized culture?

Reflection point 2: Is national identity a passive embodiment of a predetermined cultural template as conventional frameworks of culture dictate?

Reflection point 3: Are the terms 'intercultural' and 'international' interchangeable?

Reflection point 4: Do we need to address culture at different levels (for instance, national, societal, regional, etc.) for optimal cultural sense-making?

Reflection point 5: Do conventional frameworks of culture explain social change?

Reflection point 6: Is culture simply an 'uncaused cause' as conventional frameworks of culture posit?

Reflection point 1: Have the conventional frameworks of culture satisfactorily conceptualized and operationalized culture?

Various frameworks that address culture at the national, societal and regional levels (see Chapter 3) emerged in business literature in the latter half of the twentieth century. Have these frameworks satisfactorily conceptualized and operationalized culture? Many scholars believe that, despite the proliferation of cultural frameworks at a variety of levels, the term 'culture' is far from a conceptual and operational consensus and that culture remains a poorly defined and operationalized term. Child and Tayeb (1983) lamented the lack of adequate definitions of culture in cross-national organizational research. Even today, in 2012, we are far from an operational consensus. Due to the excessive focus on national culture, culture has commonly become a synonym for 'nation' (Adler and Doktor 1986, Usunier 1998) and, in a circular manner, differences among national samples are sometimes ascribed to nationality. Culture is often confined to 'attitudes and opinions that abstracted from, and discouraged attention to, national institutions and socio-political systems' (Child and Tayeb 1983: 23).

Further, as more and more companies set up international business oper-ations, operationalizing culture meaningfully in the context of cross-country business collaborations, such as international strategic alliances (ISAs), becomes not only more important but also more problematic. Cross-border business collaborations, such as ISAs, experience constant restructuring, and ongoing mergers, acquisitions and takeovers, which result in ever-changing boundaries and increasing diversity of conflicting goals (Angwin and Vaara 2005). In such entities, there is a blurring of the corporate and national identities of members because members belong to different and, sometimes, overlapping national, corporate, professional, loyalty and interest groups. Therefore, attempting to explain human behaviour in ISAs solely based on national/societal origin, as many scholars have attempted to do, is inadequate (Ailon-Souday and Kunda 2009). Therefore, there is the need to find alternative approaches to conceptualizing and operationalizing culture in such entities with ways that are not grounded in geo-ethnic definitions of culture.

To sum up, despite the various definitions of culture that one can find in extant literature and despite the various frameworks of national/societal/regional culture, culture scholars can still not claim that they have acquired a satisfactory handle on conceptualizing and operationalizing this elusive term. In the following subsection, we reflect further on the validity of the static concept of 'national identity' and the different viewpoints on how this plays out, especially in the context of international business collaborations.

Reflection point 2: Is national identity a passive embodiment of a predetermined cultural template as conventional frameworks of culture dictate?

According to national culture frameworks, such as Hofstede's framework discussed in Chapter 3, national identity imprints a value-based and cognitively constraining 'culture' or collective 'software' in people's minds (Hofstede 1991, Ailon-Souday and Kunda 2003). Using Hofstede's framework (Hofstede 1980, 1991), many experts (for example, Erez and Earley 1993, Harzing and Hofstede 1996, Kanungo and Mendonca 1996, Olk and Earley 1996) have argued that cultural identities manifest themselves in organizations through stubbornly distinctive behavioural patterns. Many sociologists and anthro-pologists (Ailon-Souday and Kunda 2003) have contradicted such a static national culture concept. In the sociological and anthropological traditions, national identity is considered to be a symbolic resource that is actively mobilized by members for different social goals. Early interactionist scholars, such as Mead (1934), conceptualized identity as a collectively defined, dynamic and symbolic process. Later, Goffman (1959) explained that identities are constructed for the purpose of managing impressions in everyday life, and these identities shift and change from one interaction to another (Van

Maanen 1979). On the same lines, Stone (1962) explained that identities are flexibly cast as fluid social objects in accordance with the interpretational mood in the interaction. For postmodernist scholars, identities are not only multiple (for example, Featherstone 1990, 1995) but also mobile constructs (Sarup 1996). They represent infinite combinations of cultural possibilities that can be picked up and chosen like clothes from shelves (see Mathews 2000). For a more complete review of sociology and an anthropology-based understanding of national identity, we invite readers to refer to the works of Galit Ailon-Souday and Gideon Kunda (see additional reading at the end of this chapter).

In line with the sociological and anthropological tradition, Ailon-Souday and Kunda (2003) have argued that, despite their popularity in business studies, conventional frameworks of culture are overly static and minimalist (Roberts and Boyacigiller 1984, Tayeb 1994, 2001). These frameworks treat national identity 'as a passive embodiment of a predetermined cultural template and fail to take into account the freedom that members have in defining what national belonging means' (Ailon-Souday and Kunda 2003: 1074). In their subsequent paper, Ailon-Souday and Kunda (2009) showed that managers display substantial discretionary power in deciding when to activate and when to suppress national identity in global organizations. Through the study of an Israeli-American merger, they showed that Israeli employees often chose to play out their 'Israeli identity' explicitly while undermining it at other times. In each of these instances, they demonstrated considerable flexibility in defining what national identity meant to them and how their strategic interests guide their decisions. Following Ailon-Souday and Kunda (2003, 2009), we conclude that national identity is not merely an objective essence, it is a social construct. Belonging to a certain nationality does not automatically imply that one would mechanically embody the cognitively constraining cultural outlook dictated by one's national association. We agree that there is a need to create a better understanding of the agency of members in constructing their identities and the relation between this agency and resulting social processes.

This subsection reveals that for many scholars, both from the field of business studies as well as from sociology and anthropology, the notions of a static, unchanging national culture and a passive, predetermined national identity remain unconvincing. This leads us to our next question, to what extent is it fair to equate 'nation' with 'culture' as many scholars have done in the past?

Reflection point 3: Are the terms 'intercultural' and 'international' interchangeable?

Following the work of Hofstede (1980), many scholars have been using the terms 'international' and 'intercultural' interchangeably. This implies that (1) they are equating nation with culture and (2) in the process, they are negating intra-national differences and international similarities. In this subsection, we explore to what extent it makes sense to equate 'intercultural' with 'international'.

Brendan McSweeney has been particularly eloquent in his critique of national culture scholars and their tendency to conflate nation and culture. McSweeney (2009) has explained that one would reasonably suppose that 'national culture' is the culture of a 'nation'. However, frameworks of national culture (such as the one proposed by Hofstede 1980) have conflated the word 'nation' with the terms 'country' or 'state'. These terms, McSweeney (2009) argued, should not be used interchangeably because some states such as the United Kingdom include many nations. In this case, the nation and the state are not one and the same. It is also possible that a nation may extend beyond the borders of a single state, as seen in the case of the Kurds. According to Gellner (1983), there are about 8,000 nations and only 159 states. While national culture frameworks treat each country as having one national culture, a country is not in fact a single nation but a cluster of nations within a single state (McSweeney 2009).

We find that McSweeney is neither the only nor the first expert to question the validity of equating nation with culture. Over a decade before McSweeney (2009), Jean-Claude Usunier (1998) explained that nationality is a delimitation of individuals belonging to a large group, which is operational and, obviously, convenient. However, the direction of causality between the concepts of nationality and culture is not self-evident. He has argued that an attempt to equate culture directly with the nation-state or country would be misguided for a number of convergent reasons. First, some countries are deeply multicultural, for example, India, which is made up of highly diversified ethnic, religious and linguistic groups. Second, some nation-states are explicitly multicultural, for example, as with Switzerland, with a strong emphasis on the defence of local particularism in the political system. Third, over the years, colonization and decolonization have resulted in borders that are sometimes straight lines on a map with little respect for cultural realities. For African countries, 'ethnic culture' matters, whereas 'national culture' is in many cases meaningless.

In this subsection, we have offered points of view from different scholars, notably Usunier (1998) and McSweeney (2009), who have challenged the practice of equating culture with nation. We agree with these viewpoints. Additionally, we note that the same arguments would also apply to the practice of equating culture with other geo-ethnic entities. For instance, it would be just as incorrect to equate the terms 'culture' and 'regions'. While the practice of equating culture with geographic regions is less prevalent than the practice of equating culture with nations or countries, both suffer from the same underlying drawback – they wrongly juxtapose culture with a geographic entity. This leads us to ask another question: Is it imperative to address culture at the level of geo-ethnic entities (country, nation, society, region, etc.) for cultural sense-making? Is there no framework that surpasses geo-ethnically grounded conceptualizations of culture? An attempt to answer these questions follows in the next subsection.

Reflection point 4: Do we need to address culture at different levels (national, societal, regional, etc.) for optimal cultural sense-making?

As seen in earlier chapters of this book, many scholars have conceptualized culture at the level of geo-ethnic entities. Based on the similarities observed between countries or nations on a variety of cultural dimensions, these scholars have categorized them into clusters, societies and/or regions. But do these categorizations convince other scholars? For instance, the GLOBE study categorized Canada as a member of the 'Anglo' cluster along with New Zealand, Australia, England, Ireland and South Africa (partly). This implies that Canada shares certain cultural similarities with these other countries. This categorization reveals the underlying assumption that a single and unique Canadian culture exists that fits with the other members of the 'Anglo' cluster. However, as Rosalie Tung (2008) has pointed out, Canada is a highly diverse nation, and there are clear distinctions between the Anglophone Canadians and the Francophone Canadians. It is believed that the former share more cultural similarities with their American counterparts than with their French-speaking compatriots. There is also a third group of people whom Tung (2008) has called Allophones, a group composed of people who are neither Anglophones nor Francophones. In light of this discussion, one is compelled to question the merit of simplistically categorizing Canada in the Anglo cluster as the GLOBE scholars have done.

Similar questions can also be raised concerning more recent works of Hofstede. Hofstede (2005) grouped many countries from the Middle East into one cluster called the 'Arab World' or 'Arab-speaking countries'. This cluster includes Egypt, Iraq, Kuwait, Lebanon, Libya, Saudi Arabia and the United Arab Emirates. Hofstede attributed a relatively high score to this cluster on power distance (PDI = 80), masculinity (MAS = 52) and uncertainty avoidance (UAI = 68) with a relatively low score on individualism (IDV = 38). This categorization indicates Hofstede's (2009) underlying assumption of cultural homogeneity across these countries. Hofstede also extrapolated the findings from the 'Arab-speaking countries' cluster to other countries such as Jordan. In contrast, recent studies by Alkailani, Azzam and Athamneh (2012) revealed a different set of scores for Jordan as compared to those proposed by Hofstede. Alkailani *et al.* (2012) found that, on masculinity versus femininity and on individualism versus collectivism, Jordan is close to the scores attributed by Hofstede to Arab countries, but, on uncertainty avoidance versus risk-taking and on power distance, Jordan has a much lower score than other Arab countries. The authors attributed the low power distance score to the high level of education in Jordan and to the availability of a highly skilled workforce. They also drew our attention to the work of Al-Nashmi and Syd Zin (2011) who contested the broad generalizations regarding Arab countries as offered by Hofstede. Instead, these scholars suggested that the Arab region needs to be studied as different territories according to their cultural proximity. For instance, they suggested that Yemen, Iraq and all the Arab Gulf countries should be explored as one cultural territory; Syria, Lebanon, Jordan and Palestine as another one; Egypt as a separate territory; and so on. Al-Nashmi and Syd Zin (2011) conclude that Arab people from different Arab countries differ in terms of their national cultural values. The works of Tung (2008), Al-Nashmi and Syd Zin (2011) and Alkailani *et al.* (2012) have revealed that not everyone agrees with the country clusters that the GLOBE study and Hofstede (2005) have offered.

Now, we revert to the original question: Is addressing culture at the level of different geo-ethnic entities (country, nation, society, region, etc.) imperative for optimal cultural sense-making? To answer this question, we refer to the work of Anne Tsui and her colleagues. Tsui *et al.* (2007) reviewed culture litera-ture from 16 leading management journals over a period of 10 years from 1997 to 2007. They noted that much progress had been made in terms of understanding of cross-cultural management.[1] However, the fact that the fundamental concept of culture has not been systematically examined has overshadowed this progress. In addition, scholars have not paid attention to the proliferation of cultural framework with overlapping dimensions, and they have neglected the fact that national-level variables other than culture can also have an impact on how one country differs from another. Grounding our reflections in the work of Tsui *et al.* (2007), we feel compelled to ask whether the varied cultural frameworks with overlapping dimensions are in fact required for optimal cultural sense-making. We are also prompted to question whether students and scholars of culture really need to address culture at so many different geo-ethnic levels: nations, societies, regional clusters, etc. We wonder whether it is possible to conceptualize culture in ways other than those grounded in geo-ethnic entities. If such alternative frameworks of culture exist, then these could be used to study cultures across a variety of geo-ethnic entities because they would not be constrained to specific geo-ethnic entities in their definition and application. Finally, many scholars such as Barth (1978) and Tsui *et al.* (2007) have believed that there are cultural phenomena that span across levels. Such phenomena have been largely neglected by culture scholars, especially those in business studies, due to lack of appropriate frameworks. We reckon that a cultural framework that is not limited to specific geo-ethnic entities in terms of its application would facilitate the investigation of such cross-level and cross-scale cultural phenomena.

To conclude, we remain unconvinced by the categorization of certain countries into clusters. As seen in the example of Canada and the 'Arab-speaking countries' cluster, there are often significant differences within a nation and/or cluster of nations. These differences are often too significant and too numerous to be ignored. Furthermore, we remain unconvinced that culture must inevitably be addressed at the national, societal or regional levels. We reckon that, if we had a more innovative framework of culture, we would not necessarily be obliged to address culture at so many different levels nor would cultural scholars be compelled to use so many different frameworks, each purportedly addressing culture at a different level.

Reflection point 5: Do conventional frameworks of culture explain social change?

As mentioned earlier in this book, the frameworks of national culture (as well as many other frameworks of societal and regional culture) popular in business literature treat culture as a static set of characteristics distinguishing one nation (society or region) from another. Culture has been largely treated as reflecting a shared knowledge structure that attenuates variability in values, behavioural norms and patterns of behaviour (Erez and Earley 1993). If cultures change, they do so very slowly (Hofstede 2001). Many scholars support this stable conceptualization of culture, which is understandable considering that such a conceptualization helps reduce ambiguity and facilitates a better control over expected behavioural outcomes (Weick and Quinn 1999). Such frameworks demand a fit between a given culture and managerial practices. A high fit means high adaptation of managerial practices within the culture in question and, therefore, high effectiveness (Erez and Earley 1993). Although business literature has studied organizational change as an outcome of environmental change, the issue of change at the national level has rarely been addressed (Leung *et al.* 2005). In fact, few frameworks in business literature address the dynamic aspect of culture. Nevertheless, the stable conceptualization of culture has invited much criticism from scholars who believe that cultures change and evolve continually. For instance, Kwok Leung and his colleagues (2005) argued that the assumption of cultural stability is valid only as long as there are no environmental changes. We support Leung *et al.* (2005) in their attempt to challenge the notion of stable cultures, but we are compelled to point out that a situation of no environmental changes rarely exists. One need only look at the events since the 1940s on social, cultural, economic and political fronts for evidence.

Among the theories that do address the dynamic aspect of culture, the ecocultural model of Berry *et al.* (2002) and Kitayama's (2002) systemic view are noteworthy. Berry *et al.* (2002) conceptualized culture as evolving adaptations to ecological and socio-political influences. This eco-cultural model views individual psychological characteristics, in a population, as adaptive to their cultural context, as well as to the broader ecological and socio-political influences (Leung *et al.* 2005: 362). On the same lines, Kitayama (2002) proposed a systemic view to expose the dynamicity of culture, as opposed to the entity view that sees culture as static. The systemic view suggests that each person's psychological processes are organized through the active effort to coordinate one's behaviour with the pertinent cultural systems of practices and meaning. Yet, concurrently, many aspects of the psychological systems develop rather flexibly as they are attuned to the surrounding socio-cultural environment and are likely to be configured in different ways across different sociocultural groups (Leung *et al.* 2005: 362). These dynamic views of culture are supported by empirical evidence. For example, Inglehart and Baker (2000) examined cultural change as reflected through changes in basic values in 65 societies. They found that (1) economic development is accompanied with a shift away from traditional norms and values towards values that are increasingly rational, tolerant, trusting and participatory; and (2) the broad cultural heritage of a society (e.g. Protestant, Orthodox, Confucian, etc.) have an enduring impact on traditional values notwithstanding modernization.

As seen in this subsection, the fact that conventional frameworks treat culture as a set of stable characteristics at the national/societal/regional levels has indirectly resulted in their inability to explain social change. There are other unintended consequences of these frameworks; for instance, they have led to culture being treated as an 'uncaused cause', which will be discussed next.

Reflection point 6: Is culture simply an 'uncaused cause' as conventional frameworks of culture posit?

In recent times, culture has become a broad umbrella encompassing a wide variety of beliefs, norms, actions, practices, routines, etc. Angwin and Vaara (2005: 1447) pointed out that 'the cultural perspective has become an overall explanation to which it is far too easy to return when trying to understand post-merger problems, difficulties and failures' (see also Vaara 2002). Due to the excessive focus on national culture, scholars have tended to treat human behaviour as a passive embodiment of a static national culture. Also, due to their excessive focus on national culture differences, scholars have tended to neglect the possibility of potential similarities between national cultures. This has led to treating culture as an 'uncaused cause' (Thompson and Ellis 1997) that implies that, while culture is considered to be the source/cause of many problems, it can itself not be explained. Thompson and Ellis (1997) explained that, as long as culture is defined solely in terms of national, religious, ethnic, racial or corporate distinctiveness, culture must remain a fancy name for what we do not understand. They further state that, as long as culture is treated as an 'uncaused cause', it will only be invoked to explain failures when all other forms of explanation (bad planning, poor design, inadequate resources, etc.) have been found wanting. Our experiences in the field support the observations of Thompson and Ellis (1997). International managers are quick to attribute blame to culture when their alliances fail, but they are unable to explain culture itself or how it influences their success (see Patel 2007a, 2007b). Thompson and Ellis (1997) expounded that those that treat culture as an 'uncaused cause' assume that we live in a world in which values are disembodied and unattached to human subjects. In contrast, they explained that a convincing framework of culture would be one that explains the link between people's underlying values, their social relations and behavioural preferences (Thompson and Ellis 1997). A convincing framework of culture does not simply place people into categories, but it uses those categories to explain certain social phenomena. Finally, a convincing framework of culture also satisfactorily explains social change. Although conventional frameworks of culture give us broad generalized patterns of behaviour at the national/

societal/regional levels, they do not explain how these behavioural patterns are created and sustained, nor do they explain social change. Hence, there is a need for alternative frameworks that better address these issues than the conventional frameworks of culture discussed so far in this book.

In light of the six points of reflection presented in this section, it is evident that, notwithstanding the simplicity and resulting popularity of conventional frameworks of culture, many scholars remain unconvinced of their merit. Many adherents of these conventional frameworks have recognized their limitations and are actively engaged in addressing them with efforts that have led to significant advances in the field, some of which are summarized in the next section.

Recent advances in national culture frameworks: A shift from a static to a dynamic conceptualization of culture

Having recognized some of the limitations of the national culture framework, many adherents to this school of thought are now working towards refining or expanding them. Leung *et al.* (2005) informed us that current research on culture in business literature is developing along two, almost diametrically opposed, axes:

1. research on new trait-like static cultural dimensions similar to those proposed by Hofstede; and
2. research inspired by breakthroughs in cognitive psychology, which increasingly portrays the human mind as dynamic and flexible.

As an illustration of the first axis of development, Leung *et al.* (2002) attempted to expand the dimensional map of culture on a large scale. These scholars created a social axiom survey based on items from psychology literature and from qualitative research conducted in Hong Kong and Venezuela. This has resulted in a five-factor structure, and the robustness of which was subsequently confirmed through a study of over 40 cultural groups (Leung and Bond 2004). This five-dimensional structure captured the attention of culture scholars and was applied at the individual level to investigate influence tactics in international business (Fu *et al.* 2004). A culture-level factor analysis of this model has yielded only two factors: (1) a dynamic externality (the belief in fate, the existence of a supreme being, the positive impact of religion; also, a belief in effort and knowledge, as well as the complexity of the social world); and (2) a societal cynicism (a negative view of human nature and a mistrust in social institutions). This area of research is still in its infancy and may yield many interesting insights in the years to come.

The second axis of development in the field of culture studies treats the human mind and, consequently, human behaviour as dynamic and flexible. This viewpoint contrasts sharply with the conventional view of culture that conceptualizes culture as a stable set of characteristics manifested at the national, societal and/or regional levels. The dynamic viewpoint is influenced by the current research in cognitive psychology that shows that the human mind is fluid and adaptive and interacts dynamically with the environment. In line with this school of thought, Tinsley and Brodt (2004) provided a cognitive analysis of cultural differences in conflict behaviours through a discussion of frames, schemas and scripts. Since the content and salience of frames, schemas and scripts are sensitive to environmental influences, they can and do evolve. Hong *et al.* (2000) conducted another study that illustrated the dynamicity of culture. Conventional culture literature shows that, unlike members of individualistic cultures, members of collectivistic cultures tend to attribute the cause of other people's behaviours to external causes (such as situational demands), as opposed to internal causes (such as personality traits). Through an interesting experimental study involving Chinese subjects from Hong Kong, who as we know are categorized as collectivistic by conventional culture scholars, Hong *et al.* (2000) showed that the way subjects attribute people's behaviours to internal or external variables can be made to change. This shows that cultural change is much easier to achieve than has been believed in the past.

With gradually growing literature in the field (see Oyserman *et al.* 2002), Leung *et al.* (2005) explained that more research in this promising direction may be expected. Studies supporting the dynamic nature of culture offer many important implications. For instance, such studies imply that cultural differences are easier to overcome than previously assumed. If mental processes associated with national culture are relatively fluid, then they can be changed by appropriate situational influences. Leung *et al.* (2005) have proposed that this is an exciting new avenue to pursue in international business research on culture. Many scholars (see Leung *et al.* 2005, Taras, Kirkman and Steel 2010) also have suggested that, rather than questioning whether or not national culture matters, it is now time to address the issue of how and when national culture makes a difference. For example, through a meta-analysis of 598 previously published studies, Taras *et al.* (2010) showed that the predictive power of Hofstede's cultural values is significantly lower than personality traits and demographics for certain organizational outcomes, but it is higher for others. They also found that cultural values are more strongly related to organizational outcomes for certain kinds of samples than for others; for example, the correlation was stronger for managers than for students and for older male and more educated respondents. Thus, Taras *et al.* (2010) have placed boundary conditions within which Hofstede's framework may be used effectively. On the same lines, Gibson, Maznevski and Kirkman (2009) showed that there are individual level (e.g. the people's attachment to their own national culture), group levels (e.g. the level of team cooperation) and situational (e.g. the level of uncertainty about, say, technology) factors, which moderate the impact of national culture on individual outcomes. Such studies provide greater precision in cultural theoretical models (Leung *et al.* 2005). Leung *et al.* (2005) suggested that future cultural research must include multiple potential moderators at various levels of analysis, whenever possible.

While we recognize that significant advances have been made in demonstrating the boundary conditions under which national culture frameworks may be used effectively (see Taras *et al.* 2010), and while we applaud such efforts, we feel it is important to remind readers that the concept of 'national culture' itself has been challenged by other scholars (Usunier 1998, McSweeney 2009). Therefore, we suggest that it might well be time for students and scholars of culture to make a conscious shift away from the national culture concept and towards alternative conceptualizations of culture. This is a possibility that we explore in Part III of this book. More precisely, in Chapters 7 and 8 of this book, we review past and current literature from anthropology in search of alternative conceptualizations of culture. Fortunately, we are not alone in this endeavour. Many other culture scholars (e.g. Leung *et al.* 2005) have also resorted to disciplines such as cognitive psychology, economics, sociology and anthropology in search of alternative conceptualizations of culture.

Concluding remarks

In conclusion, previous research on culture in international business takes a simplistic view of culture and examines the static influence of a few cultural elements in isolation from other cultural elements and contextual variables (Leung *et al.* 2005). Much of the research inspired by Hofstede's dimensions falls into this category. Literature that is more recent favours instead a multi-layered, multifaceted, contextual and systems view of culture (Leung *et al.* 2005). These recent works also suggest that some cultural elements are stable, whereas others are dynamic and changing. Therefore, recent scholars have focused their attention towards developing mid-range dynamic frameworks of culture that are sensitive to the nuances of different contexts (Leung *et al.* 2005).

In addition to the national, societal and regional levels of culture that we have discussed in Chapters 3 and 4 of this book, many culture scholars (see Hofstede 1991, Trompenaars and Hampden-Turner 1997) have suggested that culture also manifests itself at the corporate level. In the next chapter, we explore some of the frameworks that address the corporate level of culture to ascertain if these can provide managers with more appropriate tools for cultural sense-making than the frameworks evoked so far. We discern two schools of thought in corporate culture literature. The first views corporate culture as static and homogeneous within a company; the second treats corporate culture as dynamic and plural. Both these schools of thoughts and their strengths and weaknesses are discussed in the next two chapters.

Note

1 Tsui *et al.* (2007) noted that we now have a better understanding of negotiation, conflict behaviour, ethical orientations, job attitudes, leadership, etc. in different

nations. Also, research design in cross-cultural research has become more rigorous in recent years.

Additional reading

G. Ailon-Souday and G. Kunda (2003) 'The local selves of global workers: The social construction of national identity in the face of organizational globalization', *Organization Studies* 24(7): 1073–96.

G. Ailon and G. Kunda (2009) 'The One-Company Approach: Transnationalism in an Israeli-Palestinian Subsidiary of an MNC', *Organization Studies* 30(7): 693–712.

5 Understanding corporate culture
The integration perspective

We are much too much inclined in these days to divide people into permanent categories, forgetting that a category only exists for its special purpose and must be forgotten as soon as that purpose is served.

Dorothy L. Sayers, *Are Women Human?*

What you will learn in this chapter:

- different definitions of corporate culture;
- different perspectives and schools of thought in corporate culture literature;
- Joanne Martin's integration perspective of corporate culture;
- different frameworks of corporate culture adhering to the integration perspective;
- limitations of the aforementioned frameworks.

Introduction

In previous chapters of this book, we have noted that, despite the proliferation of academic literature on culture in business studies, the term 'culture' remains complex and elusive. While many scholars have chosen to focus on the national, regional and/or societal levels of culture (as discussed in Chapter 3 of this book), other scholars have identified different levels of culture such as corporate culture, professional or occupational culture, ethnic culture, etc. Hofstede (1991) and Levinson and Asahi (1995) defined occupational or professional culture as the set of values and beliefs that come from an occupation and its training. Yet other scholars have attempted to uncover the different layers of culture. For instance, in his onion model, Hofstede (1991) separated culture into four layers: symbols, heroes, rituals and values. In the same way, Trompenaars and Hampden-Turner (1997) divided culture into three complementary layers: explicit products, norms and values, and assumptions about existence. In this chapter and the next, we focus on what we can learn from extant literature about corporate or organizational culture.

Much of our knowledge about organizational culture comes from other disciplines like anthropology (Geertz 1973), sociology (Durkheim 1965) and social psychology (Festinger 1957, Hartnell, Ou and Kinicki 2011). While corporate or organizational culture emerged as a concept in business and management literature in the early 1970s through the works of scholars like Clark (1972) (Hassan, Shah, Ikramullah *et al.* 2011), it really gathered momentum as a research topic after Pettigrew's (1979) seminal paper in which he effectively brought together insights from sociology and anthropology to inspire business scholars to explore organizational culture. Since then, inspired by the belief that organizational culture influences many individual-, group- and organizational-level behaviours (Hartnell, Ou and Kinicki 2011), there have been over 4,600 articles published in academic journals on the topic.

Corporate culture is believed to play an important role in determining an individual's commitment, satisfaction, productivity and longevity within the company (Holland 1985, Kilmann *et al.* 1985, O'Reilly *et al.* 1991). This is because individuals tend to select groups that they perceive as having similar values to their own and try to avoid others that are dissimilar (Schneider *et al.* 1995). Further, corporate culture may explain differences in managerial styles and organizational practices (e.g. Bhagat and McQuaid 1982 as quoted by Nahavandi and Malikzadeh 1998) and may affect the success (e.g. Peters and Waterman 1982 as quoted by Nahavandi and Malikzadeh 1998) and performance (Kotter and Heskett 1992) of organizations. Some researchers have suggested that a fit between company culture and strategy is essential for organizational effectiveness (Schwartz and Davis 1981 as quoted by Nahavandi and Malikzadeh 1998, Ackerman 1984). In mergers and acquisitions, corporate culture may influence the implementation of strategic decisions (Schwartz and Davis 1981, Davis 1984, Shrivastava 1986 as quoted by Nahavandi and Malikzadeh 1998). Therefore, organizational or corporate culture is believed to have an impact on many individual-level, organizational-level and inter-organizational level outcomes in companies. Since corporate culture seems to play such an important role in both domestic and international businesses, we begin our present chapter by defining this key concept.

Definitions of corporate culture

Just as there is a plethora of definitions found in business literature for the term 'culture' (see Chapter 1), the terms 'corporate culture' or 'organizational culture' have also been variously defined by business scholars. For instance, Siehl and Martin (1981) defined corporate culture as the social or normative glue that holds a company together (see also Tichy 1982). For Louis (1980), corporate culture expresses the values and beliefs that organizational members come to share (see also Siehl and Martin 1981). Symbolic devices, such as myths (Boje, Fedor and Rowland 1982), rituals (Deal and Kennedy 1982), stories (Mitroff and Kilmann 1976), legends (Wilkins and Martin 1980) and specialized language (Hirsch and Andrews 1983 as quoted by Smircich 1983), manifest these values or patterns of belief. Corporate culture may help individuals to understand an organization and provide them with norms for behaviour (Weick 1985, Deshpande and Webster 1989). Deshpande *et al.* (1993) distinguished organizational culture from organizational climate. Grounding their argument in the earlier work of Schneider and Rentsch (1988), Deshpande *et al.* (1993) explained that culture is about 'why things happened the way they do', whereas organizational climate is about 'what happens around here'.

Mats Alvesson (1987) provided an excellent overview of the various definitions of corporate culture found in business literature, some of which we reproduce in this section (see the additional reading cited at the end of this chapter for a full reference of Mats Alvesson's work). As Alvesson (1987) explained, Bate (1984) conceptualized corporate culture as a set of ideas, meanings and values that is implicit in people's minds and to which they subscribe collectively. Trice and Beyer (1984) offered a similar definition, but they distinguished between the substance of culture (i.e. networks of meanings contained in its ideologies, norms and values) and its forms (i.e. practices whereby these meanings are expressed, affirmed and communicated to members). Pettigrew (1979) explained that culture gives people a sense of what the reality in a particular setting means and of how they should act in relation to it. Finally, Morgan (1986) explained that

> shared meaning, shared understanding, and shared sensemaking are all different ways of describing culture. In talking about culture we are really talking about a process of reality construction that allows people to see and understand particular events, actions, objects, utterances, or situations in distinctive ways.
>
> (Alvesson 1987: 5)

Alvesson (1987) conceded that extant literature presents a somewhat confusing picture of corporate culture. Nevertheless, it also presents a realistic picture of what organizational scholars are required to deal with when they study organizational culture. Alvesson (1987) concluded that, barring a few exceptions, most organizational scholars accept that shared values are an important feature of organizational culture.

As we can see from Alvesson's (1987) review of extant literature, corporate culture continues to be a term that simultaneously intrigues and challenges business scholars. The discourse around corporate culture becomes even more complex due to the variety of perspectives and schools of thought that have emerged around the topic during the latter part of the twentieth century. We begin by outlining some of these different perspectives in the next section of this chapter. While some of these perspectives will be elaborated upon in subsequent sections of this chapter, a more comprehensive understanding of these perspectives and the way they contradict and complement one another will be realized in Chapter 6 of this volume.

Corporate culture: Differing perspectives and schools of thought

Over the years, various schools of thought regarding corporate culture have emerged in business literature. In an attempt to systematize theoretical approaches to corporate culture, Linda Smircich (1983) produced a classification that distinguished three basic perspectives on the issue. According to this classification, culture can be dealt with as an external variable, as an internal variable or as a root metaphor. The first two perspectives treat culture as a stable set of characteristics that distinguishes an organization, but the last approach admits that an organization, as a social phenomenon, is a culture. This last perspective, culture as a root metaphor, adopts a view of culture specific to anthropology. 'In anthropology, culture is the foundational term through which the orderliness and patterning of much of our life experience is explained' (Smircich 1983: 341). According to this perspective, each member of a specific organization is affected by the organization's culture through socialization. At the same time, each member takes an active part in re-creating the culture through daily networking with the other members of the organization. As Nowicka (2000: 60) noted, 'Human beings create culture, are culture's bearers and recipients and also manipulate culture as a tool in social life' (Czarzasty 2002). Unfortunately, many authors in international business subscribe to the first two perspectives that Smircich (1983) identified, i.e. culture as an internal or external variable. Hence, for these scholars, corporate culture represents a stable set of characteristics that characterize and describe an organization. We find that this approach is very similar to what Joanne Martin (2002, 2004) referred to as the 'integration' perspective. We discuss Martin's (2002, 2004) review of corporate culture literature and her classification of corporate culture frameworks next.

Like Linda Smircich (1983) before her, Joanne Martin (2002, 2004) has offered an excellent summary of the different schools of thought in corporate culture literature. She outlined three main perspectives in corporate culture literature: integration, differentiation and fragmentation. Martin (2004) classified the corporate culture frameworks discussed in subsequent sections of this chapter (such as the frameworks proposed by Hofstede *et al.* (1990) and Trompenaars and Hampden-Turner (1997)) as falling under the integration perspective. Martin (2004) explained that such integration frameworks (see also Schein 1985, Collins and Porras 2002) assume that consistency, organization-wide consensus and clarity characterize culture. Consistency occurs because the top management announces a set of espoused values that the employees of the firm accept and that the management reinforces by selectively recruiting people with similar values and through subsequent socialization. This assumes that firm members know how and under what circumstances to follow a course of action. If deviances are observed, these are depicted as 'not part of the culture' or as failure to achieve a 'strong' culture. Within the integration perspective, cultural change becomes an organization-wide transformation, whereby a new way of doing things replaces the old way. As Martin explained, the integration perspective has acceptance in part because it paints a picture of clarity and harmony in organizations. Such a view is attractive to practitioners, who need to believe that they can create such consensual and harmonious cultures in their companies. Consequently, within this perspective, any behaviour that does not conform to the mainstream viewpoint is either neglected or excluded. While frameworks adhering to the integration perspective are very popular, understandably, they also have the least empirical support. We focus on some of these frameworks in the next section of this chapter. In Chapter 6 of this volume, we will elaborate on frameworks adhering to the differentiation and fragmentation perspectives of corporate culture (Martin 2002, 2004).

Corporate culture: Frameworks adhering to the integration perspective

This section offers an overview of some of the corporate culture frameworks that adhere to the integration perspective (Martin 2002, 2004). Proponents of these frameworks treat culture as static and unchanging in companies. These frameworks assume that top management of a company dictates the corporate culture that members of that establishment adopt and follow systematically. Subsequently, recruiting candidates with similar values maintains a stable corporate culture and orientates these new recruits in line with the values espoused by the top management. According to this perspective, corporate culture is homogenous within a company, and any ambiguities or deviations point to instances of failure to achieve a strong corporate culture. This section commences with those frameworks that have received maximum recognition and popularity in extant business literature.

When Geert Hofstede (1980) conducted his original study on national cultures (see Chapter 3 for details), he collected data across different branches of IBM. The underlying assumption guiding his work was that, since the same company was being explored across different countries, any differences in people's behaviours would be the outcome of differences in national cultures. This revealed the underlying assumption that the IBM culture across different branches would be the same. Although Hofstede (1980) started with the idea of one overarching organizational culture, in his later work, he acknowledged that this assumption was flawed. In a subsequent study, Hofstede and his colleagues stated that corporate culture differences are composed of elements other than those that make up national culture differences (Hofstede, Neuijen, Ohayv and Sanders 1990). Hofstede *et al.* (1990) found considerable differences in values among national cultures; the opposite was the case among corporate cultures; there they found several differences in practices for people

Table 5.1 Hofstede *et al.*'s (1990) six-dimensional model of corporate culture

Cultural dimension	Description
Process-orientated versus results-orientated	Concern with means versus concern with goals.
Employee-oriented versus job-oriented	Concern for people versus concern for getting the job done.
Parochial versus professional	Employees deriving their identity from the organization versus people deriving their identity from the type of job they do.
Open system versus closed system	Is the communication climate open or closed?
Loose versus tight control	The amount of internal structuring in the organization.
Normative versus pragmatic	Normative organizations perceive their task towards the outside world as the implementation of inviolable rules, while pragmatic organizations are market driven.

Source: Hofstede et al. (1990)

holding the same values. A major outcome of the research by Hofstede *et al.* (1990) was the six-dimensional model of corporate culture presented in Table 5.1.

According to the framework of Hofstede' *et al.* (1990), the classification along the six cultural dimensions shown in Table 5.1 characterizes an organization's culture. Within this framework, an organization can be either employee-oriented or job-oriented, but it cannot be both. Similarly, it is either normative or pragmatic, but not both. We disagree with such categorizations and contend that sometimes it may be neither feasible nor meaningful to categorize organizations into such dichotomous categories. For instance, sometimes being employee-oriented might lead the organization to also get the job done (i.e. to become job-oriented). Therefore, in such a case, being employee-oriented and job-oriented may go hand in hand. In the same way, we are not convinced that organizations need to be categorized as either normative in their orientation or as market driven. Surely, a normative organization also needs to recognize the importance of being pragmatic or market driven and vice versa. Therefore, we find the framework of corporate culture by Hofstede *et al.* (1990) overly static, and it may be too categorical to offer a realistic reflection of organizational life.

In the same tradition, other scholars have proposed additional classifications of corporate culture. Wilkins and Ouchi (1983) have offered three types of corporate cultures – namely clans, markets and bureaucracies. In the same way, Denison and Mishra (1995) categorized organization cultures into four types: involvement, consistency, adaptability and mission. Finally, Trompenaars and Hampden-Turner (1997) offered a four-fold typology of organizational cultures: the Eiffel Tower, the Guided Missile, the Incubator and the Family. Table 5.2 briefly outlines these.

Table 5.2 Trompenaars and Hampden-Turner's (1997) typology of corporate culture

The Family Culture	Culture that is not only personal, with close face-to-face relationships, but also hierarchical in the sense that the 'father' of a family has experience and authority greatly exceeding those of his 'children', especially when they are young.
The Eiffel Tower Culture	The organizational structure is steep, symmetrical, narrow at the top and broad at the base, stable, rigid and robust. Like the formal bureaucracy for which it stands, it is very much a symbol of the machine age.
The Guided Missile Culture	It differs from both the Family and the Eiffel Tower by being egalitarian, and differs also from the Family and resembles the Eiffel Tower in being impersonal and task-oriented.
The Incubator Culture	The Incubator culture reflects the existential idea that organizations are secondary to the fulfilment of individuals.

Source: Trompenaars and Hampden-Turner (1997)

Trompenaars and Hampden-Turner's (1997) framework of corporate culture is similar to the framework of Hofstede *et al.* (1990), offering a static and internally consensual conceptualization of corporate culture. In line with the integration perspective (Martin 2002, 2004), Trompenaars and Hampden-Turner's framework (see Table 5.2) relies on the underlying assumption that most employees largely buy into the central premise of a company's culture. For example, in a company with a 'family' culture, most employees would accept the corporate leader as the 'father' figure who shares both a relational as well as a hierarchical bond with his 'children' (i.e. the employees). Inversely, Alvesson (1990) pointed out that expecting all individuals to relate to organizations through a commonly defined and accepted organizational identity is becoming less likely in modern organizations. The link between organizations and employees is becoming weak,[1] and the idea of corporate culture being the way to unify all the employees under one roof no longer holds. We agree with Alvesson's (1990) observation, and we reckon that two shifts are required: a conscious shift towards more flexible and realistic frameworks of corporate culture and a simultaneous shift towards a more dynamic understanding of human behaviour in organizations.

Having introduced some corporate culture frameworks that subscribe to the integration perspective (Martin 2002, 2004), we now offer a more in-depth critique of the same in the following section.

Critiquing corporate culture frameworks that adhere to the integration perspective

This chapter has outlined different frameworks of corporate culture subscribing to the integration perspective. Nonetheless, these frameworks suffer from some key drawbacks. First, none of these frameworks tells us whether the cultural types or dimensions proposed are exhaustive; it is unclear whether these frameworks successfully deal with the full range of human behaviours observed in companies.

Second, the corporate culture frameworks discussed in this chapter share some of the structural weaknesses of the conventional culture frameworks discussed in Chapter 3 of this book (i.e. frameworks addressing culture at national, societal or regional levels). Most of the corporate culture frameworks discussed in this chapter treat corporate culture as homogenous and static in a company. This contrasts significantly with real-life experiences in companies. Anyone who has ever been involved with an exercise of organizational change will attest to the fact that the same change is perceived differently by different groups of employees in the company. While some see the change as a threat, others might perceive it as an opportunity. While some react to protect what they perceive as their own interests, others may act in the interest of a larger group with which they identify. Therefore, the assumption of a homogenous and static culture throughout an organization is just as debatable as the notion of internally homogenous and stable national cultures.

Third, just as there are many scholars who have supported the idea that companies have homogenous and static corporate cultures, there are an equal number of researchers (e.g. Smircich 1983, Sathe 1985, Alvesson 1990) who have disagreed with the idea of a common overarching corporate culture in an organization. Sathe (1985) explained that, although the term 'corporate culture' connotes organizations have a monolithic culture, most organizations have more than one set of beliefs influencing the behaviour of employees. These various subcultures within one organization may be divided along occupational, functional, product or geographical lines; such subcultures may be enhancing, orthogonal or counter to one another (Sathe 1985). On the same lines, Smircich (1983) commented that the extensive literature grounded in the assumption of one overriding corporate culture in an organization makes one lose sight of the likelihood that there are in fact multiple corporate subcultures, or even countercultures, competing to define the nature of situations within organizational boundaries. Finally, as explained earlier in this chapter, Alvesson (1990) has also rejected the idea that corporate culture represents a common set of rules that unify individuals in a company.

In conclusion, we draw readers' attention to a fundamental question we have raised in Chapter 4 of this volume: if a cultural framework were really sound, would it not be possible to apply the same framework to make sense of culture at different levels? We maintain that, if we could identify such a sound cultural framework, it would become possible to use the same framework for cultural sense-making at and across a variety of levels, including the corporate level. Such an innovative framework would indirectly render the various frameworks cited in this and the previous chapter obsolete and/or redundant.

Concluding remarks

As mentioned in earlier sections of this chapter, Joanne Martin (2002, 2004) outlined three main perspectives in corporate culture literature: integration, differentiation and fragmentation. The corporate culture frameworks discussed in this chapter (such as the frameworks proposed by Hofstede *et al.* (1990) and Trompenaars and Hampden-Turner (1997)) fall under what Martin (2004) has referred to as the integration perspective. Although frameworks adhering to the integration perspective are very popular among business scholars and practitioners, they also have the least empirical support. There is therefore a need for cultural scholars to seek alternative perspectives to corporate culture. Fortunately, many other frameworks of corporate culture do not adhere to the overly simplistic integration perspective. These alternative frameworks support the idea that multiple cultures coexist in the same time and space and that these cultures evolve. These frameworks adhere to what Martin (2004) has called the differentiation and fragmentation perspectives of corporate culture. Such frameworks form the focus of attention in Chapter 6 of this book.

Note

1 Alvesson explained that societal changes have led to the creation of identities that are weaker and more vulnerable than those that existed in the past. Due to ongoing sociocultural changes, people are becoming more open-minded and culturally flexible than former generations. Similar sociocultural fragmentation is also brought about by increased complexity, turbulence and technocratization of the world.

Additional reading

M. Alvesson (1987) 'Organizations, culture, and ideology', *International Studies of Management and Organizations* 27(3): 4–18.

6 Understanding corporate culture

The differentiation and fragmentation perspectives

Scientific thought, then, is not momentary; it is not a static instance; it is a process.

Jean Piaget

What you will learn in this chapter:

- the dynamic conceptualization of corporate culture;
- Joanne Martin's differentiation and fragmentation perspectives of corporate culture;
- different frameworks of corporate culture adhering to the differentiation and fragmentation perspectives and their critique;
- ongoing debates in corporate culture literature;
- locating different perspectives of corporate culture along different epistemological stances.

Introduction

In the previous chapter, we wrote of the scholars who have chosen to focus on the corporate level of culture rather than the national, societal or regional levels. Many scholars also have believed that companies carry within themselves one set of values or guiding principles that control the behaviour of all the employees in the company. In other words, they have supported the idea of homogenous and static corporate culture in companies. This perspective of corporate culture is what Joanne Martin (2002, 2004) has referred to as the integration perspective. Chapter 5 of this volume elaborates on such frameworks (e.g. frameworks offered by Hofstede *et al.* (1990) and Trompenaars and Hampden-Turner (1997)) and points out the limitations of frameworks adhering to this perspective. Fortunately, cultural scholars and practitioners have recourse to other frameworks that adopt very different approaches to corporate culture. The proponents of these alternative frameworks have conceptualized and defined corporate culture as dynamic.

Consider Ogbonna and Harris's (2002) conceptualization of organizational culture. Their definition of corporate culture draws from the views of Schein (1992), DiBella (1993) and Hatch (1993) and states that organizational culture is the dynamic set of assumptions, values and artefacts, whose meanings are collectively shared in a given social unit at a particular point in time. Much before Ogbonna and Harris (2002), Gray, Bougon and Donneilon (1985) expressed dissatisfaction with the static conceptualization of corporate culture. They complained that, in focusing on what is stable and permanent about organizations, one loses sight of the dynamicity of organizational life. Instead, Gray *et al.* (1985) preferred to conceptualize organizations as construction and deconstruction of meaning. The advantage of this conceptualization is that, rather than viewing organizations as being static and stable entities, it draws attention to the contradictions and changes of meanings and power struggles observable in all organizations. Thompson and Wildavsky (1986: 293) also have a similar conceptualization of corporate culture. They described an organization as follows:

> An organization is not so much a conceptual scheme as a structure that is sustained and transformed by a multiplicity of conflicting and contradictory conceptual schemes. In all but the simplest of such structures (and perhaps not even there), the clear faith in a single well-defined organizational goal soon runs out into the sands of diverse conflicting goals; as it does, the unitary information culture that characterizes the upper reaches of an organization's structure rapidly gives way to the seething plurality of conflicting information cultures that so enriches life among the lowerarchs.

Broadly speaking, Joanne Martin (2002, 2004) (for full reference to the work of Martin 2002, see the additional reading section) categorized such pluralistic frameworks of corporate culture as falling within the differentiation and fragmentation perspectives. The present chapter will discuss these frameworks.

Corporate culture frameworks adhering to the differentiation perspective

Martin (2004) has explained that unlike frameworks adhering to the integration perspective (see Chapter 5), frameworks adhering to the differentiation perspective support cultural plurality in organizations. According to this perspective, subcultures often appear along lines of functional, occupational and hierarchical differentiation (see Smircich 1983, Van Maanen in Frost *et al.* 1991). Sometimes subcultural differences also reflect demographic differences (e.g. race, ethnicity, age and gender). Martin and Siehl's (1983) work on organizational cultures deserves a special mention here as they have supported the idea that organizational cultures are composed of at least three types of subcultures: enhancing, orthogonal and countercultural. An enhancing subculture exists when members of an organization choose to adhere to the core values of the dominant culture rather than those found in other pockets of the organization. In an orthogonal subculture, members simultaneously accept core values of the dominant culture while maintaining a separate set of values of their own. Conversely, in a counterculture, some core values of a counterculture present a direct challenge to the core values of a dominant culture. In such a context, a dominant culture and a counter-culture might exist in an uneasy symbiosis, taking opposite positions on value issues that are critically important to each of them. Many differentiation scholars (Willmott 1993, Alvesson 2002) conceptualized culture as a partially successful attempt by management to exercise hegemonic control over lower-ranking employees. This will result in an environment where some employees choose to comply with the demands of the management, while others resist such demands (Martin 2004).

Martin (2004) provided many examples of frameworks adhering to the differentiation perspective. She reviewed the study by Bartunek and Mock (in Frost *et al.* 1991) in which they showed that there is a variety of subcultures within a food production firm and that consensus exists within subcultural boundaries. Similarly, in Van Maanen's (in Frost *et al.* 1991) study, several cultures were found to coexist in Disneyland. Largely, hierarchical status dictated cultural distinctions. For example, food vendors had a lower status, and ride operators enjoyed a higher status. A similar cultural typology was also observed in Young's (in Frost *et al.* 1991) study of 'bag ladies' in a British manufacturing plant. In this case, they observed that two distinct subcultures split the younger and older employees. While we refrain from discussing frameworks adhering to the differentiation perspective in detail, from the examples cited in this paragraph, it is clear that scholars supporting the differentiation perspective have recognized the cultural plurality in organizations. However, while differentiation studies have attempted to question the oversimplified coherence of the integration view, they have continued to emphasize consistency, consensus and clarity, this time within a subculture, and they have continued to relegate ambiguities to the interstices among subcultures (Martin 2004). In comparison, scholars adhering to the fragmentation perspective have gone much further in exploring cultural plurality, cultural change and ambiguity. Next, we discuss the fragmentation perspective of corporate culture.

Corporate culture frameworks adhering to the fragmentation perspective

Similar to the scholars who adhere to the differentiation perspective (see the previous section), followers of the fragmentation perspective have also argued that, although the term 'corporate culture' is often used as if companies have an internally homogenous and stable culture, in fact, most companies house a variety of belief systems that leads to the emergence of a variety of cultures, each with its own preferences and characteristics. However, unlike differentiation scholars, fragmentation scholars have argued that corporate culture affects each employee of a company and, in turn, the employee takes an active part in re-creating the corporate culture through daily networking with other employees (Smircich 1983). According to this viewpoint, corporate culture is dynamic and evolving (Martin 2004). Martin (2004) has explained that, in fragmentation studies (for example, see Feldman in Frost *et al.* 1991, Meyerson in Frost *et al.* 1991, Weick in Frost *et al.* 1991, Robertson and Swan 2003[1]), claims of clarity, consensus and consistency are believed to be oversimplifications that fail to capture the complexity of today's companies. Rather than neglecting ambiguity (as integration scholars do) or relegating ambiguities to subcultural interstices (as differentiation scholars prefer), fragmentation studies treat ambiguity as an integral feature of organizational culture.

Fragmentation scholars, therefore, take a much more dynamic approach to culture than differentiation scholars. According to the fragmentation perspective, if consensus exists, it is issue-specific. Networks emerge when an issue emerges, and they disappear as soon as the issue disappears. These networks are therefore in a constant state of flux. From this perspective, 'culture looks less like a monolith and less like a collection of subcultural islands, and more like a roomful of spiderwebs, constantly being destroyed and rewoven' (Martin, 2004: 10–11).

According to fragmentation studies, change is a constant flux rather than an intermittent interruption in an otherwise stable state. Since environmental factors or other factors beyond the individual's control can trigger change, fragmentation scholars have offered few guidelines for controlling the change process. We find the following description of the fragmentation perspective by Meyerson and Martin (1987: 638) to be particularly eloquent:

> Individuals are nodes in the web, temporarily connected by shared concerns to some but not all the surrounding nodes. When a particular issue becomes salient, one pattern of connections becomes relevant. That pattern would include a unique array of agreements, disagreements, pockets of ignorance, and hypocrisy. A different issue would draw attention to a different pattern of connections. ... patterns of attention are transient and several issues and interpretations – some of which are irreconcilable – may become salient simultaneously. ... the web itself is a momentary and blurred image, merely a single frame in a high speed motion picture.

Considering that fragmentation scholars consider culture to be a set of transient patterns that link people together, it is logical that cultures change continually. This contrasts with the differentiation perspective whose proponents conceptualize cultural change as a one-time event involving an organization-wide shift from one way of being to another. While both the integration and differentiation perspectives ignore ambiguity, proponents of the fragmentation perspective ignore patterns of stability. For them, cultural change is ongoing and virtually beyond the control of managers. Thus, fragmentation scholars offer a much more dynamic conceptualization of culture and a more realistic representation of organizational life compared to integration and differentiation scholars. However, since these fragmentation scholars focus excessively on awareness of ambiguity, it becomes nearly impossible to make sense of social change. According to this perspective, since cultural change is perceived as never-ending and chaotic, it becomes difficult for the culture scholar systematically to study cultural change and to discern a clear pattern in the change process. This leads us to ask another question: is there a cultural framework that allows for a dynamic conceptualization of culture and simultaneously permits a systematic explanation of social change? We hope to revert to this question in subsequent chapters of this book.

For now, we present two examples of corporate culture frameworks: Quinn and Rohrbaugh's (1983) Competing Values Framework (CVF) and Max Boisot's (2000) I-Space framework. We would like to point out that these frameworks meet many but not all the criteria described in this section of the fragmentation perspective. Hence, strictly speaking, we would locate these two frameworks (CVF and I-Space framework) between the differentiation and fragmentation perspectives.

Quinn and Rohrbaugh's Competing Values Framework

The Competing Values Framework (CVF) was developed by Quinn and Rohrbaugh in 1983. These scholars offered two value dimensions to explain organizational effectiveness: (1) internal versus external focus and (2) flexibility versus stability and control. Plotting these two dimensions against one another resulted in four cultures: clan, adhocracy, market and hierarchy. The four cultural types of CVF are discussed in Table 6.1.

As Braunscheidel, Nallan and Boisnier (2010) have explained, CVF offers cultural types that are modal and not mutually exclusive (Cameron and Quinn 1999, Deshpande, Farley and Webster 1993). This is a very important point of distinction between CVF and other integration and differentiation frameworks discussed earlier in this book. The fact that the cultural types of CVF are modal and not mutually exclusive implies that movements are possible along the underlying dimensions (i.e. internal versus external focus and stability versus flexibility). Unlike the static categorizations of the integration frameworks, the cultural types of CVF are flexible. Some scholars have supported the concept that, although the four cultures proposed by CVF are present in an organization, only one dominates at a point in time (Deshpande *et al.* 1993). Cameron and Quinn (1999) have explained that one or more of the four culture types offered by the framework have characterized more than 80 per cent of the thousands of organizations they have studied. Cameron and Quinn (1999) have gone so far as to claim that those organizations who do not reveal a dominant cultural type are either unclear about their culture or

Table 6.1 The four cultures of the Competing Values Framework (Quinn and Rohrbaugh 1983)

The Hierarchy Culture	As Cameron and Quinn (2006) have explained, this culture (also called the bureaucratic culture) has an internal organizational focus, and it emphasizes control and stability. The cherished values are order, uniformity, efficiency and rules and regulations. Leaders in this kind of culture are cautious, and they are good coordinators and organizers. The strategic emphasis in such a culture is on permanence and stability.
The Market Culture	According to Cameron and Quinn (1998), the market culture has an external organizational focus. In other words, it focuses attention on external constituencies such as suppliers, customers, contractors, licensees, unions, regulators and others. However, at the same time, it stresses stability (as opposed to flexibility). Goal achievement, productivity, profitability, efficiency and competitiveness are valued, and these are achieved through a strong emphasis on external positioning and control. Leaders are identified as directive, decisive and instrumental. The strategic focus is on competition and performance (Cameron and Quinn 2006).
The Clan Culture	For Cameron and Quinn (2006), a clan culture stresses internal focus and flexibility. A clan is characterized by teamwork, employee involvement programs and corporate commitment to the employee (Cameron and Quinn 1998). Loyalty, trust, cohesiveness, participation, sense of family, affiliation, involvement and tradition are valued. Leaders demonstrate mentoring, facilitating and supportive and participative styles. The strategic focus is on human development, teamwork, morale and organizational commitment (Cameron and Quinn 2006).
The Adhocracy Culture	As Cameron and Quinn (2006) have explained, the adhocracy culture emphasizes external positioning and flexibility. The core values of its members are innovation, entrepreneurship, adaptability, dynamism, creativity and development. Leaders demonstrate the ability to take risks, to be entrepreneurial and to be innovative. The strategic focus is on growth and on obtaining new resources.

Source: Quinn and Rohrbaugh (1983)

emphasize the four types equally. Another salient feature of CVF is that it allows scholars to measure organizational culture based on competing choices. This is consistent with the fact that, when faced with competing demands regarding the marketplace, firms have to make competing choices arising from competitive pressures.

In our understanding, what makes CVF interesting is that it allows for cultural plurality in organizations. While other scholars (Hofstede *et al.* 1990,

Trompenaars and Hampden-Turner 1997) have claimed that a company may have only one type of corporate culture commonly held by all its employees (see Chapter 4 for a discussion of integration frameworks of culture), Quinn and Rohrbaugh (1983) have suggested that cultural plurality in organizations is inevitable. This makes CVF significantly different from and much more flexible than the integration and most of the differentiation frameworks of corporate culture. Further, CVF proponents have elucidated that the cultural type might not be consistent across different units of the firm. For example, while an organization might be a market type on leadership styles, it could be a clan type on strategic emphasis (Deshpande *et al.* 1993). As Braunscheidel, Nallan and Boisnier (2010) have explained, one major advantage of this framework is that it allows for systematic cultural comparisons across different levels, including organizations and nations. The framework has already been applied to explore culture in a wide variety of areas such as healthcare (Gregory, Harris, Armenakis and Shook 2009), manufacturing (McDermott and Stock 1999), libraries (Shepstone and Currie 2008) and the military (Yardley and Neal 2007). It has also been used to study culture across countries (Ubius and Alas 2009) and across a variety of different scenarios (Quinn and Kimberly 1984). The fact that CVF can be used to study culture across different levels and different scenarios implies that it meets one very important criterion we have evoked in earlier chapters of this book: if an innovative framework of culture were identified, then that would make it possible for us to use the same framework across a variety of levels and scales and alleviate the need to rely on a plethora of frameworks. Based on our discussion so far, it would seem that CVF meets this criterion. Further, over the years, proponents of CVF have contributed much towards consolidating its credibility as a framework of culture. As Cameron and Quinn (2006) have explained, the validity of CVF has been assessed through studies conducted in over 10,000 organizations globally. Another advantage of CVF is that, although it allows for a systematic study of a dominant culture in an organization, it does not undermine the simultaneous existence of other cultures in organizations.

However, CVF also has certain drawbacks. For instance, we find that, although it meets many of the criteria of the fragmentation perspective, its proponents do not explicitly focus on cultural ambiguity and on cultural change. This, however, does not mean that CVF does not have the capacity to explain cultural change. For example, the framework dictates that a market culture emerges when the focus is on external stakeholders and on stability. However, one may argue that, prompted by internal and external factors, agents may decide to shift the focus towards flexibility, while retaining the focus on external stakeholders. This implies that a shift from a market to an adhocracy culture can occur by changing one's position on the underlying dimensions. We do not wish to imply that bringing about this cultural shift is an easy task. Instead, the point we wish to make is that the framework itself has the potential to explain cultural change, and this has not yet been fully exploited. Second, Hartnell *et al.* (2011) explained that reducing the discussion of the four cultural types offered by this framework to only one or more dominant cultural types may be a mistake. Focusing on dominant cultural types decreases the usefulness of the framework because these dominant cultural types cannot account for the full range of cultures seen in organizations. Denison and Spreitzer (1991) also have explained that an organization may have a unique combination of different cultural types. Therefore, reducing the discussion of organizational culture to a few dominant cultural types implies ignoring the synergistic interactions between the different value systems that make up the organization.

Following the original framework exposed in Quinn and Rohrbaugh's (1983) study, Deshpande and his colleagues (1993) explored the impact of corporate culture on performance in Japanese firms. They found that Japanese companies in which market and adhocracy cultures dominated outperformed those firms that had a dominant clan or hierarchical culture. Deshpande *et al.* (1993) explained that the market culture characterized by its emphasis on competitive advantage and market superiority is likely to be the best in business performance, and the hierarchical culture with its emphasis on order would perform unsatisfactorily. In the same vein, they argued that they could expect adhocracies with their focus on entrepreneurship to perform better than clans whose loyalty, tradition and focus on internal maintenance could lead them to ignore market needs. In effect, they demonstrated that each cultural type in CVF has its strengths and weaknesses. They also found that, although the most predominant self-reported cultural type is a clan, all four types of cultures are well represented in the sample. They claimed that, in all cases, the self-reported cultures of individual firms contained elements of more than one cultural type. They concluded that organizational cultural plurality is more a matter of degrees of variations rather than whether or not the different cultures are present in the organization. In particular, the Japanese firms studied showed characteristics of both clans and markets. Although we agree with Deshpande *et al.*'s (1993) observation that all four cultures can coexist in organizations and that each has certain strengths and weaknesses, we find the argument that effectiveness is highest with the market culture and lowest with hierarchies to be less convincing. We believe that a variety of contingency variables contribute to the effectiveness of a firm. Therefore, the culture that drives effectiveness and performance could change over time as a function of different contingency variables (see Patel and Patel 2008 for further details). Rather than assuming that one cultural type is more effective than the other is, we support that a firm may need to support a variety of cultural strategies at different stages of its evolution if it aims to remain effective over a long period.

Max Boisot's I-Space framework

Boisot (2000) has defined organizations[2] as data processing and data sharing entities. He has explained that corporations contain agents who need to structure and share information to suit both the insiders (whom he calls the hierarchies) and the outsiders (meaning the markets). In so doing, Boisot has referred to two forms of cultures often evoked in past literature: markets and hierarchies (see Williamson 1975). Citing his own earlier work (Boisot 1998) and that of other experts (see March and Simon 1958), Boisot has explained that, due to lack of time, agents often minimize the amount of data they need to process and transmit. Moreover, agents prefer structured data since it is easy to transmit. Boisot (2000) then raised a very interesting question: how is data processed into meaningful structures? He explained that data processing has two dimensions: codification and abstraction. He defined codification as the creation of categories to which phenomena can be assigned together with the rules of assignment. By contrast, uncodified categories and rules of assignment are fuzzy and ambiguous. Abstraction is about establishing the minimum number of categories required to make such an assignment meaningful.

Relative to different levels of codification and abstraction and relative to whether or not data is diffused, Boisot explained that different kinds of information environments or cultures can be generated in companies. Further, differences in the possibilities of structuring and sharing data can bring forth distinctive cultural practices and institutional arrangements. In other words, different information cultures can be generated based on how agents choose to structure and share data. Boisot identified the four kinds of information environments diagrammatically represented in Figure 6.1.

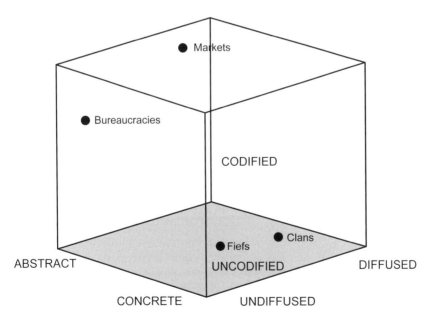

Figure 6.1 The four information cultures of Boisot's I-Space Model
Source: Boisot (2000)

Table 6.2 Characteristics of the four cultures of Boisot's I-Space framework

Markets	Bureaucracies
• Information widely diffused, no control • Relationships impersonal and competitive • No superordinate goals, each individual for himself • Hierarchical coordination through self-regulation • No necessity to share values and beliefs	• Information diffusion limited and under central control • Relationships impersonal and hierarchical • Submission to superordinate goals • Hierarchical coordination • No necessity to share values and beliefs
Fiefs	*Clans*
• Information diffusion limited by lack of codification to face-to-face relationships • Relationships personal and hierarchical (feudal/charismatic) • Submission to superordinate goals • Hierarchical coordination • Necessity to share values and beliefs	• Information diffusion limited by lack of codification to face-to-face relationships • Relationships personal but non-hierarchical • Goals are shared through a process of negotiation • Horizontal coordination through negotiation • Necessity to share values and belief

Source: Boisot (2000)

Table 6.2 describes the characteristics of each of the four cultures of Boisot's (2000) framework.

Boisot further explained that these four information cultures (i.e. bureaucracies, markets, fiefs and clans) act as what mathematicians call attractors in the I-Space – pulling in and shaping any transactions located in their neighbourhood. In other words, Boisot has treated these information cultures as dynamic with each one trying to attract more adherents within its own space. Another interesting point that distinguishes the work of Boisot from that of other researchers in the field of corporate culture is that, although beginning at the level of corporate culture, his approach does not end there. Like CVF, Boisot's I-Space framework can also be applied at and across different levels: corporation, nation, societies, industries, etc. Boisot has now moved his argument about the four kinds of information cultures found in companies to the level of functional or professional groupings as seen in specific departments. He explained that people involved in different professions also exhibit cultural traits of each of the four kinds of information cultures (see Figure 6.2). The firm itself, as Boisot has explained, would accommodate the four information cultures. Doing this would require some integration efforts because if one of the four cultures is allowed to dominate at the expense of the others, then dysfunctional behaviours are likely to appear. He has given the classic example of the commonly cited conflict that occurs in companies between the Marketing and Sales (M&S) teams with their counterparts in the Research

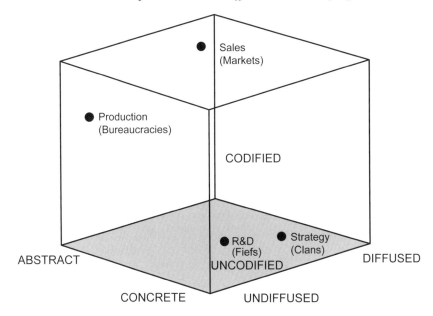

Figure 6.2 Functional or professional manifestations of different cultures in the
           I-Space framework
Source: Boisot (2000)

and Development (R&D) departments. A strong sales department focused on
well-identified customer needs in a competitive environment often works
under strict time frames. The R&D departments often have a more long-term
and 'blue skies' approach. If the sales department dominates, it is likely to
undermine the interests of the R&D department. In the same way, those
involved with production often have a preference for the bureaucratic information culture and those involved in the creation and implementation of
strategies are often members of clans (see Figure 6.2).

Figure 6.2 shows that members of different functional or professional
groups might exhibit cultural traits of different information cultures and that
the four cultures exist in every company. Next Boisot (2000) extended the
argument to the level of industries (see Figure 6.3). He explained that, while
emergent industries might exhibit the cultural traits of fiefs, oligopolic industries would behave as clans. While monopolistic industries would act like
bureaucracies, competitive industries would exhibit cultural traits of markets.

Boisot's (2000) framework of information cultures goes far beyond the
frameworks of corporate culture discussed in earlier sections of this chapter
and in Chapter 5 of this volume. It is an excellent example of a dynamic
framework of culture that allows for cultural plurality within an organization
and allows for cultural change. However, its biggest advantage is that it can
be applied to varied levels: company, intra-company or interdepartmental,
industry, etc. It is therefore an example of a framework of culture that goes

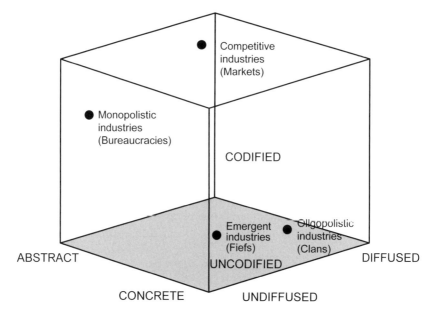

Figure 6.3 Industry structures in the I-Space framework
Source: Boisot (2000)

beyond the geo-ethnic definitions of culture. We believe that Boisot's framework
has the ability to provide us many more insights than have been presently
exposed. For instance, Boisot stopped short of discussing how, if an information
culture were allowed to dominate, it would undermine other information
cultures and the overall system. He did not explain how each culture competes with the others to establish its dominancy within the social system. In
addition, he did not explicitly explore the relationship of interdependence that
exists between members of the four cultures. If we consider Boisot's earlier
example of the ongoing competition between members of the M&S department
and those of the R&D department of a company, we agree with Boisot that
allowing any one of these departments (and thereby the cultures they represent)
to dominate would lead to dysfunctional relationships. Nonetheless, we also
believe that, despite their mutual rivalry, these two information cultures need
one another for their survival. For example, the M&S department would not
be able to make sales if the R&D personnel did not go beyond the immediate
needs of the market and imagine new products and services that consumers
might use in the future. On the other hand, if R&D people were left to
themselves, they would no doubt produce amazing products. However, without
the timely orientation of these efforts towards the needs of the customers,
which is inherently the focus of M&S personnel, the most imaginative and
creative products would remain on the shelf forever. For a company to be truly
competitive, it needs both these information cultures to coexist despite their
inherent differences and rivalry. The same argument can also be extrapolated

to the other two information cultures, i.e. bureaucracies and fiefs. Boisot's I-Space framework thus offers many advantages over the frameworks adhering to the integration and differentiation perspectives of corporate culture (see Chapter 5 and earlier sections of Chapter 6).

In the previous sections of this chapter, we have introduced two different perspectives of corporate culture found in extant literature: the differentiation and fragmentation perspectives. We have also offered examples of frameworks adhering to each of these perspectives. In the next section, we conclude our discussion on corporate culture by eliciting some of the unresolved debates in corporate culture literature.

Unresolved debates in corporate culture literature

In Chapters 5 and 6 of this volume, we have focused on addressing culture at the corporate or organizational level. We have reviewed frameworks that adhere to three different perspectives (integration, differentiation and fragmentation), which allow for different degrees of dynamicity and plurality in addressing corporate culture. However, this does not imply that the domain of corporate culture studies is now free from disagreements. If anything, the field is rife with unresolved debates; we now discuss some of them.

The first unresolved debate in the study of corporate culture concerns the conceptualization of an organization or a company as a cultural entity. As Alvesson (1987) has explained, many scholars exploring culture at the corporate level have made the mistake of juxtaposing organization and culture. In other words, they have viewed organizations as a unit whose boundaries surround a type of cultural entity. This implies that a member of said organization shares cultural similarities with other members of that organization and differs significantly from members of other organizations. However, another stream of literature on meanings, sense-making and symbols in organizations contradicts this viewpoint. Proponents of such literature have not referred explicitly to corporate or organizational culture and have not conceptualized organizations as a kind of cultural entity. They have pointed out, however, that complex organizations contain a number of different groups, social classes, professions, interest groups and departments/subunits (see Morey and Luthans 1985). Other scholars from this school of thought (such as Pfeffer 1981) have pointed out that organizations may have several subunits, which each have their own shared meanings, ideologies and sub-paradigms. They have also suggested that the arguments applicable to total organizations can also be made, though to a lesser degree, with respect to subunits within those organizations. Still other scholars have questioned even the idea of addressing culture at the level of subunits. They have argued that even people within a subunit do not always share common values, and, even within specific subunits or departments, there may be groups with different cultural attributes. Consistent with this line of arguments, scholars such as Van Maanen and Barley (1984) proposed the concept of 'occupational communities'[3] as an alternative way of making sense of culture in organizations. For Van Maanen and Barley (1984), distinctive work cultures characterize these occupational communities that promote self-control and collective autonomy for their members. Such communities do not exist only within the boundaries of a specific organization, but they may be found in various organizations and, possibly, also outside them, e.g. among physicians and lawyers. They often have interest organizations of their own, such as unions or professional societies, which may put pressure on the organizations in which the members are employed. To sum up, the question of whether or not an organization or company is the right level of focus when attempting to understand culture is far from resolved.

Another very important debate concerns whether or not corporate cultures can really be 'managed' by managers and to what extent managers control cultural change. Although it is tempting to believe that companies can and do manage their cultures, many scholars (many of whom support the fragmentation perspective of corporate culture) believe that corporate cultures are so dynamic that attempting to control them is a futile exercise. As an example of the latter school of thought, Martin and Siehl (1983: 53) have explained,

> It is likely that cultural development, like other aspects of organizational functioning, is not as responsive to direct managerial attempts at control as many would like to believe. It may be that cultures cannot be straightforwardly created or managed by individuals. Instead, cultures may simply exist and managers may capitalize on cultural effects they perceive as positive or minimize those perceived as negative. Perhaps the most that can be expected is that a manager can slightly modify the trajectory of a culture rather than exert major control over the direction of its development.

Taking a more balanced viewpoint, Ogbonna and Harris (2002) explained that, whilst the view that organizations can easily change their cultures may be overly optimistic, the opposite viewpoint that organizational culture cannot be changed at all might be overly rigid. Both extremes of the culture management debate suffer from 'cultural schizophrenia' (Fiol 1991: 192). Instead, Ogbonna and Harris (2002) have argued that, although organizational culture can and does change, the direction and impact of the change cannot be subject to conscious action of management.

Concluding remarks

To sum up, we find that, over time, researchers have proposed different frameworks of corporate culture by building on the strengths of existing frameworks and attempting to overcome the limitations of their predecessors' work. In this summary section, we relate our observations regarding the evolutions in corporate culture literature with shifting epistemological stances in culture studies. Broadly speaking, we find that, similar to our observations regarding conventional frameworks explored in Chapters 3 and 4 of this volume, corporate culture literature also seems to be going through a gradual shift from a functionalist to a more postmodernistic epistemological standpoint.

As explained in Chapter 1 of this book, functionalist researchers have defined culture as the static and unchanging characteristics of a group. Stability is widely emphasized in the functionalist tradition and often considered intrinsic to the definition of culture itself. For instance, Schein (1991: 245–48) declared that 'culture implies stability' and that 'if things are ambiguous, then, by definition, that group does not have a culture'. In line with this discussion, it seems logical to say that the frameworks adhering to the integration perspective of corporate culture seem to follow the functionalist tradition. Not only do proponents of the integration perspective support the idea of organization-wide cultural stability, uniqueness and homogeneity, they also underplay ambiguity and reject any behaviour that does not fit into the so-called corporate culture (Martin and Meyerson 1988). As seen in our earlier discussion, proponents of the differentiation perspective have acknowledged cultural plurality in organizations, but they continue to conceptualize subcultures as internally homogenous and stable entities and to channel ambiguity towards the interstices between subcultural groups. Hence, differentiation scholars also seem to adhere to the functionalist tradition. Out of the three perspectives towards organizational culture, only the fragmentation perspective acknowledges ambiguity and supports the idea of cultural dynamicity and plurality in organizations. As a perfect illustration of the fragmentation perspective, Baudrillard (1988) conceptualized culture as a 'network of floating signifiers that offers momentary seduction rather than the ability to store and transmit meaning' (Poster 1988: 3). We find that this standpoint is more in line with the postmodernist tradition where the focus is 'on the processual as opposed to structural character of human institutions' (Cooper and Burrell 1988: 100 as cited by Schultz and Hatch 1996). However, note that the fragmentation frameworks that we have cited in this chapter (CVF and I-Space framework) do not take the same extreme postmodernist stance that one finds in the work of Baudrillard (1988). Therefore, they can be located somewhere between the interpretive[4] and postmodernist traditions. Interpretive researchers, as we know, focus on the interrelated cyclic processes of interpretation, sense-making, understanding and action (Weick 1979, Smircich and Morgan 1982, Czamiawska-Joerges 1992, Hatch 1993) rather than on the ruptures, discontinuity and fragmentation of sense-making (cf. Clifford and Marcus 1986). We find that, in line with the interpretative tradition, CVF and the I-Space framework both offer at best a static representation of a dynamic process. However, in line with the postmodernist tradition, both the frameworks have the inherent potential of explaining cultural change as a never-ending and unpredictable phenomenon. Hence, we place these frameworks between the interpretative and postmodernist standpoints.

Having located the different corporate culture frameworks covered in Chapters 5 and 6 of this volume along different epistemological standpoints, we now present our own take on corporate culture. For us, culture is the outcome of ongoing interactions between individuals and their social contexts. We also believe that people's behaviours change as they move from one context to another. While we support the idea of cultural change as an ongoing and never-ending process as opposed to cultures as stable and unchanging, we do not believe that cultural change is as chaotic and unpredictable as some postmodernist scholars (see Baudrillard 1988) claim. We believe that there are certain discernible systematic patterns of human behaviour despite the semblance of chaos and volatility in the process of cultural change. In other words (and to answer the question raised earlier in this chapter), we do believe that, if a credible framework of culture is identified, then we might be able to conceptualize culture as dynamic and plural, while simultaneously allowing for a systematic explanation of social change. We will elaborate more on this in Part III (Chapters 7, 8 and 9) of this book. However, in order to do this, we need to transcend the disciplinary boundaries of business studies and seek help from other disciplines. Therefore, in Part III of this volume, we turn towards the discipline of anthropology. In anthropology, the idea of unique cultures and the notion of individuals as passive recipients of culture has long since been rejected (McSweeney 2009). Hence, we believe that business scholars have much to gain from a review of anthropology literature on culture.

Notes

1 Robertson and Swan (2003) have explained that managerial attempts to develop a strong consensual corporate culture have little to do with generating real commitment on the part of the employees and more to do with the management attempting to exercise hegemonic control over its employees. Based on this understanding, a 'strong culture' largely serves the management's purpose by limiting the independence and autonomy of the employees to choose the values they wish to adopt, as opposed to those imposed on them by the management.
2 Boisot (2000) uses the terms organizations and corporations interchangeably.
3 For Van Maanen and Barley (1984), an occupational community is a group of people who are involved in the same kind of work. Hence, these people share common values, norms and perspectives. The bonds that members of an occupational community share are by no means limited only to the work context; their relationships expand into the social spheres of their lives.
4 Interpretive researchers stress instability or fluctuation in culture research (Meyerson and Martin 1987, Martin 1992, Hatch 1993) and criticize functionalist scholars for ignoring ambiguity (Frost *et al.* 1991: 8) and 'that which is unclear, unstable, and disorderly' (Meyerson 1991: 255).

Additional reading

J. Martin (2004) *Organizational Culture: Mapping the terrain*, Sage Publications: London, New Delhi.

Part III

Alternative cultural paradigms and their comparison to conventional cultural paradigms

7 Introducing the transactional culture approach

We need to see our empirical work as an obligation, to acquit as best we can by critically using the variety of methods and concepts available to us at any one time, not by only performing the operations that are most fashionable or refined. But we equally need to regard every new empirical finding as a provocation, to rethink our assumptions and redesign our models. Pursued in this fashion, social anthropology promises to be as exciting in the future as it has been in the past.

Fredrik Barth

What you will learn in this chapter:

- Fredrik Barth's dissatisfaction with the structural-functional approaches popular in his time;
- Fredrik Barth's transactional approach, his concept of rationalities and his understanding of social change;
- the contribution of other transactional culture theorists towards engendering a better understanding of culture;
- the strengths and weaknesses of the transactional culture approach.

Introduction

In Part II of this book (Chapters 3–6), we selectively focused on cultural frameworks that have gained popularity among business scholars in past decades. In contrast, in Part III (Chapters 7–9), we resort to anthropology literature in search of alternative cultural frameworks. In the present chapter, we draw on Bruce Kapferer's (1976) *Transactions and Meaning*, in which he provided an excellent synopsis of the work done in the domain of transactional culture theory or exchange theory by different anthropologists. Kapferer (1976) explained that approaches to the study of transactional and exchange behaviour are extremely diverse. In their broadest usage, the terms 'transaction' and 'exchange' refer to patterned transference of 'items' both material (shells, animals, food and labour) and immaterial (status and power) between individuals and groups (Kapferer 1976). Gilsenan (1976) added an interesting element to the transaction theory. He underlined that it is important to examine the process of communication and meaning in transactional activity because what is apparently transacted or communicated is not necessarily what is received or understood. The transactor cannot be separated from what is transacted. Actors, as Mauss argued, also transact aspects of their own identity via the transaction. Transactions are symbolic and their symbolic properties themselves control and direct action. Many transactional theorists proposed that meaning sets are not immutable but are fluid, and that ambiguities in symbolic activities and in the rules underlying behaviour emerge in the process of interaction (see Gilsenan in Kapferer 1976). In other words, they supported that cultural rules have a dynamic quality, capable of changing meanings and redirecting behaviour along new paths.

Ekeh (1974) categorized different approaches in transactional theory into 'individualistic' and 'collectivistic' theories. While individualistic theories derive from the British and American social anthropological tradition, collectivistic transactional theory emerges from the European sociological tradition and is best typified by the early work of Levi-Strauss, which is itself influenced by the works of Durkheim and Mauss (Kapferer 1976). There is much concern on the part of many American and British anthropologists about the individualistic turn of transactional theory and what they view as the neglect of the structure of the cultural and social systems in which exchanges and transactions take place. Despite this concern, most of the work using transactional theory in Britain and America has continued in the individualistic tradition. One name that surfaces very often in transactional theory circles is that of Fredrik Barth, a Norwegian social anthropologist. Barth is commonly acknowledged as one of the most widely read transactional scholars. The next section summarizes some key highlights of Barth's work.

Fredrik Barth's contributions to transactional culture approach

Fredrik Barth's contributions to the domain of transactional analysis remain unparalleled. According to Kapferer (1976), Barth's Model of Social Organization (1966b) can be conceived as marking a 'paradigm shift' in British social anthropology. In this work, Barth attacked the dominant orthodoxies of normative consensus and structural-functionalism for a variety of reasons (see next subsection for details). Barth's early research on Kurdish tribes had already made him realize the futility of identifying a community or a place as an 'object of study'. Therefore, he recommended that social scientists needed to shift their focus to those underlying processes that lead (or not) to the emergence of certain behavioural patterns and to the intellectual task of conceptualizing variation. We find this approach championed by Barth to be in direct contradiction to the conventional (national/regional/societal) frameworks of culture discussed in Chapter 3 of this book. Barth (1956, 1959a, 1959b) argued that, rather than assuming that culture is a structurally integrated whole, anthropologists should concentrate on both the process where various institutional elements within a society become integrated and the conditions and processes that do or do not produce generally shared meanings and understandings. Four decades after Barth's writings, Thompson and Ellis (1997) reiterated the same viewpoint and explained that a convincing theory of culture is also a theory of social relations that should be able to explain what types of social relations shape which preferences in what kinds of ways and vice versa. In the following subsections, we elaborate on various aspects of Barth's work and relate them to topics evoked in earlier chapters of this book. We begin by explaining Barth's dissatisfaction with the structural-functional orthodoxies popular in his time.

Barth's dissatisfaction with structural-functional orthodoxies of his time

In 1966, Barth (1966b) identified many limitations of the normative and structural-functional orthodoxies popular at that time. His points of disagreement with these approaches are very similar to some of the complaints levelled against conventional frameworks (static frameworks of national, regional and societal culture) that have been popular in business literature, more so since the first appearance of Hofstede's work in 1980. For instance, Barth challenged the structural-functional approaches because these approaches regarded society as a system of morals, logically prior to behaviour, and did not depict any 'intervening social process between the moral injunction and the pattern' (Kapferer 1976: 2). He found that a map depicting the world as divided into separate yet internally cohering 'societies' was an oversimplification of the terrain of social relations. He also questioned the credibility of schemas that represent society as a whole composed of parts. He argued that, if individuals form the elementary parts of any social setting, they can and will hold memberships not only in a variety of groups across different levels and scales but also in groups that span across levels and scales. Building on this argument, he further challenged the notion that smaller social entities (companies, clubs, etc.) are determined by the larger framework within which they are located (social, national and global). Instead, he explained that social entities like companies also exercise their own autonomy within these larger frameworks. Hence, it would be unfair to apply the generalizations drawn at higher levels to entities existing at lower levels and vice versa. It would be more meaningful to think of those paths by which rules and norms at one location in society interact with rules and norms in another without necessarily imagining these as smaller concentric circles embedded within larger ones.

Barth's dissatisfaction with normative and structural-functional approaches of people's behaviour also emanated from the fact that these approaches could not satisfactorily deal with a major problem area in anthropology – the matter of social change. He explained that the reason behind this was the inherent inability of these approaches to treat social behaviour as a process (Kapferer 1976). Soon other transactional scholars, such as Leach (1954), joined forces with Barth in his criticism of static models of structural-functional anthropology. In subsequent decades, other scholars like Buckley (1960), Van Velsen (1964) and Geertz (1973) also joined Barth in his criticism of modes of anthropological analysis that assumed a close integration of standardized modes of thought with observed patterns of social activity. These scholars stressed the need for a more dynamic anthropological analysis and an approach that accounted for variation as well as conformity of observed behaviour.

In the 1980s, Barth and his wife and colleague, Unni Wikan, began studying the cultural pluralism in Southern Arabia. This study further encouraged Barth to definitively abandon the simple part/whole scheme that anthropologists tended to use when discussing local and regional distribution. He concluded that some situations can be described only in terms of a much more complex schema in which parts of the local system connect in diverse and criss-crossing ways to higher levels. This encouraged Barth (see also Barth 1978) to problematize the issue of 'scales' in comparative analysis of social systems (Barth 2007).

In light of his dissatisfaction with structural-functional explanations of human behaviour, Barth began exploring other ways of cultural sense-making. This search led him to the transactional approach and the concept of 'rationality', which is discussed in the next subsection.

Barth's transactional culture approach and his concept of 'rationality'

In light of growing recognition of the limitations of normative and structural-functional explanations of human behaviour, Barth called for developing an alternative approach that would overcome these limitations and lead to the development of a 'science of social life' with hypotheses capable of being tested. By focusing on human transactions, he believed that one would be able to overcome the tendency in comparative anthropology to engage in a 'morphological matching of forms so as to locate differences' (Kapferer 1976: 3) and be better equipped to explain how cultures are generated and how they change. Barth, therefore, proposed the concept of transactions in order to analyse the construction of those social relations that are inherently built on confrontation, strategy and cooperation. As Barth (1966: 4) puts it, 'Transaction is the process which results where the parties in the course of their interaction systematically try to assure that the value gained for them is greater or equal to the value lost'. The cumulative effects of how people shape their decisions and actions in the relationship by a transactional accounting, he explained, determine many factors of human relations. Barth's transactional framework provided a way to model micro- (e.g. interpersonal) and macro- (e.g. social systems) level relationships. From this perspective, enacted behaviour of the actors is more important than the informants' accounts of patterns and customs. The keynote of Barth's approach was the emphasis he laid on explaining how various social forms, such as political alliances, units of economic production, etc., are generated. This could be achieved, Barth said, by focusing explicitly on transactional behaviour. The transaction would be viewed as subject to the rules of strategy put forward in decision and game theory models (Kapferer 1976).

Further, in attempting to explain how actors realize where their interest lies in a transaction, Barth proposed the concept of 'rationality'. He explained that, in the beginning, individuals do not really know what they want. They have a repertoire of disparate values that help them to discern the world around them, assess the courses of actions available and decide which course of action will be the most advantageous. If they perceive that there is a match between their choices and that of those around them, then this will reinforce that behaviour. However, if there is a mismatch, then they will have to readjust their values in order to do better next time. Through more experience, the repertoire of values becomes systematized and consistent with those around them (Thompson 1996).

Finally, Barth encouraged social anthropologists to focus on underlying processes that may or may not lead to certain outcomes, rather than on merely describing observed patterns and functions. He called for constructing generative models that can explain how social forms come about, rather than simply summarizing and characterizing such forms. We quote from Barth's (2007: 8) work in the following excerpt:

> A generative model seeks to identify a set of factors that, through specified operations will produce a determined output. ... A generative model is thus of a different order from the structural-functional models that were favoured at that time and even now. The structural-functional model seeks to generalize the overt form of a society and show its coherence with people's own cultural representations. A generative model tries to identify sets of regular events, processes that lend toward the emergence of such an observed form in a local or regional social system.

We believe that Barth's call for developing generative models or frameworks of culture holds even currently. As we have noted in Parts I and II of this volume, structural-functional approaches to understanding human behaviour continue to dominate business literature. We contend that business scholars who wish to conceptualize culture as dynamic have much to gain from Barth's notion of generative culture frameworks. Further, in an attempt to overcome one of the key limitations of the structural-functional approach, Barth delved into understanding the process of social change. A summary of Barth's work on social change follows.

Barth's elucidation of 'social change'

As seen in earlier sections of this chapter, one of the many reasons that led Barth to criticize the structural-functional orthodoxies of his time was their inability to explain social change. The same criticism can also be levelled against the static models of culture so popular in business studies in the latter half of the twentieth century. In his work, Barth (1967) attempted to address this challenge by emphasizing the needed attention towards studying social change empirically, towards exposing the continuity in a sequence of change and towards studying change as an ongoing process. Barth (1967) explained that, if we look at social behaviour as an allocation of time and resources, we can study the patterns where people allocate their time and resources to specific activities and any subsequent changes in the proportion of these allocations. New allocations can be observed as concrete events that may generate important change. He quoted Sharp's (1952) example of the Vir Voront women of Australia. Unlike their predecessors, Vir Voront women in the 1950s did not need to be submissive to their husbands because they no longer needed to go to them to obtain axes. Since the resource allocation is handled differently, the relation between men and women in this community has also evolved. Change in the system of resource allocation could thus be an important indicator of cultural change. As another example of social change, Barth explained that the tribal people he studied allocated less time and resources to festivals than they did before because they no longer depend on festivals to obtain certain tools. Comparing the conceptualization of social change in conventional literature with his viewpoint, Barth (1967: 663) explained that:

> In one case [i.e. in conventional literature], a social form or a whole society is seen as a morphological creature with certain requirements that need to be ascertained, in the functionalist tradition, the better to under-stand how it is put together. In the other case [in Barth's approach], a social form is seen as an epiphenomenon of a number of processes and the analysis concentrates on showing how the form is generated. Only the latter view develops concepts that directly promote the understanding of change (brackets our own).

Barth (1967) urged social anthropologists to further our understanding of social change by using concepts that make the concrete events of change available to observation and systematic description. He also added that a social anthropologist should be able to specify the nature of continuity between the situations discussed under the rubric of change. For instance, taking the example of a household, he explained that we should not rest satisfied with observing which household body has been replaced by another household body; instead, our focus should be on those circumstances in which the husband–wife set chooses to arrange their lives differently. Barth stated that any hypothesis about social change is inadequate unless it takes all the constraints of continuity into account.

Barth (1967) also addressed the question of adoption of change. He asked the question: How do people decide which change to adopt and which to reject? He explained that people make these decisions based on the pay-offs or outcomes they hope to obtain, and, more often than not, these judgements are based on their own or others' past experiences. The innovativeness of a new idea does not facilitate adoption of change; the allocation of rewards (or lack thereof) facilitates (or not) the adoption of change. If multiple options are available to the individual, the rates and kinds of pay-offs of alternative allocations within that system will determine the adoption of a certain option. Sometimes individuals misjudge the pay-offs, but such errors are reduced with increased experiences. If outcomes are in line with one's expectations or if the pay-offs are gratifying, other members of the community will attempt to engage in the same behaviour. However, if the pay-offs are below expectations or not desirable for the actor, they will desist from that behaviour and will revert to the previous set of behaviours. Finally, the allocation of rewards or pay-offs in one unit will also affect other units who are now exposed to new opportunities or feel the need for countermeasures. Therefore, the overall outcome will be the aggregate result of this ongoing competition between units and their mutual constraints.

Although Barth's work on social change does answer many questions that structural-functional scholars failed to address, he has not been able to meet all the criteria he had set for studies exploring cultural change. He had called for studies exposing the continuity in a sequence of change and of change as an ongoing process. Despite the many advances Barth has made towards our understanding of cultural change, he has not been able to address the never-ending nature of social change. Therefore, we contend that a framework of culture that better explains the non-linear, never-ending nature of social change is desired. We return to this challenge in subsequent chapters of this volume.

As seen in this section, Barth made many significant contributions towards our understanding of human behaviour. Not only did he challenge the dominance of normative and structural-functional approaches, but he also offered an alternative way of making sense of human behaviour through his discussion of transactions and rationalities. He advanced our understanding of social change and called for generative models capable of explaining the emergence of behavioural patterns. Thus, Barth made significant contributions towards advancing transactional culture literature. Yet, his work is subject to some criticism. The next section discusses the limitations in Barth's work.

Critique of Barth's transactional framework

In this section, we discuss three of the most commonly cited criticisms to Barth's transactional framework. First, Barth is often accused of overly focusing on actors pursuing 'self-interest' and 'maximization of profit' in the explanation of his transactional model and his concept of rationalities. Other proponents of the transactional approach have argued that cultural contexts are likely to govern behaviours differently. In other words, not all people define 'self-interest' in the same way. Consider, for example, individuals who define self-interest through meeting their own needs and those of their immediate kin, as opposed to those who see their self-interest inherent in the larger good of the country and the society. A second criticism of Barth's model is that it seems very likely to intrude consciously or unconsciously on the process of data selection and the recording of behaviour. For example, Asad (1972) has reanalysed Barth's early work among the Swat Pathans (1959a, 1959b), and a key point emerged from Asad's criticism of Barth's work. Since a political system at any point in time is an outcome of a different combination of factors operating at different times, it is inappropriate to specify a single mechanism leading to the generation of a political structure. Kapferer (1976) speculated that perhaps only reanalysis would provide the necessary corrections and indications as to where assumptions have intruded into ethnographic description and where significant data were excluded. Another common criticism of Barth's approach is that the empirical determination of individual or group motives and value preferences might not be easy. People do not always have clear objectives nor is it likely that they organize and rank their objectives through a means–end schema. In addition, it is very difficult to separate an actor's values from the relationship that the transactional activity produces. As we commonly observe in day-to-day life, actors often reinterpret their own motives and readjust their perspectives on commitments and relationships. Rather than generating the relationship in question, the declared motives and values may themselves be a product of the relationship. Finally, a transactional orientation such as Barth's is at once too broad and too restrictive (Kapferer 1976). While the all-encompassing nature of the model and the looseness of the definition of some of its concepts lead to tautological argument, compromising the explanatory power of the framework, it is also restrictive in the sense that it attempts to explain behaviours as transactions using a uni-dimensional model.

Barth and other researchers have understood these limitations and have attempted to overcome them. For instance, Skvoretz and Conviser (1974) devised a set of exchange rules based on whether individuals organize their actions in the form of rules pertaining to 'individualism', 'competition', 'group-gain', 'equity' or 'reciprocity' (1974: 60). In so doing, they distinguished between relationships in which individuals pursue self-interest and relationships in which individuals pursue benefits for the group. Skvoretz and Conviser (1974) also suggested a clearer definition of the concept of 'interest' and recommended that the assumption that individuals orient their activity to obtaining satisfactory benefit replace the notion that individuals pursue maximal benefit. All this constitutes a valuable revision of Barth's initial model, but it still confines the analysis of transactional activity to a restrictive idea of 'rationality', and activity continues to be in terms of receiving benefits or gain (Kapferer

1976). Therefore, we conclude that more work on the variety of rationalities and the social contexts that provoke these different forms of rationalities is desired.

As seen in this section, although Barth helped overcome many of the limitations of structural-functional approaches of culture, his work like any other conceptual framework has some limitations. Nevertheless, Barth's work inspired several other scholars. While some of the subsequent work in the field enriched transactional culture literature, some other studies also attracted further criticism. The contribution of other transactional culture scholars to the field follows in the next section.

Contributions of other transactional culture scholars and resulting challenges

The previous section shows us that the transactional culture approach, especially the work of Barth (1956), helped to overcome some of the underlying problems with the structural-functional orthodoxies of human behaviour. This inspired many other scholars to follow in the footsteps of Barth. Some of this work has led to developing and enriching the transactional culture school, and other work has generated new intellectual challenges for and debates among transactional scholars. The well-known transactional theorist Clifford Geertz stated in his famous book *The Interpretation of Cultures* (1973: 2) that culture is 'a system of inherited conceptions expressed in symbolic forms by means of which people communicate, perpetuate, and develop their knowledge about and attitudes toward life'. The function of culture is to impose meaning on the world and make it understandable. The role of anthropologists is to try to interpret the guiding symbols of each culture. Since the meaning attached to each action or symbol in every culture is different, it follows that each culture is unique and, hence, not comparable to another culture. In 1980, Geertz wrote *Negara: The Theatre State in Nineteenth-Century Bali* in which he stated that the Balinese state defies easy conceptualization by any of the familiar models popular among Western political theorists. To reduce the Balinese culture to such categories compels one to neglect what is unique about its culture. Although we appreciate Geertz's frustration with Western anthropological models, which when applied inappropriately only result in a distorted understanding of reality, we disagree with his underlying assumption that each cultural entity is so unique that it cannot be compared with any other entity. We believe that, in arguing in favour of cultural uniqueness, Geertz might have made two errors: first, he offered support to the idea of cultural infinity, thereby rendering cultural comparisons impossible; and second, he inadvertently contributed towards a widening of the east–west divide, rather than overcoming it.

Kapferer (1972), another strong champion of the transactional approach, studied Zambian workers in an Indian-owned factory. In his study, which is an excellent example of the transactional approach, he questioned why a group of workers who had been divided in one action against the management became united in another and how social relations emerge between workers through participation in urban and national environment of Kabwe and Zambia. In this study, Kapferer tried to break free from Western social scientists' obsession with dualities. Although Kapferer's work is much appreciated, some scholars are dissatisfied with it because it does not provide a consistent and systematic tool that can be applied in other cultural contexts or in other studies. In light of Kapferer's work, Boswell (1975: 787) criticized the transactional culture approach with the following observation:

> Transactional analysis takes several forms, and it is not always clear that these share anything apart from a focus on the sequence and meaningful content of interpersonal interaction. Some attempt to document empirically the utilitarian thesis of classical economics … others are concerned with symbolic interactionism. Finally, there are those whose primary concern is with the process by which regular or recurring patterns of behaviour give rise to form a social structure.

Kapferer clearly adhered to this last approach. In his own words,

> I demonstrate that the social composition of the factory is not simply a product of the processes general to the environment but that processes specific to the factory context mediate and control the extent to which general environmental processes influence its emergent structure.
>
> (Kapferer 1972: 65)

Although Kapferer (1972) made an effective use of the transactional approach, he could not provide us with a systematic approach applicable to other sociocultural contexts. However, he did acknowledge that

> An individual's behaviour is not only governed by the structure of the context within which he acts … individual behaviour is also channelled in certain directions and not others in accordance with the particular constructs or perceptions of relevant aspects of the context made by individual participants.
>
> (Kapferer 1972: 206–7)

Although he hinted here that there could be more than one direction for an individual to follow, Kapferer could not tell us how many precise directions there are and which direction an individual will choose to follow in a specific context. We will revisit this point in Chapter 8 which deals with the Douglasian Cultural Framework (DCF).

Edmund Leach (1954, 1961), another well-known transactional anthropologist, rejected Levi-Strauss's emphasis on universal properties of the human mind and insisted that similarities of patterns across cultures be understood in their ethnographic context (Tambiah 2002). Leach (1954) also identified two contrasting ideal types of political organization that alternated historically between egalitarianism and hierarchical modes (rather like the swing of a pendulum). Even though we appreciate Leach's advice to locate the cultural reality within its ethnographic context, we wonder whether there are ways to compare across cultures that take into consideration the transactional aspect and yet are not self-limiting through excessive reliance on Western dualistic typologies. We find that, through his famous pendulum metaphor, Leach (1954) may have inadvertently reinforced Western dualistic typologies, which already seem to have been very popular among anthro-pologists at that time. In other words, Leach's work revealed the underlying belief that there are only two possible states to fall back upon: either the right end of the swing of the pendulum or the left end. Like many other social scientists of our time (e.g. Durkheim's (1893) 'organic' versus 'mechanical' solidarities, Williamson's (1975) 'market' and 'hierarchies' and others), Leach reinforced the use of two-fold schemes of human behaviour. We ask whether there are transactional frameworks that allow for sense-making of cultural plurality without having to rely on such dualistic categories.

We have found our answer in McKim Marriott's (1976) *Hindu Transactions: Diversity Without Dualism*. In this extraordinary work, Marriott criticized Western social scientists of his time for having distorted the reality of the Indian subcontinent in their work by trying to reduce it to dualistic categories popular in the West. Using the simple example of the practice of food-giving and food-receiving in the Hindu caste system, Marriott proposed a four-way model to explain four strategies in ranked transactions, one for each caste in the Hindu society. These included Brahmans (optimal strategy and asymmetrical exchange), Ksatriya (maximal strategy and symmetrical exchange), Vaisya (minimal strategy and symmetrical exchange) and Sudra (pessimal strategy and asymmetrical exchange). Although Marriott did an excellent job of providing a four-fold transactional explanation of the famous Indian diversity without falling back to the self-limiting dualistic categories, he did not explicitly provide a systematic instrument to carry out the same exercise in other social systems. While Marriott admitted that transactional models, such as the one he proposed in his study, can also be generated to study other problems in other social entities, he himself did not go so far as to offer such a broadly applicable four-fold framework.

Based on the review of the contributions of different scholars to the trans-actional culture literature, we conclude that, on the positive side, the transactional analysis approach has successfully challenged the fallacies of structural-functional models of anthropological analysis available at that time. For instance, they have challenged the dominance of Western dualistic categories, which when used unwisely to make sense of culture only lead to a distorted representation of reality. By challenging such dualistic categories, transactional scholars have called for alternative and pluralistic models of culture grounded in the cultural setting in question. Conversely, on the negative side, we are now faced with transactional scholars (Geertz 1973, 1980) who sometimes assume that there are as many cultures as there are social entities. In attempting to overcome the limitations of frameworks propagating one overarching homogenizing culture (such as the structural-functional frameworks from anthropology or conventional culture frameworks from business literature), we face the dilemma of unlimited or infinite cultural types. In other words, in attempting to minimize the evils born out of the concept of 'unity', we have now ended up with the problem of 'infinity'.

Further, other limitations still plague the transactional approach. For example, although Barth has criticized the structural-functional approaches for failing to satisfactorily address social change and has attempted to rectify this error, transactional experts, including Barth, have not been able to explain change as a non-linear never-ending process. Second, neither Barth himself nor other transactional theory experts have been able to explain how individuals decide where their interests lie. Third, and as has been pointed out in earlier sections, although valuable revisions have been made to Barth's initial models, transactional analysis still remains limited to the idea of 'rationality' and activities continue to be seen in terms of receiving benefits or gains. We therefore need a framework that will be capable of explaining human behaviour in all its diversity, while simultaneously explaining the different kinds of rationalities and the social contexts that activate them. Finally, as Kapferer explained, little attention (except for Handelman 1976) has been focused on the way social relationships emerge from transactional activity 'feedback', either sustaining the relationships or obliging the actors to redefine them. Kapferer concluded that attention should be focused in transactional analysis on the structure, form and content of social relationships produced through transactional activity and on the processes of flow and feedback between the organizations and institutions, which either leads to strengthen the relationship or to dissolve it.

Concluding remarks

In this chapter, we have offered an overview of the vast and extensive literature on the anthropology-based transactional culture approach. In addition to Fredrik Barth's transactional culture framework and his concept of rationality, we have also reviewed the works of prominent scholars like Geertz, Kapferer, Leach and Marriott who have all contributed towards enriching the transactional culture approach. In reviewing transactional culture literature, we find that some transactional scholars, such as Barth, seem to adhere to an interpretive epistemological standpoint. Like interpretive scholars cited earlier in this book (Schultz and Hatch 1996), these transactional scholars are interested in the interrelated cyclic processes of interpretation, sense-making, meaning creation, understanding and action. Historically, interpretive researchers have had little patience for their functionalist colleagues whom they criticize for ignoring ambiguity (Frost *et al.* 1991: 8) and all 'that which is unclear, unstable, and disorderly' (Meyerson 1991: 255). This is another characteristic that we find common among transactional scholars such as Barth and other culture scholars adhering to the interpretive tradition.

In conclusion, as explained in the previous section of this chapter, while the transactional culture approach has helped overcome many of the limitations of the structural-functional approaches, it is still subject to certain limitations. We wonder whether there are cultural sense-making tools that, while adhering to the overall guidelines of Barth's transactional framework, also overcome some of its limitations. In other words, we are interested in identifying a cultural framework that conceptualizes culture as emerging from human transactions but, at the same time,

1. explains social change as a never-ending process;
2. offers a feedback mechanism to explain the continuity of social relationships;
3. offers a richer explanation of rationality and the social contexts that stimulate them;
4. explains the diversity of human behaviour without resorting to dualistic categories found in Western literature; and
5. supports the plurality of cultures without relying on the 'infinity' argument of culture.

Meeting all these criteria is a formidable challenge. Yet, we believe that one framework might meet these criteria satisfactorily. The framework that we refer to as the Douglasian Cultural Framework (or DCF) has its roots in the transactional culture approach and its origins in the work of Mary Douglas (1970). Although DCF has its roots in anthropology (Douglas 1978, 1982, Thompson and Ellis 1997), it has been applied in a wide variety of disciplines such as ecology (Douglas and Wildavsky 1983), political science (Thompson *et al.* 1990, Coyle and Ellis 1994, Thompson *et al.* 1999), public administration (Wildavsky 1987, 6 and Peck 2004) and business studies (Patel 2007a, 2007b, Patel and Patel 2008, Patel and Schaefer 2009, Patel and Rayner 2012a, 2012b). We present this framework in the next chapter of this book.

Additional reading

B. Kapferer, (Ed.) (1976) 'Introduction' in *Transaction and Meaning: Directions in the anthropology of exchange and symbolic behaviour*, Philadelphia, PA: ISHI.

8 Introducing the Douglasian Cultural Framework as a tool of the transactional culture approach

Each culture is a way of organizing; each is predatory on the other for time and space and resources. It is hard for them to co-exist peacefully, and yet they must, for the survival of each is the guarantee of the survival of the others. Hostility keeps them going.

Mary Douglas

What you will learn in this chapter:

- Mary Douglas's Cultural Framework (DCF);
- what makes DCF a dynamic framework of culture;
- whether and to what extent DCF meets the criteria set forth at the end of the previous chapter.

Introduction

Previously, in Chapter 7 of this volume, we outlined the contributions of anthropology-based transactional culture scholars towards cultural sense-making. We have also identified many strengths and weaknesses of the transactional culture approach. We conclude that an ideal instrument of cultural sense-making would be one that adheres to the guidelines of Fredrik Barth's transactional framework and simultaneously offers a better explanation of rationalities than Barth's concept of individuals pursuing self-interest. An ideal instrument of cultural sense-making should also be able to offer a better explanation for social change as a never-ending non-linear process than has been offered this far by transactional scholars. Similarly, it should be able to explain the feedback mechanism to illustrate the continuity of social relations. Finally, this framework should also be able to explain cultural plurality or diversity without relying on the dualistic approaches so popular among Western scholars and without automatically resorting to the infinity argument of culture. Our search for a cultural sense-making tool that would meet these criteria leads us to Mary Douglas's cultural framework.

In this chapter, we begin by introducing the work of Mary Douglas. Although many experts have referred to Douglas's work as 'Cultural Theory', Douglas herself always insisted that her framework is a heuristic device, not a 'theory'. Hence, we choose to refer to her work as the Douglasian Cultural Framework or DCF. Using DCF as a label also helps avoid confusion with other cultural frameworks and theories, which abound in business literature (see Chapters 3–6 of this volume for examples). Next, we explain how DCF was transformed over time from a somewhat static to a more dynamic framework of culture because of sustained efforts of DCF scholars, notably Michael Thompson (1996) (Thompson and Wildavsky 1986). In explaining this transition, we also present Thompson's (1996) elaboration of the impossibility theorem, the requisite variety condition and multiple rationalities. We draw our discussion of DCF to a close in Chapter 9 of this volume by comparing DCF with the conventional frameworks of culture presented in earlier chapters (Chapters 3–6) of this book, and we tease out the comparative strengths and weaknesses of each of these frameworks.

Introducing the Douglasian Cultural Framework (DCF)

Mary Douglas introduced the Douglasian Cultural Framework (DCF) in *Natural Symbols* (Douglas 1970) and expanded it in *Cultural Bias* (Douglas 1978). Since then, DCF has been applied in a wide variety of disciplines, including ecology (Douglas and Wildavsky 1983), political science (Thompson *et al.* 1990, Coyle and Ellis 1994, Thompson *et al.* 1999), public administration (Wildavsky 1987, 6 and Peck 2004) and business studies (Patel 2007a, 2007b, Patel and Schaefer 2009, Patel and Rayner 2012a, 2012b), and to explore a wide variety of topics such as perceptions towards risks (Rayner 1986), workplace crimes (Mars 1982), sports-related hooliganism (Frosdick 1995a, 1995b), and learning and innovation in organizations (Patel and Patel 2008). The basic principle in Mary Douglas's work is that people structure their ideas about the (natural and) social world in ways that are compatible with the social structures in which they find themselves at a point in time. In *Natural Symbols*, Douglas (1970) compared bodily rules of behaviour or the system of natural symbols across different cultures. Douglas explained that people's social interactions influence the system of symbols they use to make sense of the world. She hypothesized that the more value people set on social constraints, the more importance they attribute to symbols of bodily control. Thus, there is a relationship between the concepts people use to understand the world and the systematic social constraints or structures to which these people are exposed – this is the central premise of DCF. The overall aim of DCF is to serve as a tool that cultural analysts may use in order to relate differences in organizational structures to the strength of values that sustain them (Gross and Rayner 1985).

Douglas (1970) offered two social dimensions in order to classify cultures called 'group' and 'grid'. These two dimensions make up the horizontal and the vertical axes of a system of coordinates. Gross and Rayner (1985) explained that the horizontal group axis represents the extent to which people are restricted in thought and action by their commitment to a social unit larger than the individual. High group strength results when people devote a lot of their available time to interacting with other unit members. Group strength is low when people negotiate their way through life individually on their own, neither constrained by nor reliant upon any significant group. The low group experience is a competitive, entrepreneurial way of life (Gross and Rayner 1985). On the other hand, the vertical grid axis is a composite index of the extent to which people's behaviour is constrained by role differentiation, whether within or without membership of a group (Gross and Rayner 1985).

As we move along the right of the group dimension on the grid–group axis, the individual is more and more deeply committed to a group, so choices are more standardized (Douglas 1996). Gross and Rayner (1985) maintained that a high group score shows that people devote a lot of available time to inter-acting with members of a group, that the group's boundaries are clearly defined and that the group is fairly exclusive. In their book *Measuring Culture: A Paradigm for the Analysis of Social Organization*, Gross and Rayner (1985) described five predicates of the group dimension:

- Proximity: a measure of the closeness between unit members.
- Transitivity: a relationship R is considered transitive if whenever aRb and bRc, it follows that aRc.
- Frequency: the proportion of members' time during which they interact with other unit members.
- Impermeability: a measurement of the likelihood that a non-member who satisfies the requirements for membership and wants to join will actually attain membership.
- Scope: a person's involvement in the activities inside the unit, relative to the total number of activities within the unit.

The grid dimension, in turn, registers increasing complexity of discriminating rules (Douglas 1996). Gross and Rayner (1985) indicated that a high grid score occurs whenever roles are distributed on the basis of explicit public social classification, which may be based on criteria such as sex, colour, position in the hierarchy, holding a bureaucratic office, belonging to a clan or lineage or progression through an age-grade system. Conversely, grid is of low strength when these distinctions are weak and do not limit the range of available alternatives. Gross and Rayner (1985) identified the following four predicates for the grid dimension:

- Specialization: the proportion of possible roles that a member actually assumes during a typical time span.
- Asymmetry: the lack of symmetry in role exchanges among unit members.

- Entitlement: the proportion of ascribed roles compared to all roles.
- Accountability: the proportion of role interactions in which people are dominant or subordinate.

Douglas's (1970) consideration of high and low strength of grid and group gives rise to four cultures – each with its specific values, preferences and behavioural patterns, which the next subsection discusses.

The four cultures of DCF

When one plots the high and low strengths of grid and group against one another, the following four cultural types emerge at the four quadrants of the grid–group matrix:

1. Low grid–low group quadrant (commonly referred to as 'Competitive' or 'Individualist' culture).
2. High grid–high group quadrant (often called 'Hierarchical' or 'Bureaucratic' culture).
3. Low grid–high group quadrant (variously referred to as 'Egalitarian', 'Sect' or 'Enclave' culture).
4. High grid–low group quadrant (sometimes called 'Fatalistic' or 'Isolate' culture).

A more detailed explanation of these four quadrants is now presented:

1. Low grid–low group quadrant (competitive or individualist culture): The competitive culture emerges when people attribute low importance to both group and grid dimensions in their social interactions. On the grid–group matrix, this culture is plotted on the lower left-hand corner. For Gross and Rayner (1985), the low grid–low group culture allows the maximum options for negotiating contracts or choosing allies. This culture is characterized by individual spatial and social mobility. Ancestry or history is irrelevant; individuals are responsible for themselves. Since restrictions on behaviour are weak, members of this culture impose few restrictions over others. Douglas (1996) and Coyle and Ellis (1994) argued that, in such a culture, all boundaries are provisional and subject to negotiation. Self-regulation and the respect for individual rights are the order of the day. The prototypical structure where the competitive culture comes to the fore is the free market.
2. High grid–high group quadrant (hierarchical or bureaucratic culture): Unlike the competitive culture, the hierarchical culture emerges when people attribute a lot of importance to both the grid and group dimensions. On the grid–group matrix, this culture is plotted on the top right-hand corner, i.e. diagonally opposite to the competitive culture discussed before. In this hierarchical culture, Gross and Rayner (1985)

contended that one might find tradition-bound arrangements in which everyone knows his place but in which that place might vary with time. This culture values security and obtains it by forsaking opportunities for competition and social mobility. Gross and Rayner (1985) cited bureaucratic organizations and some tribal societies as examples of hierarchical culture, which imply both compulsion and inequality. Coyle and Ellis (1994) stressed that, in hierarchies, unequal members have unequal roles and that behaving in a 'noble' manner is expected of those who hold superior positions. The tight rules and restrictions that characterize hierarchy also introduce an element of accountability for both the superior and the subordinate. Like Rayner (1982), Schwarz and Thompson (1990) also supported that members of the hierarchical culture are oriented towards processes and are more concerned with who does what rather than with outcomes.

3. Low grid–high group quadrant (egalitarian, sect or enclave culture): The egalitarian culture emerges when people attribute low importance to the grid dimension and high importance to the group dimension. On the grid–group matrix, this culture is plotted on the lower right-hand corner. While the hierarchical and competitive cultures have received a great deal of attention in the social sciences, (e.g. Weber 1930, Williamson 1975), the two other cultures of DCF (i.e. the egalitarian and the fatalist) have not been subject to as much scientific analysis. According to Gross and Rayner (1985), the egalitarian culture is a social context in which the external group boundary is typically the dominant consideration. All other aspects of interpersonal relationships are ambiguous and open to negotiation. Later, Douglas (1986) gave a similar interpretation of Taylor's (1982) 'communities'. She explained that a community is by definition small, face-to-face in the interactions and many-sided in its relationships. Participation in its decision-making process is widespread. Members of the egalitarian culture hold beliefs and values in common, and a network of reciprocal exchanges binds them together. In an egalitarian culture, there are few constraints, yet the group consciousness is high, and there is a voluntary respect for concerns of others (Coyle 1997). The egalitarian culture is not very different from Ouchi's (1980) 'clan'.

4. High grid–low group quadrant (fatalistic or isolate culture): The diametrical opposite of the egalitarian culture is the fatalistic culture, and it emerges when people experience little group support while they are subject to high social classification or discrimination. On the grid–group matrix, this culture is plotted on the top left-hand corner. The fatalistic culture represents an environment in which people's socially assigned classifications strongly regulate their behaviour (Gross and Rayner 1985). This culture emerges when people in strongly hierarchical structures have been excluded from decision-making or when highly competitive individuals are no longer allowed to compete. For some scholars, like

Gross and Rayner (1985), the fatalistic culture implies an element of coercion – people are not in this culture by their own free will. In line with Gross and Rayner's (1985) exposition of the fatalistic culture, Douglas (1986) offered her interpretation of Olson's latent groups. She explained that members join such groups not because they believe it serves a purpose but because they do not wish to be sanctioned against; the choice of joining the group is not of their own free will. However, not all scholars have agreed with the viewpoint that fatalism is an involuntary state of existence. We will revisit this point later in this section. Coyle and Ellis (1994) characterized fatalism as a cultural context in which individuals have little choice how they spend their time, whom they associate with, what they wear or eat or where they live or work. The fatalist endures the social isolation of the competitive culture without its autonomy – the constraints of hierarchy without the support of a loyal group. Coyle preferred to label fatalism as 'despotism', because that accounts for the nature of leadership in such a culture (Coyle and Ellis 1994). The leader's power under despotism is exceptional, arbitrary and limitless. One finds that fatalism has also been discussed in the works of other scholars such as Etzioni (1975)[1] and Hirschman (1970).[2] We contend that, while fatalism is not a widely advocated culture, organizations facing problems may tend in this direction or, at least, may be viewed as such by their members.

While Douglas has derived four cultures: competitive, hierarchical, egalitarian and fatalism, Thompson and Ellis (1997) distinguished a fifth type, born out of the disagreement regarding whether belonging to the fatalistic culture is always the result of coercion or whether it is the result of voluntary choice. This fifth culture, which Thompson calls the hermit, is characterized by deliberate withdrawal from social influences and is located in the centre of the grid–group matrix (Thompson and Ellis 1997). Although Thompson, Grendstad and Selle (1999) have said that the hermit is a curious sort of culture because it stabilizes itself by the deliberate avoidance of all coercive involvement, many social scientists have argued that, in rejecting social involvement, the hermit has removed itself from the social stage and has thereby rendered itself irrelevant to the concerns of social scientists (Thompson 1997a, 1997b, 1997c). Therefore, notwithstanding the intrigue that it inspires, the hermit has unfortunately not received much attention from DCF scholars in recent years.

Having introduced the four cultures of DCF, we now summarize their key characteristics in Table 8.1, which we have borrowed from the works of Perri 6 (2003). In this table, 6 has plotted two dimensions: social regulation (i.e. grid) and social integration (i.e. group). Social regulation is the basis of the power structure on which the control of authority is established, and social integration is the network structure of ties between people. The table also sets out the strengths and weaknesses of each culture. While Table 8.1 provides a

Table 8.1 The basic forms of social organizations

Social regulation (grid)	Social integration (group)			
	Fatalistic: Strong regulation, weak integration	Hierarchy: Strong regulation, strong integration	Individualism: Weak regulation, weak integration	Egalitarian: Weak regulation, strong integration
Style of organization	Heavily constrained individuals acting opportunistically; unable to sustain trust save perhaps with close kin.	Centrally ordered community, e.g. bureaucratic organization.	Instrumental, entrepreneurial individuals – e.g. markets.	Internally egalitarian but sharply marked boundaries with others; held together by shared commitment to moral principle (e.g. sects, cults, movements and clubs).
Basis for power	Domination.	Asymmetric status; rule- and role-based authorization.	Personal control of resources.	Constant personal and collective reaffirmation commitment.
Strategy	Coping or survival-oriented behaviour; individual withdrawal.	Regulation; counterpoint between vertical and lateral boundaries internally; control through systems of status based on role.	Brokering, negotiating for control of resources.	Intense mutual support within egalitarian, confrontation of those outside.
Network	Sparse social ties.	Dense social ties at top, mainly vertical ties at the bottom.	Sparse social ties, spanned by brokers.	Dense social ties.
Authority	Weak, if any, among dominated fatalists: temporary celebrity; otherwise, temporary despotism among dominating fatalists.	Status-based, paternalistic but with rule-bound discretion (in Weberian terms, bureaucracy).	Power based: authority defined from ability to define opportunities and bestow rewards (in Weberian terms, merchant adventurer).	In Weberian terms, charismatic, based on personal demonstration of marginally greater commitment to shared principle.
Strengths	Enables valuable coping behaviour and survival during adversity; prevents excessive aspiration during periods when this might be destructive.	Enables clarity and complex divisions of labour.	Unleashes powerful motivations of aspirant self-interest; enables focused instrumental activity.	Empowers passionate principled commitment and supports integrity, unleashes powerful motivations of protection.

Table 8.1 (continued)

Social regulation (grid)	Social integration (group)			
	Fatalistic: Strong regulation, weak integration	*Hierarchy: Strong regulation, strong integration*	*Individualism: Weak regulation, weak integration*	*Egalitarian: Weak regulation, strong integration*
Weaknesses	Limited ability to sustain collective action or tackle complex problems.	Limited availability to generate prosperity and can undermine it, the system of rule and role can become so Byzantine as to be illegible; risks de-motivation of the 'lowerarchy' through denial of access to superior authority and denial of sufficient validation.	Limited ability to define the basic goods and services, rights and duties around which self-interest and instrumental activity are oriented; may eventually undermine the capacity to do so; risk de-motivation through insecurity.	Focus on distribution can undermine production and prosperity; risk schism; principle of internal equality can undermine level of authority necessary for efficacy; risks de-motivation through exhaustion, burn-out.

Source: 6 (2003)

neat summary of the key characteristics of the four cultures of DCF, the behavioural patterns it outlines are not exhaustive. In fact, those who seek a more detailed understanding of the four cultures of DCF can find a more complete list in the work of Hofstetter (1998: 55–56)[3] (Thompson, Verweij and Ellis 2005).

Before we conclude this subsection, there are two points we would like to clarify. First, much before Douglas proposed her four-fold typology, other scholars had addressed the idea of mutually contradictory thought styles cohabiting a system. Consider, for instance, the work of Weber (1905) whose basic model of society is an equilibrium between two different institutional sectors: one dominated by the competitive mind-set and the other by a bureaucratic mind-set. While a practical means–ends reasoning characterizes the competitive mind-set, institutional thinking, abstraction and routinization characterize the bureaucratic mind-set (Douglas 1986). Although Weber, like Douglas, spoke of different 'institutional sectors' coexisting in a system despite their mutual differences, there is a basic distinction between the Weberian approach and DCF. Like many other scholars of the time, Weber believed that our experience of society is very different from the experience of those people who exist in the record of explorers, missionaries and anthropologists. Consequently, those contexts that cannot be described in terms of the institutional sectors that we use to describe our world are automatically neglected by Weber and discarded to obscure areas outside our realm of inquiry. In contrast, Douglas (1986) argued that Weber's distinction between our world and those of so-called 'remote' societies is not well founded. She insisted that what can be applied to Eskimos can also be applied to modern organizations. This marks a major distinction between DCF and the work of scholars like Weber.

Second, so far in this chapter, we have only discussed DCF in a static fashion. In other words, DCF's presentation in this subsection is not very different from the structural-functional models that Barth criticized (see Chapter 7 of this volume). Nor is it very different from the conventional frameworks of culture seen in business literature that we have criticized earlier (see Chapters 3–6). Indeed, for many initial followers of Douglas's work, the DCF represented a functional and static tool of cultural sense-making. It was only later, in 1996, that Michael Thompson made significant advances in the framework by exposing its dynamic potential (see full reference of Thompson 1996 in the additional reading section). Many subsequent DCF scholars, including Mary Douglas (2005) herself, credited Michael Thompson with unravelling the dynamic potential of DCF. The following subsection discusses this transition from a static to a dynamic framework.

DCF: From a static to a dynamic framework of culture

The previous section of this chapter offered a static explanation of DCF. As the framework currently stands, it neither accounts for how or why people's behaviours change with changing contexts nor explains why an individual may behave differently at different times. The four-fold static grid–group framework also does not elucidate how members of the four cultures, despite their differences, continue to interact with one another. Finally, our discussion so far has not yet exposed how DCF addresses the question of rationality, or rather 'multiple rationalities', influencing people's behaviours. In the present section, we address each of these questions.

Let us begin by exploring how DCF explains changes in people's behaviours when they are exposed to different contexts. First, we must clarify that the four cultures of DCF should not be confused with the cultural categories offered by conventional culture frameworks (see Chapters 3–6 of this volume). While conventional cultural frameworks explain people's behaviours based on their national, regional, or societal origin, DCF explains people's behaviours as a function of their grid–group preferences. Since people arrange themselves along different grid–group configurations at different times and in different contexts, the four cultures of DCF are not rigid categories (Mars 2001) but are shifting patterns of preferences. Following Barth (1967), DCF scholars explained that people may be temporarily forced to alter their preferences and behaviours to fit with those around them, either due to the internal reasons or due to external stimuli (Thompson 1996). Price and Thompson (1996) provided an excellent example of how people's behaviours shift because of an external stimulus. They found that Swiss villagers who normally behave in a competitive way with one another with regard to their forest and pasture lands immediately shift to egalitarian behaviours when avalanches threaten their homes (Price and Thompson 1996).

Now, let us address the question of why the same individual may behave in different ways at different times. DCF scholars have explained that individual behaviour is a function of the social pressures within which individuals find themselves within a specific context (Thompson 1996). Therefore, the same individual may experience different levels of social pressure and may behave differently in different contexts. Conversely, different individuals within a specific context may be subject to different degrees of social pressures, thereby resulting in considerable behavioural plurality within that entity. Consider the example we offered in our study of Indo-French strategic alliances (Patel 2007a, 2007b). In one of the alliances studied, we found that, although one high-level manager insisted on not being recorded by the researcher and offered the company policy as a reason behind his request, other senior managers were either unaware of the said policy or were not affected by the policy in the same way; therefore, they chose to ignore it. Even within the same company, managers experienced different degrees of social pressures that had different degrees of impact on their decision regarding conforming to or deviating from expected behaviour.

Third, DCF scholars explained that a relation of mutual competition and interdependence holds together members of different cultures. The competitive, hierarchical and egalitarian cultures are active cultures (see Mamadouh 1999, Mars 1972, 2005 for illustrations), and their members compete with each other for a dominant position in the system by converting others around them to their own worldview (Thompson 1996). They organize perceptions and knowledge in line with their way of life, and they socialize new entrants accordingly (Rayner 1991). Members of the fatalistic culture, who are passive, simply align themselves to whichever culture is strongest at the time. Members of different cultures also depend on one another for their survival, so, if one culture were to disappear, they would all disappear (Thompson 1996). For example, the principled and rule-based hierarchical culture provides a way of countering the excessive market-focused rationality of the competitive culture. While the latter helps harness opportunities for creativity and entrepreneurship (see Patel 2007a, 2007b for examples), it also counters hierarchy's excessive affinity for rules and procedures. While the egalitarian group helps members of the hierarchical and competitive cultures to bridge their differences (Thompson 1996), the fatalistic culture makes a less obvious but valuable contribution to the system by offering coping mechanisms in the face of adversity (6, 2003). Thus, each culture has its own strength and weakness, and eliminating any one would lead to the collapse of the entire system. The question, therefore, is not which one is right but rather which one is more appropriate than the other is in a specific context (Thompson and Wildavsky 1986). In light of the perpetual tension between the members of the four cultures, one may ask how they manage to transact with one another. Thompson (1996) has explained that, when forced to work with one another, members of different cultures bring forward their similarities and temporarily underplay their differences. In so doing, they attempt to create a workable coalition with one another. Not surprisingly, such alliances cannot last forever. Differences soon resurface between the members of different cultures, eventually leading to a rupture (Thompson 1996).

Finally, in order to explain the variety of rationalities that individuals resort to, Thompson (1996) has evoked the concepts of information bias and information rejection. He explained that we are all subject to biases in the way we absorb and handle information. There is absolutely no way of looking at data from all directions. At best, we pay attention to certain phenomena and reject other bits of information that do not fit our organized perception (Thompson and Wildavsky 1986). Thompson and Wildavsky (1986) asked: How many kinds of biases can there be? How does each bias affect the way in which people handle and process information? They revealed four kinds of biases and four distinct information rejection styles among members of the four cultures. We combine this with the recent work by Patel and Rayner (2012b) on the rationalities of the four cultures in order to expose both the information rejection styles as well as the rationality of members of each culture. It follows that members of each of the four cultures suffer from different kinds of biases; they choose to handle information differently; they prefer different kinds of rationality; and, consequently, they behave differently when faced with a common scenario. Consider the following interesting example provided by Schwarz and Thompson (1990): When faced with mortal danger, our instinct for self-preservation will prompt us all to seek a safe spot. However, different individuals will adopt different attitudes to save themselves. While some support the 'each for himself and the devil take the hindmost' attitude, others advocate 'women and children first' or 'follow the leader'. Still others say, 'it's no use. I'll just stay here'. Individuals act out their instinctive preferences without being aware of how this influences collective survival. Yet, not all individuals behave selfishly. Table 8.2 explains and summarizes the information rejection styles of the four cultures of DCF and their preferred rationalities.

1. Competitive culture: For members of the competitive culture, information handling/rejection is done through networking. Members of the competitive culture shift the vital discussions away from the formalized information-handling system and on to the informal 'old boy net' (Wynne and Otway 1982). Thompson and Wildavsky (1986) characterized this strategy as individualist manipulative. Further, Patel and Rayner (2012b) have reiterated that members of the competitive culture care less about status or procedures and more about the bottom line (Thompson 1996). Therefore, they pursue a pragmatic, substantive and competitive rationality, which guides their market-focused way of life.

2. Hierarchical culture: For members of the hierarchical culture, paradigm protection is the way to handle/reject information. Members of hierarchical cultures are not resistant to change itself, but they are resistant to those changes that threaten their hierarchical structure, causing information to spill out of its proper channels, shortcutting correct procedures and, most importantly, questioning the paradigm on which their whole system rests. Paradigm protection is an information rejection style, which is often diffused or depersonalized. When exposed, it is usually repackaged and presented as altruistic self-sacrifice. It is about collectivist manipulation. Grounding their arguments in the work of many DCF scholars, Patel and Rayner (2012b) reiterated that members of this culture adhere to a hierarchical and process-oriented rationality. They are more concerned with who does what rather than the outcomes.

3. Egalitarian culture: Members of the egalitarian culture take a very uncompromising and fundamentalist stand with regards to any information that threatens their fellow members. They concentrate all their defences at the boundary of the group, protecting the vulnerable 'insiders' from the predatory 'outsiders'; any threat against one member is seen as a threat against all members. The egalitarian culture protects its own members by rejecting any threatening information or by expelling deviants from the group. Egalitarian groups neither negotiate nor compromise. They cannot manipulate anyone except their own members, who, of course, do not see this as manipulation. So the members of this sort of group sustain themselves with a collective survival strategy. According to Patel and Rayner (2012b), while members of the egalitarian culture are close knit, consensual and egalitarian internally, they are unrelenting in criticizing what goes on outside their 'walls of virtue' (Thompson 1996: 10). Thus, they pursue an egalitarian rationality internally and a critical rationality externally (Thompson 1996).

4. Fatalistic culture: For members of the fatalistic culture who perceive that 'life is like a lottery', risk absorption is the only way to handle information. To the fatalistic mind-set, individuals do not control anything that happens to them. 'Strategy' is really too strong a word to use for the way of coping to which members of fatalistic groups resort. For such people, the objective is merely self-preservation. As Patel and Rayner (2012b) have pointed out, the rationality that members of the fatalistic culture adhere to is fatalistic because they do not perceive themselves as having any control on what is happening to them.

Thompson and Wildavsky (1986) concluded that the four information rejection styles of the four cultures are mutually contradictory and exhaustive. In other words, they are all the socially available strategies. Therefore, they suggest that it should be possible to disaggregate a population in these terms; thus, it should now be possible to understand all the different things that are going on simultaneously in an organization.[4] We summarize the four information rejection

Table 8.2 Information rejection styles and preferred rationality of four cultures of DCF

Culture	Information rejection style	Preferred rationality
Competitive culture	Networking	Pragmatic, substantive and competitive rationality focused on the bottom line
Hierarchical culture	Paradigm protection	Hierarchical and process-oriented rationality focused on who does what rather than on outcomes
Egalitarian culture	Expulsion	Egalitarian rationality internally and critical rationality externally
Fatalistic culture	Risk absorption	Fatalistic rationality focused on self-preservation

Sources: Thompson (1996), Thompson and Wildavsky (1986), Patel and Rayner (2012b)

styles and the preferred form of rationality of each of the four cultures in Table 8.2.

The discussion presented in this subsection reveals the dynamic potential of DCF. In converting DCF from a static to a dynamic framework of culture, Thompson (1997a, 1997b, 1997c) also addressed another very important question: What is being classified in DCF? Is it the individual or is it the pattern of social relationships (together with its supporting cultural bias and the behavioural strategy)? If it is the former case, then all the social interactions of an individual must take place in just one quadrant. If it is the latter case, then one may ask, would individuals not be leading different parts of their lives in different compartments? Rather than making a forced choice between these two obvious but incorrect options, Thompson (1997a, 1997b, 1997c) chose to completely reject the long-running dispute between methodological individualists and methodological collectivists and explained that cultural dynamics are independent of social scale. This means that, if transactions fall into a number of distinct spheres, the same individual could be a member of different cultures in different contexts. This insight adds another dimension to our understanding as to why the same individual behaves differently in different social contexts. Also, Thompson's conceptualization of cultural dynamics as being beyond social scales lends support to Barth's (1978, 2007) claim that, if individuals form the elementary parts of any social setting, then they can and will hold memberships in a variety of groups across different levels and scales as well as in groups that span across levels and scales (see Chapter 7, for details). Thus, both Barth and Thompson supported that cultural dynamics are not limited to specific levels and scales.

Having introduced the basic premise of DCF and having exposed its potential as a dynamic framework of culture, we now attempt to explore whether DCF meets the criteria outlined at the beginning of this chapter.

Does DCF meet the criteria set out at the beginning of this chapter?

As discussed in Chapter 7 of this volume, the transactional culture approach focuses on social transactions or exchanges to make sense of human behaviour. Since social transactions are not limited to specific geo-ethnic boundaries, transactional frameworks of culture can be used to study culture at all kinds of levels (both at the micro and macro levels) and across different levels and scales. Therefore, using Barth's transactional framework makes the discourse regarding different 'levels of culture' moot, thereby alleviating the need for a variety of cultural frameworks at different levels. It is also possible to use Barth's transactional framework for comparing cultures not only across similar kinds of social entities (for example, between two nations or two companies) but also for comparing cultures across different kinds of social entities (such as between a company, a local football club and local authorities; see Frosdick 1995a, 1995b) because social transactions can be observed in, across and between all kinds of social entities. Drawing from our discussion in Chapter 7 and as outlined at the beginning of the present chapter, we are now looking for a cultural framework that follows Barth's transactional framework, and also meets the following criteria:

1. It extends the discussion of rationalities beyond Barth's idea of 'self-interest'.
2. It explains social change as a never-ending non-linear phenomenon.
3. It satisfactorily explains the diversity/plurality of human behaviour without relying either on dualistic categories (popular among Western social scientists in the last century) or on the infinity argument of culture.[5]
4. It provides a feedback mechanism to explain the continuity of social relations.

In this subsection, we explore whether DCF meets these criteria.

1. Does DCF extend the discussion of rationalities beyond Barth's idea of self-interest?

In *Inherent Relationality: An Anti-Dualistic Approach to Institutions*, Thompson (1996) explained that Barth (1966a, 1966b) had tried to answer the one question that has troubled many social scientists: How do individuals decide where their best interests lie? Barth (1966a, 1966b) explained that people do not know at the outset where their best interests lie, but they have a 'rag-bag' of values from which to choose. When they make an arbitrary choice from this rag-bag, they are either rewarded or punished by the outcome. With more and more experiences, people's behaviours consolidate with those sets of values that they feel are rewarded in their context, and they start transacting in accordance with these values. Although Barth suggested that the choices of values made by the individual are ad hoc,

Thompson (1996) argued that there are precisely four sets of values and behaviours to choose from, which are consistent with the four cultures of DCF. Thompson (1996) stressed that there is one major difference between Barth's transactional framework and DCF: the former has no directions. It only has 'this systematizing, integrating and homogenizing process, and the idea ... that we start off all over the place and we all end up at the same place' (Thompson 1996: 18). In contrast, DCF scholars have argued we have precisely four directions from which to choose. 'Of course, we do not all stay where we end up – there is always some movement of people between these places – but social life is absolutely not a one-way journey to a single destination' (Thompson 1996: 18).

Further, choosing to consciously pursue a certain direction implies that the individual makes rational decisions in the process. As explained earlier, despite valuable revisions to Barth's initial framework, transactional analysis still remains limited to the idea of 'rationality' and activities continue to be seen in terms of receiving benefits. On the other hand, DCF scholars such as Thompson (1996) have suggested that, as long as we limit ourselves to Herbert Simon's (1978) concept of bounded rationality or even Cyert and March's (1963) idea that our rationality is limited by our physiological apparatus, we will be restricted in our understanding because we will continue to treat rationality as singular. DCF scholars have proposed instead that there are four ways of rationalizing: one for members of each culture. They also have argued that people stop way short of their physiological limits of information processing and that not everyone stops short at the same point. In order to stop short, one is required to effectively reject information, not just avoid collecting information. Thompson (1996) then proposed four different ways of information rejection based on the four cultures of DCF (see Table 8.2 in this chapter). Subsequent scholars, notably Patel and Rayner (2012b), exposed the different rationalities of members of the four cultures. They explained that, consistent with a process-oriented rationality, members of the hierarchical culture are guided in their behaviour by rules, regulations and procedures rather than by individual or communal gains. Following a communal and critical rationality, members of the egalitarian culture behave in ways that support the communal interest of their group members, even if this implies challenging non-members. The substantive rationality of members of the competitive culture encourages them to behave in ways that optimize self-gains, even if this occasionally leads to compromising rules or communal interest. Interestingly, competitive individuals may support communal gains if doing this increases gains for all, including themselves. Finally, people adhering to the fatalistic rationality pay lip service to whatever measure contributes to self-preservation. Thus, through the discussion of four different kinds of information rejection and four kinds of rationalities, DCF meets the first criteria set out at the beginning of this chapter: it does indeed expand our understanding of rationality beyond the idea of individuals serving their own interests.

(2) Does DCF explain social change as a never-ending, non-linear phenomenon?

As Kapferer (1976) has admitted, structural-functional scholars who dominated the discipline of anthropology in the last century did not pay attention to the process of social change. This trend was challenged by Barth, who contributed significant efforts towards generating a deeper understanding of social change. However, even Barth's work failed to meet one objective he had identified: understanding social change as a never-ending, non-linear phenomenon. Let us now see how DCF scholars have explained social change and whether or not they have met Barth's objective.

In *Man and Nature as a Single but Complex System*, Thompson (2003) provided several examples in social sciences where a change from state A implies an automatic landing in state B. Consider, for instance, a shift from mechanical to organic solidarity (Durkheim 1893), from community to society (Tönnies 1887), from traditional to modern (Weber 1930), from status to contract (Maine 1861), from capitalism to communism (Marx 1859) or from markets to hierarchies (Williamson 1975). Thompson explained that the problem with these two-fold models is that, if one is dislodged from state A, their only option is to fall into state B, and this can only allow for temporary change. Tipping out of one state invariably implies falling into the other, thereby inviting a self-inflicted dead end in the process of change. In contrast, DCF has provided an alternative four-fold model in which change is a never-ending permanent feature. A four-fold model means that dislodgement from state A no longer implies falling into state B. There are several possible transitions – twelve to be precise (three possible transitions for members of each culture). Dichotomous frameworks such as those proposed by Weber (1905), Durkheim (1895) or Williamson (1975) rely largely on two-fold categories, but DCF has offered a much richer scope of understanding human behaviour by offering two additional quadrants: the egalitarian culture and the fatalistic culture. This, Thompson (1996) contended, enables us to treat change as a complex, never-ending, non-linear and non-equilibrium process as opposed to a simple linear Newtonian mechanism leading to some sort of equilibrium. Thompson (1996) compared the social change phenomenon with the flight of a flock of starlings. We find this analogy to be particularly eloquent:

> The appropriate analogy is not the arrow (as favoured by Durkheim, Weber, Marx) not is it even a pendulum (Spencer, Leach, etc.). It is the flock of starlings, endlessly transforming itself (otherwise it could not stay a flock) yet never going anywhere. Such a system is certainly ordered, and that orderliness is achieved only by continuous change, but you can predict nothing about that change beyond the prediction that things will not stay as they are.
>
> (Thompson 1996: 57)

Further, Thompson (1996) explored whether a tiny movement from one quadrant to another results in a change in cultural affiliations. Conversely, he also asked what happens when individuals move within a quadrant without crossing its boundary. He explained that tiny movements that lead to crossing cultural borders do result in a cultural change (because they bring the person under the influence of a different attractor). On the other hand, much larger movements within a quadrant that do not involve crossing cultural borders imply minor cultural shifts (which are more or less ongoing) but not major cultural changes (see Thompson 1996: 18–19). Further, each culture applies pressure on members of other cultures in order to influence them to change their cultural preferences. Each culture competes with other cultures to get as many adherents as possible, thereby attempting to gain dominance in the system. This internal competition leads to an ongoing cultural change from within the system (Thompson 1996).

One logical question that emanates from the above discussion is the following: if cultural change is an unpredictable as DCF scholars claim, how can managers bring about a cultural change in their companies. Some scholars (see Martin and Siehl 1983) believed that it is not possible for managers to develop or change corporate cultures at will. The best a manager can hope to do is to understand the cultures at play in their companies and to capitalize on those cultural effects they perceive as positive. While managers cannot bring about major cultural changes, it may be possible for them to slightly modify the trajectory of a culture. DCF scholars explained that minor cultural modifications can be brought about by altering the grid–group components of the interaction in question. Consider the hypothetical example of an employee who has been feeling disillusioned because the employee's concerns are not being given due attention, and the employee no longer has a 'voice' in the workplace, leading to feelings of despondency and to the use of fatalistic strategies at work. There might be other employees in the company who also find themselves in the fatalistic quadrant for other reasons (being thrown out of competition, being forced to accept decisions with which they do not agree, etc.). Our employee finds some solace in the company of other fatalistic members, although there is little real support they can actually get from one another. If the manager of the employee in question is observant enough, these fatalistic tendencies will be recognized and can be overcome by ensuring that the employee in question is offered opportunities to be more involved in decisions affecting both the employee and the employee's department. The manager could accomplish this by encouraging open expression of concerns, by allowing competition in a fair and transparent manner for the employee's professional progress and by offering the employee patient and empathetic hearing. Such an open and collaborative environment may strengthen the 'group' dimension in the relation between the employee, the manager and other colleagues and weaken the 'grid' dimension that poses barriers to communication. As a result, the employee may gradually move away from the fatalistic quadrant towards one of the other quadrants. This shift may lead to a ripple effect, inspiring other fatalists to seek similar solutions. Support for such efforts throughout the organization might set a social change in motion. Having said this, it is important to point out that, while such minor changes may be easy to achieve, actors may well revert back to their previous fatalistic tendencies if they lose their newly gained voice, visibility and support. In addition, while such minor changes seem easy to bring about, more profound and long-lasting cultural changes where members significantly change their values, perceptions and behaviours are much more difficult to achieve. For such changes to occur, supporting policies and rewards may be necessary to complement managerial efforts. Such changes will occur only when there is enough incentive for individuals to make the shift (Douglas 1996).

(3) Does DCF satisfactorily explain cultural diversity/plurality without relying either on dualistic categories or on the infinity argument?

As seen in the previous chapter and in earlier sections of the present chapter, many social scientists in the twentieth century heavily relied on dualistic categories to make sense of human behaviour. The use of such dualistic categories or dichotomies fails to provide a complete and satisfying explanation of cultural diversity in certain contexts. It was this dissatisfaction with dichotomous categories that inspired scholars like McKim Marriott (1976) to propose alternative four-fold models to explain the diversity of food-giving and food-receiving practices between four castes of the Hindu society (see Marriott's 'Hindu Transactions: Diversity without Dualism'). However, Marriott's four-fold typology was restricted in its application to the specific context and did not lend itself to other questions that social scientists may wish to explore. Therefore, we reckon that a cultural framework that can explain the plurality of culture without relying on dualistic categories, and which can be applied to a broad range of questions, is desired. DCF partially meets this criteria due to its reliance on four cultural types and to what DCF scholars refer to as the impossibility theorem and the requisite variety condition. DCF's impossibility theorem and requisite variety condition are discussed next.

Thompson (1996) explained that, if you were to set up a social system in which individuals had to maximize their transactions, they could either form themselves into groups or choose to engage in networks. Let us imagine a scenario wherein these individuals are forbidden to form groups. In such a scenario, they would organize themselves into networks – either as network centralists (competitive culture, i.e. those who are free to forge relationships without restrictions) or as network peripheralists (fatalist culture, i.e. those for whom many relationships are 'foreclosed' by their prior involvement with other networks). On the other hand, if individuals were free to organize themselves as groups, they might form groups whose members maximize transactions by keeping their groups apart from others (egalitarian culture) or as groups whose members maximize their transactions by arranging their groups into orderly and ranked relationships with other groups (hierarchist culture). Thus, DCF has given us four cultures, each defining itself against the others. 'The whole thing, therefore, is a self-organizing system that cannot be simplified. If one way of organizing is there, they will all be there and if one of them were to disappear, they would all disappear' (Thompson 1996: 56). Therefore, there are four and only four cultures[6] – a situation that DCF scholars have referred to as the impossibility theorem. Further, these four cultures of DCF need to depend on one another for their survival – a condition that DCF scholars have referred to as the requisite variety condition (originally proposed by Ashby 1947). Thus, DCF has offered a four-fold self-organizing system that satisfactorily explains cultural diversity/plurality without relying on dualistic or dichotomous categories. In addition, its basic dimensions – group and grid – are so broad in their scope that DCF can be (and has been) applied to a wide variety of questions that social scientists might wish to explore.[7]

Another problem that the discussion of the transactional approach left us with in the previous chapter was the 'unity' versus 'infinity' dilemma. While structural-functional scholars in anthropology have supported the 'unity' argument (much like current conventional culture scholars in business literature) by claiming that societies are culturally integrated wholes, some transactional scholars, such as Geertz (1973, 1980), Saïd (1979) and Leach (1954, 1961), have taken the diametrically opposite standpoint and have argued that cultures in their own ethnographic contexts are so unique that there can be no systematic comparison across cultural entities. These transactional scholars support the 'infinity' argument of culture, and they believe that there are as many cultures as there are social contexts and, hence, cultural comparisons are impossible.[8] In 'Why and How Culture Matters', Thompson, Verweij and Ellis (2005) resolved this 'unity' versus 'infinity' dilemma. They explained that culture is subject neither to unity nor to infinity. Culture is in fact subject to 'constrained relativism'. Thompson *et al.* (2005) explained that, contrary to structural-functional orthodoxies, which emphasize singular forms of culture, DCF scholars propagated the idea of plural forms of culture. Plurality of anything obviously introduces the concept of relativism. However, this should not necessarily be taken to imply that this relativism is absolutely unconstrained; rejecting unity should not automatically mean supporting infinity. In line with their idea of constrained relativism, Thompson *et al.* (2005) explained that comparisons across cultures can be made on the basis of the four cultures of DCF, which can be observed in all social entities. What differs, however, is the strength of these cultures in each case. Thus, DCF scholars overcame the unity versus infinity dilemma through their concept of constrained relativism.

(4) Does DCF offer a feedback mechanism to explain continuity of social relations?

As seen in Chapter 7 of this volume, transactional scholars have called for a better explanation of feedback mechanisms for the continuity of social relations.

However, as Kapferer (1976) reported, very few among them (with the exception of Handelman (1976)) have actually been able achieve this. We now explore whether DCF explains the continuation of social relations. Following the call of transactional scholars such as Buckley (1960), Van Velsen (1964) and Geertz (1973), DCF scholars have focused on variations as well as conformity in behavioural patterns. By explaining how individuals and groups with similar preferences on grid and group dimensions have similar behavioural preferences, DCF scholars have explained the conformity of human behaviour. On the other hand, by showing how different cultures coexist in every system and how people shift from one culture to another in different contexts, DCF scholars have clarified variations in human behaviour. DCF scholars also have explained that the four cultures are not only contradictory to one another but also sustain the system through their contradictions. The four cultures are in constant competition with each other to gain more adherents and thereby more dominance in the system. Choosing to favour one culture implies rejecting the other cultures (Douglas 1996), thereby contributing to the hostility between the four cultures. However, interestingly, each culture also needs to depend on the other for its survival. This is because, although each culture has its strengths, it also has its weaknesses, which can only be overcome by collaborating with members of other cultures. Each culture has blind spots, and members of the four cultures need to combine forces in order to optimize the system's chances of survival. The four cultures thus need to depend on one another to define and reproduce themselves – cognitively as well as institutionally. Thus, the conflict between the four cultures is also a source of social stability, and the four cultures sustain themselves through their mutual contradistinctions. Through this discussion of ongoing competition and simultaneous mutual interdependence, DCF has provided a feedback mechanism for the continuity of social relationships. Douglas (1996) summarized this perfectly, when she explained that each of the four cultures is predatory on the other. The four cultures constantly compete with one another for resources and dominance in the system. While this rivalry makes it difficult for the four cultures to exist side by side harmoniously, this coexistence is also necessary because excluding any one implies the automatic elimination of all of them.

Our discussion in this section reveals that to some extent DCF does meet the four criteria that we have outlined at the beginning of this chapter. This does not, however, imply that DCF is without criticisms. Like every theoretical framework, it has its weaknesses. Chapter 9 will summarize some of the criticisms leveled against DCF.

Concluding remarks

In this chapter, we have introduced DCF as a tool of the transactional culture approach. Additionally, we have presented arguments to show how it overcomes some of the critiques of Barth's transactional framework and, more generally, of the transactional culture approach. In so doing, we believe that DCF contributes towards enriching transactional culture literature. Readers should note, however, that our discussion of DCF is not exhaustive. Numerous scholars have enriched this literature in past years, and, despite best efforts, it is nearly impossible for us to do justice to their varied contributions within the constraints of the present chapter.

This might be a good moment to stop and recap what we have covered so far in this book. We began this book with an overview of culture and how it impacts businesses (Chapters 1 and 2). In Chapters 3 and 4, we attempted to understand and critique various conventional (national/societal/regional) frameworks of culture. Following the same trend, Chapters 5 and 6 covered the different schools of thought in corporate culture literature and many corresponding frameworks adhering to these schools of thought. Having understood the limitations of the static frameworks of culture, we then moved towards anthropology literature in search of alternative ways of addressing culture. This search led us to the transactional culture approach in Chapter 7 and, more precisely, to the work of Fredrik Barth. While the transactional approach overcomes many of the limitations of the structural-functional orthodoxies of anthropology and of currently popular frameworks in business literature, it also has its own weaknesses. This realization brings us to the present chapter where we offer DCF as a transactional tool – one that follows Barth's transactional tradition and simultaneously overcoming many of its weaknesses. In the next chapter, we will review how DCF compares with the conventional frameworks of culture (see Chapters 3 and 4 of this volume). The next chapter therefore concludes our discussion of the varied cultural frameworks evoked in this volume.

Notes

1 Etzioni (1975) characterized the dual nature of repressive leaders and subjugated followers in his 'coercion/alienation' model.
2 Hirschman's (1970) framework referred to scenarios in which members are incapable of changing their lot. They can neither transform the system nor leave the system and go elsewhere.
3 Hofstetter (1998) has created a list of sixty norms, beliefs and perceptions for each of the four cultures.
4 As previously stated, for Thompson and Wildavsky, an organization is not so much a conceptual scheme as a structure that is sustained and transformed by a variety of conflicting and contradictory worldviews. As readers will recognize, this approach to organization is more in line with the fragmentation perspective of corporate culture as proposed by Joanne Martin (see Chapter 6 for details). Thompson and Wildavsky (1986) explained that it is highly unlikely that a single well-defined organizational goal will be sustained for long in any structure. Soon it will be in conflict with differing goals, so much so that the structure will give way to several different mutually contradictory cultural groups. Not only does this viewpoint support the plurality of cultures, but it also reveals the dynamicity of culture.
5 Point (3) combines two criteria raised in Chapter 7 of this volume: (1) it explains the diversity of human behaviour without resorting to dualistic categories found in

Western literature, and (2) it supports the plurality of cultures without relying on the 'infinity' argument of culture.

6 This is true unless, of course, we are also including 'the hermit' in our discussion.
7 Consider Rayner's (1986) study of perceptions towards risks, Mars's (1982) study of workplace crimes, Frosdick's (1995a, 1995b) study on sports-related hooliganism and Patel and Patel's (2008) study of learning and innovation in organizations. These are just a few examples of studies that have used DCF.
8 Thompson (1997) called this 'the veto on comparison'.

Additional reading

M. Thompson (1996) *Inherent Relationality: An anti-dualistic approach to institutions*, Bergen: LOS Centre Publication.

9 Comparing the Douglasian Cultural Framework with conventional frameworks of culture

A theory should be judged not against an impossible standard of perfection but by how well it performs in comparison with rival theories.

Aaron Wildavsky

What you will learn in this chapter:

- whether and to what extent DCF overcomes the limitations of conventional frameworks of culture (see Chapters 3–6 of this volume);
- whether and to what extent DCF is a more appropriate tool for cultural sense-making than conventional frameworks of culture in the specific context of international business entities;
- critique of DCF.

Introduction

In Chapter 8, we compared DCF with Barth's transactional framework and with the contributions of other transactional scholars. We demonstrated that, while following in the footsteps of Barth, DCF scholars have addressed some of the limitations of his framework and of the transactional school in general. In this chapter, we revisit some of the questions raised in earlier chapters of this volume. We compare DCF with the conventional frameworks of culture (see Part II of this volume: Chapters 3–6), which include static frameworks grounded in national, societal and regional origin and/or corporate affiliations and call to mind the following six reflection points we evoked earlier in Chapter 4:

Reflection point 1: Have the conventional frameworks of culture satisfactorily conceptualized and operationalized culture?

Reflection point 2: Is national identity a passive embodiment of a predetermined cultural template as conventional frameworks of culture dictate?

Reflection point 3: Are the terms 'intercultural' and 'international' interchangeable?

Reflection point 4: Do we need to address culture at different levels (for instance, national, societal, regional, etc.) for optimal cultural sense-making?

Reflection point 5: Do conventional frameworks of culture explain social change?

Reflection point 6: Is culture simply an 'uncaused cause' as conventional frameworks of culture posit?

Aaron Wildavsky (as quoted by Grendstad and Selle, 1997), the famous American political scientist, believed that no theory or framework is perfect. Therefore, comparing frameworks from the impossible standards of perfection is a futile exercise. On the other hand, comparing frameworks from the perspective of their usefulness in exploring the problem at hand might be a more feasible and meaningful exercise. Taking Wildavsky's advice, we now compare DCF with conventional frameworks of culture. In order to prevent our discussion from becoming overly broad and dispersed, we adopt a three-fold strategy. In subsequent sections of this chapter, we

1. focus on the same six reflection points that we evoked in Chapter 4 of this volume;
2. compare the conventional frameworks of culture with DCF on each of these reflection points; and
3. locate our discussions within the backdrop of international business, thereby furnishing a specific problem/context within which DCF and conventional frameworks may be assessed.

Therefore, our discussion is not about 'which framework is better than the other' in an ideological sense. Nor is it about demonstrating that one framework is better than another in a broad decontextualized and/or theoretical sense. Rather, our discussion is about 'which framework would make better sense as compared to others in the specific context of international business entities'. It is important to focus on the context of international business for a variety of reasons, which have been elaborated in Chapter 1. International business collaborations such as inter-organizational alliances, international markets and multinational corporate structures seem to be proliferating at an increasing rate, in part due to increasing globalization (Martin 2002 see Chapter 1 of this volume for a detailed discussion). Ease of air travel, easy access to information technology and the proliferation of international alliances (such as the European Common Market, the Organization of Petroleum Exporting Countries and the International Monetary Fund) have facilitated cooperation between nations and have blurred national boundaries (Martin 2002, Tung 2008). International business forms a major area of focus for students of business studies. Therefore, we choose to locate our discussion using the backdrop of international business entities and begin with reflection point 1, upon which we now elaborate in light of our present focus.

Reflection point 1: The conceptualization and operationalization of culture

In this subsection, we compare the conceptualization and operationalization of culture offered by conventional scholars with those advanced by proponents of DCF. We also explore which conceptualization of culture makes more sense in the context of international business entities.

As seen in Chapter 4, despite the emergence of a wide variety of cultural frameworks in past decades, many scholars (see Child and Tayeb 1983, Usunier 1998, Angwin and Vaara 2005) have remained dissatisfied with the way proponents of these frameworks have conceptualized and operationalized culture. Even in the twenty-first century, the field remains far from an operational consensus on the term 'culture'. Further, culture is now commonly employed as a synonym for 'nation' (Adler and Doktor 1986, Usunier 1998), and differences among national samples are sometimes ascribed to nationality in a circular manner. The dissatisfaction seems to be even more profound when one considers the way culture has been operationalized and applied to studies of international business entities. Static frameworks of national culture tend to treat people's behaviour as the outcome of predetermined cultural templates (Ailon-Souday and Kunda 2009). We find that operationalizing culture meaningfully in the context of cross-country business entities, such as international strategic alliances (ISAs), is problematic from the perspective of conventional frameworks of culture. This is because constant restructuring, evolving corporate boundaries, and ongoing mergers and acquisitions and takeovers characterize such entities, resulting in ever-changing boundaries and increasing diversity of conflicting goals (Angwin and Vaara 2005). Further, as explained in Chapter 4, in such entities, corporate and national identities of members blur because members belong to different and sometimes overlapping national, corporate, professional, loyalty and interest groups. Therefore, attempting to explain human behaviour in international business entities solely based on national/societal/regional origin as proponents of conventional frameworks of culture have attempted to do is inadequate (Ailon-Souday and Kunda 2009). One of the reasons behind this overall dissatisfaction with conventional frameworks of culture is that most of these frameworks fail to capture the dynamicity of culture – the fact that people (irrespective of their origin and affiliations) can and do behave differently at different times and in different contexts.

DCF, as seen in Chapter 8, offers a different conceptualization of culture. In line with the transactional culture approach, it focuses on cultural transactions between people and the patterns emerging from these transactions. It does not categorize people based on their geo-ethnic origin, but rather it explains people's behaviours as a function of their interactions with one another and as influenced by their own values, biases and rationalities within a specific context. DCF also explains that the same individual can hold membership in a variety of social groups at different times and, hence, might behave differently in different contexts. Thus, DCF offers a conceptualization of culture that is both dynamic and plural. The dynamic and pluralistic coexistence of the four cultures of DCF is well illustrated by Thompson (1997c) through the example of the Brent Spar Saga. In this case, the main protagonist, Shell, adopted a competitive stance. The government experts who approved the deep ocean disposal behaved in line with the hierarchical culture. Greenpeace (whose last-minute intervention seriously upset this negotiated outcome) was the egalitarian culture, and those who found themselves totally convinced by whomever they last heard arguing the case on television (including Thompson himself) were the fatalists. Further, the four rival cultures coexist in the system and actively influence each other in a contentious and competitive fashion, yet they also depend on one another for their own survival. We find this conceptualization of culture to be more compelling in the context of international business entities than the conceptualization offered by conventional and static frameworks of culture.

Reflection point 2: National identity: Passive and static versus fluid and constructed

In this subsection, we use insights gleaned from a variety of literatures to reflect on whether national identity is indeed a passive embodiment of a pre-determined cultural template as proponents of conventional frameworks of culture imply. We then explore how proponents of DCF treat the question of cultural identity. Finally, we reflect on which of these two conceptualizations is better suited to the context of international business entities.

In Chapter 4, we demonstrated that proponents of conventional culture frameworks consider that cultural identities manifest themselves in organizations through stubbornly distinctive behavioural patterns (for example, Erez and Earley 1993, Harzing and Hofstede 1996, Kanungo and Mendonca 1996, Olk and Earley 1996). In contrast, sociologists and anthropologists have a much more flexible understanding of cultural identity (Ailon-Souday and Kunda 2003). Many of these scholars have argued that national identities are a symbolic resource that are actively mobilized by members for different social goals, are constructed for the purpose of managing impressions during everyday life performances or are situated and flexibly cast as fluid social objects in accordance with the interpretational mood in the interaction. There is, therefore, a disagreement between conventional frameworks of culture from business literature and literature grounded in sociology and anthropology, on the topic of how national identity plays out in social interactions.

In line with the sociological and anthropological tradition, transactional scholars have supported the idea that people's cultural identities and, hence, their behaviours are flexible. They also support that cultural identities are multifaceted. In other words, many identities cohabit within an individual (for example, an individual may be a father, a son, a professor, an employee, a sportsman and may play many other roles). Each individual is affected by a variety of influences in his environment (for instance, family, school, professional group, friends and social circle, national group and others) that contribute to the emergence of a multifaceted and complex identity, with national origin being just one such factor. Consistent with this viewpoint, DCF scholars have shown that people can and do change their behaviours when they find themselves in different contexts. Following Barth (1967), proponents of DCF have explained that people may be temporarily forced to alter their behaviour to fit with those around them, either due to internal reasons (competition and interdependence between members) or due to external stimuli (Thompson 1996). As an example, consider Price and Thompson's (1996) example of Swiss villagers who switch from competitive to egalitarian behaviours in their forest management when avalanches threaten their homes. Following Barth (1992), proponents of DCF have also explained that, when social transactions fall into a number of distinct spheres, the same individual may display different grid–group preferences and therefore different behaviours in each sphere (Thompson 1997a, 1997b, 1997c). For instance, it may be acceptable to say that individuals may behave in a competitive way in the workplace and in a much more egalitarian way with their family members. This is because people assume different identities in the workplace (that of a manager seeking access to a limited pool of resources) as compared to those they assume at home (that of a parent trying to ensure an equal distribution of family resources between two children). Further, even within a context, one identity may dominate at a certain point in time as a function of certain situational variables (e.g. being a parent might dominate at a point in time, and being a professional might dominate at another time). Convinced by the dynamic and pluralistic conceptualization of culture as proffered by DCF scholars, we agree that cultural identity is not a passive embodiment of a predetermined cultural template. Rather, people consciously choose to act out (or not) their so-called national and other identities, and these choices may change from one context to another. In our earlier studies (Patel, 2007a, 2007b), we have illustrated this through the example of a manager who recognized a change in the environment from hierarchical to competitive culture, when he changed his job from a public sector organization to an international alliance. The manager quickly adapted his behaviour to match the new social and cultural context in which he found himself, just as he had done in his previous job. As this example shows, one's identity (either national or otherwise) is fluid, and actors choose to act out certain aspects of their multifaceted identities based on their assessment of the context within which they find themselves. We find that the dynamic and multifaceted conceptualization of cultural identity is a much more realistic representation of human behaviour as observed in modern business entities than the static conceptualizations offered by conventional frameworks of culture.

Despite the fact that DCF scholars support that people can and do shift their cultural identities and hence their behaviours from one context to another, this should not be taken to mean that cultural change is easy to achieve. In fact, Patel and Rayner (2012b) made a distinction between transient and temporary cultural switches and more profound cultural changes. Since proponents of DCF have conceptualized culture as patterns of behavioural preferences connecting people in a specific context, they believe that people move in and out of cultures frequently and with relative ease; therefore, ongoing cultural shifts are almost inevitable. In contrast, profound cultural changes are less frequent and more difficult to bring about. Often individuals spend their lives in different spheres. Individuals 'compartmentalize' themselves and do not question contradictory beliefs for as long as these are manifested in different spheres. This compartmentalization helps them cope with the different cultures governing activities in these spheres (Thompson *et al.* 1999). However, the 'compartmentalization of the self' cannot continue forever – individuals will eventually make a choice, at which time, both the individuals and the concerned groups will experience a certain amount of trauma and shock (Hendry 1999).

Reflection point 3: 'Intercultural' and 'international' as interchangeable

In this subsection, we explore whether the terms 'intercultural' and 'international' are a proxy for one another. Additionally, we question whether, like conventional scholars, DCF scholars also use the two terms interchangeably.

Many culture scholars in international business studies rely on conventional frameworks of culture and use the terms 'intercultural' and 'international' interchangeably, as seen in Chapter 4. This practice of using the two terms as a proxy for one another leads to two main problems: (1) it equates nation with culture; and (2) it negates the possibility of intra-national cultural differences and international cultural similarities. Hence, the practice of using these two terms interchangeably has received much criticism from scholars such as McSweeney (2009) and Usunier (1998). McSweeney (2009) drew a distinction between nation-states and countries, and Usunier (1998), through the example of countries like India and Switzerland, has shown that there could be several cultures within the same country (see Chapters 1 and 4 for detailed discussion).

In contradiction to conventional frameworks of culture, both transactional scholars, such as Barth, and DCF scholars, such as Thompson, have challenged the geo-ethnically grounded conceptualization of culture. As explained in Chapter 7 of this volume, Barth's early research on Kurdish tribes made him realize the futility of identifying a community or a place as an 'object of study'. Instead, he preferred to focus on underlying processes that lead to the generation of cultures and on conceptualizing cultural variation. In the same way, DCF scholars such as Thompson and Wildavsky (1986) argued that cultures are not countries, customs, myths, races or ethnicities. Rather, cultures are ways of life, which are continually tested for social viability. Thus, DCF scholars do not agree with the practice of equating nation (or any geographic entity for that matter) with culture.

Now, let us explore whether or not DCF scholars negate intragroup cultural variations in the same way as proponents of conventional frameworks of culture have inadvertently done. Our review of DCF literature reveals several examples where DCF scholars have exposed the cultural plurality found in a society, an organization or a country. For instance, using DCF, Rayner (1986) showed the existence of a variety of cultures and a matching variety of risk perceptions in American hospitals. In the same way, grounding our work in DCF, we (Patel 2007a) showed that all four cultures can be found in Indo-French alliances and that these cultures do not coincide with specific national groupings (see Chapter 10 for a more elaborate discussion of Rayner's 1986 and Patel's 2007a work). Patel and Schaefer (2009) demonstrated that even within one country (in their case, India), there is considerable cultural variety, which results in varied strategies of ethical decision making in companies. Thus, DCF scholars neither support the practice of equating nation with culture nor do they negate cultural plurality/diversity within a social entity. DCF scholars aim to expose the four cultures within a social entity and the ongoing interactions between members of these cultures. Additionally, since DCF supports that any two entities with similar scores on grid and group may be expected to behave in similar ways, it is capable of explaining the potential similarities that one encounters between collaborating entities in cross-border business ventures. Hence, we conclude that DCF is better equipped than conventional frameworks of culture to address the intra-group diversity and potential intergroup similarities that one encounters in the study of international business entities.

Reflection point 4: The different levels of culture

In this subsection, we address a question that has intrigued us from the outset: Do we need to address culture at its different levels (for instance, national, societal, regional, etc.) for optimal cultural sense-making? We also explore the viewpoint of DCF scholars on this question. Finally, we expose the implications that this reflection offers for the study of international business entities.

As observed in Chapter 4 of this volume, many scholars who adhere to conventional culture frameworks have chosen to address culture at specific levels. This means that they chose to address culture at the group, corporate, national, societal cluster, regional or other levels. This also means that, when they choose to address culture at one level (say, at the corporate level), they cannot address culture at another level (such as at the national level) simultaneously. Other scholars (including us) have remained unconvinced of the merit of addressing culture at specific levels. Some of the reasons behind this resistance are the following:

1. As seen in earlier chapters of this volume, Hofstede's (1980) national culture framework can only be applied to compare the cultures of two or more nations. In the same way, Hofstede (1991) and Trompenaars and Hampden-Turner's (1997) corporate culture frameworks can only be applied to compare cultures across two or more companies. However, neither of these frameworks can be used to explore cultural phenomenon between entities at different levels and scales. For example, these frameworks cannot be applied to explore the cultural interactions between a multinational firm, the local community that is affected by the firm's actions, and the national government that sets the laws governing the operations of the firm. Since conventional frameworks of culture can only be applied to a specific level of culture, they have limited applications, and they inadvertently undermine those cultural transactions that occur across levels and scales. In other words, phenomena that do not fit into specific levels of culture fall out of their meshes of inquiry, thereby generating voids in the knowledge of culture.

2. Following their 'level focused' approach to culture, some conventional culture scholars engage in grouping countries (i.e. lower levels of cultural manifestation) into larger clusters at the societal level (i.e. higher levels of cultural manifestation) and offering broad generalizations at the level of country clusters. In this case, what applies to the cluster level is assumed to apply to every country included in that cluster. However, these categorizations are not always convincing because they tend to ignore intra-country and intra-cluster (i.e. inter-country) variations. Consider the case of Canada. Although the GLOBE study has categorized Canada in the 'Anglo' cluster, there is a wide variety in Canada with English-speaking Canadians sharing more cultural similarities with their American neighbors than with their French-speaking compatriots (Tung 2008). Therefore, categorizing Canada as one homogenous country in the Anglo cluster implies neglecting its internal diversity. In the same way, even though Hofstede (2005) categorized many countries into one cluster called the 'Arab-speaking cluster', other scholars (Al-Nashmi and Syd Zin 2011) have shown that there is a wide cultural diversity within this cluster. To sum up, we find that cluster-level generalizations do not provide a sufficiently accurate representation of the cultural reality in such cases. Also, as mentioned earlier in this book, the practice of drawing inferences about lower levels from higher-level data, and vice-versa, is a mistake. Relationships identified at one level of analysis may be stronger or weaker at a different level, or they may even be in the reverse direction (Ostroff 1993, Klein and Kozlowski 2000 as cited by McSweeney 2009).

3. Finally, it is important to note that there is an inherent contradiction in holding these different levels of culture simultaneously. For instance, holding both the national and corporate cultural approaches simultaneously (Barth 2007, McSweeney 2009) would imply little difference between corporate cultures in the same country – a practice that would

incite strong resistance and much criticism from many companies who pride themselves on their distinctive corporate cultures.

As our previous arguments reveal, we, like many other culture researchers, remain unconvinced of the need to address culture at its so-called different levels for optimal cultural sense-making. Let us now explore where DCF scholars stand in regard to this question. Our review of DCF literature suggests that DCF has been successfully applied to study culture at a variety of levels: intra-organizational, inter-organizational, national, international and others. For instance, Virginie Mamadouh (1999) applied DCF at the national level to compare political cultures among European nations. In an earlier study, Mars (1982) used DCF at the organizational level to successfully probe the issue of workplace crime. In the same way, we (Patel 2007a, 2007b) have used DCF at the inter-organizational level to explore cultural dynamics between companies that have collaborated to form international strategic alliances. In addition to the varied levels of culture, DCF has also been applied across a wide variety of disciplines. As 6 and Peck (2004) have pointed out, although DCF was originally developed in anthropology (Douglas 1978, 1982, Thompson and Ellis 1997), it has also been applied to ecology (Douglas and Wildavsky 1983), political science (Thompson *et al.* 1990, Coyle and Ellis 1994, Thompson *et al.* 1999), public administration (Wildavsky 1987, 6 and Peck 2004) and, more recently, business studies (Patel 2007a, 2007b, Patel and Patel 2008, Patel and Schaefer 2009, Patel and Rayner 2012a, 2012b). This enhances the applicability of DCF beyond what conventional frameworks of culture can claim. Further, DCF has also been used to explore cultural dynamics between and across levels and scales. For instance, Steve Frosdick (1995a, 1995b) used DCF to study safety in British football stadia. This study explored cultural interactions between various entities across a variety of levels: local authorities, local communities, local police, regional football clubs, the stadia industry, the safety industry, football players, individual fans and national-level policymakers, to name just a few (see Chapter 10 for more details). Thus, the fact that DCF can be applied across levels and scales alleviates the need to rely on the use of a variety of cultural frameworks, which each claim to address culture at a specific level.

In concluding this subsection, we wish to clarify one important point. While conventional culture literature offers a variety of cultural frameworks to culture researchers, thereby allowing them a wide variety of conceptual choices, this quality in itself does not necessarily imply more clarity or even more consensus in the field. In fact, over past decades, an indiscriminate proliferation of cultural frameworks with overlapping categories has resulted in the lack of a dominant paradigm in the field (Tsui *et al.* 2007). The fact that we question the merit of these varied conceptual frameworks should not be taken to imply that we do not value theoretical pluralism. Instead, we only wish to point out that excessive and indiscriminate theoretical pluralism leads to theoretical compartmentalization (Astley and Van de Ven 1983) and to obscuring the interrelatedness between various viewpoints (Glynn and Raffaeli 2010). Our attempt to offer DCF as an alternative framework that can be applied across levels and scales may help achieve a certain degree of commensurability and consensus in culture literature. From the perspective of the study of international business entities, we find that the use of tools like DCF would allow us to examine many phenomena left unexplored due to want of more flexible tools. For instance, it is now possible to investigate cultural dynamics between an offshore branch of an MNC, its pool of customers, the local communities affected by the MNC, the local and national government bodies and other national and international agencies.

Reflection point 5: Social change as a never-ending non-linear phenomenon

In this subsection, we compare the explanations of social change offered by DCF scholars and by proponents of conventional frameworks of culture. Additionally, we discuss the implications of this reflection for the study of international business entities.

As discussed in Chapter 4, barring the works of Berry *et al.* (2002) and Kitayama (2002), most conventional frameworks of culture largely treat culture as a static set of characteristics that manifest homogenously in a social entity. This has inadvertently led to scholars neglecting the topic of social change. In contrast, as noted in Chapter 7, transactional scholars such as Barth have done significant work on social change. Yet, Barth's discussion does not explain why social change is a never-ending, non-linear process. Conversely and as explained in considerable detail in Chapter 8 of this book, DCF scholars provide a much better explanation of social change as a never-ending, non-linear phenomenon. Thompson (2003) has explained that a major problem with two-fold models popular in social sciences in the nineteenth and twentieth centuries (see Marx 1859, Maine 1861, Tönnies 1887, Durkheim 1893, Weber 1930, Williamson 1975) is that being tipped out of one state invariably implies falling into the other state, thereby inviting a self-inflicted dead end in the process of change. In contrast, DCF has provided an alternative four-fold model in which change is a never-ending feature. A four-fold model means that being thrown out of state A no longer implies falling into state B. There are twelve possible transitions (three possible transitions for members of each culture). This, Thompson (1996) contends, enables us to treat change as a complex, never-ending, non-linear, non-equilibrium process as opposed to a simple linear Newtonian mechanism leading to some sort of equilibrium. Thus, we believe that DCF offers a much more satisfying explanation of social change than conventional frameworks of culture.

Constant change, both domestic and international, characterizes the current business environment. Consider, for instance, Baudrillard's (1988) characterization of organizational life in consumer society as being temporary and fragile. More specifically, international business entities are characterized by constant restructuring, evolving corporate boundaries, ongoing mergers, acquisitions and takeovers, resulting in ever-changing boundaries and increasing diversity of conflicting goals (Angwin and Vaara 2005). In light of the ongoing and never-ending social changes experienced by these business entities, we believe that DCF offers a much more realistic representation of organizational life in the twenty-first century.

Reflection point 6: Culture as an 'uncaused cause'

In this subsection, we discuss whether culture is simply an 'uncaused cause' as implied by some conventional frameworks of culture. We also ask whether DCF allows us to address culture differently and discuss the implications of this reflection for the cultural exploration of international business entities.

In Chapter 4, we explained that, as long as we rely on cultural frameworks that address culture as being static and manifested at the national, societal, regional or corporate levels, we will continue using culture as an 'uncaused cause'. As long as culture is solely defined in terms of national, religious, ethnic, racial or corporate distinctiveness, culture must remain a fancy name for what we do not understand, and it will only be invoked to explain failures when all other forms of explanation (bad planning, poor design, inadequate resources, etc.) have been found wanting (Thompson and Ellis 1997). This means that, while we will continue to attribute failures or 'what went wrong' to culture, we will never really be able to explain how the said culture came about in the first place. Although the cultural frameworks discussed in Chapter 3 give us broad generalized patterns of behaviour at the national/ societal/regional levels, they do not explain how these behavioural patterns are created and sustained (with the exception of Shalom Schwartz's values theory). Let us now explore whether DCF addresses this issue better.

DCF provides us with a functional link between sense-making and action bias, thereby making it possible to understand how cultures are created and recreated. The fundamental principle of DCF is that people structure their ideas about both the natural and the social worlds in a way that is compatible with their experience of the organizational structure in the social unit that constitutes the focus of their daily lives. Rayner (1991) explained that socialization into different cultural types occurs along the lines of distinct cognitive frameworks that denote four different ways of organizing perception and knowledge. Since the world is symbolically structured, cultures ensure their production and reproduction by linking perception to social structure. With the help of these cognitive schemas, individuals extract meaning from an otherwise anarchic stream of events (Rayner 1991). Thus, each culture, in order to ensure its reproduction and survival, orders perception and knowledge to suit the needs of its particular form of social organization. In this way, DCF scholars successfully explained how cultures are generated and how they are sustained over time. Hence, proponents of DCF do not feel the need to treat culture as an 'uncaused cause'.

This quality makes DCF particularly suited in the context of international business entities where one often hears complaints like, 'I just cannot work with these Indians (or Russians, French, Germans, or any other nationality for that matter). They are so different from us. The cultural differences make it difficult/nearly impossible for us to collaborate with one another in the long term'. Such a thought style is inevitable when one relies on the notion of static, predetermined cultural templates guiding the behaviour of people around us. Following such a thought style makes it inevitable to treat culture as the uncaused cause of all our problems. On the other hand, DCF allows us to break free from cultural stereotypes and assess culture and behaviours in terms of daily transactions. Thus, it allows for better cultural sense-making in the context of international business entities than those possible with conventional frameworks of culture. Also, using DCF allows us to treat human behaviour as something that can change and evolve, thereby giving us hope to keep working on the transactional aspect of human relations.

Our discussion of the six reflection points presented in this chapter shows us that DCF overcomes some of the limitations of conventional frameworks of culture. However, like every other conceptual framework discussed in this book, DCF also has its critics. We continue with some of the criticisms leveled against DCF.

Critique of DCF

Despite its popularity with scholars across a variety of disciplines, DCF also has its critics. In this section, we discuss a few criticisms that DCF has been subjected to since its debut. First, the variety of labels used for the four cultures of DCF in past literature has led to considerable confusion among researchers (Mamadouh 1999). The high grid–high group culture has been referred to as hierarchy (hierarchist or hierarchical) or bureaucracy; the low grid–low group culture has been called markets, competition, entrepreneurs or individualism (individualistic or individualists); the high group–low grid culture has been called egalitarianism or egalitarian(s), factionalism, sect, enclave, dissenting groups, communard(s) or egalitarian enclaves; and, finally, the high grid–low group culture has been labelled as fatalism (fatalist or fatalistic), isolated, insulated or atomized subordination. These different labels draw one's attention to their different connotations and undermine the importance of the underlying grid–group dimensions and their strengths (Mamadouh 1999). Also, the use of labels such as 'individualists' and 'hier-archists' have led some researchers to treat the four cultures as personality or psychological types rather than emerging cultural patterns. Not surprisingly, in their analyses, these scholars have tended to focus solely on categorizing people into the four culture types (as if they were static categories), while neglecting the social context and the constraints that these cultures place on individuals (Tansey 2004). This has somewhat weakened the presentation, application and validation of DCF (Mamadouh 1999).

Second, although DCF has proven useful in many different disciplines, its applications are vulnerable to illustrative examples and bird-spotting (Mamadouh 1999). Bird-spotting refers to the practice among DCF scholars to spot illustrative instances of the four cultures. While this practice confirms that the framework holds, it offers little by way of enriching how these cultures came about – an important aspect towards which transactional scholars like Barth have always called attention. Consequently, proponents of DCF have often found themselves caught in a crossfire between those who prefer to keep culture out of the picture and those who want to study culture but consider typologies (including those offered by DCF) to be too reductionist. We reckon that the only way to overcome this dilemma is to follow Barth's advice and focus on the underlying processes that lead to the emergence of different cultures. Doing this will give richer insights into the problem at hand compared to the reductionist and simplistic exercise of spotting the four cultures.

Some critics, such as Sjöberg (1997), have complained that DCF has not well classified a variety of human behaviours. Similarly, Renn (1992) stated that the four cultures proposed by DCF are too limited to capture the full richness of empirically observed behaviours. However, such judgements reveal that these scholars have misunderstood the purpose of the framework. It is not the objective of DCF to suggest that individuals can be definitively assigned to one of four quadrants. Instead, what DCF scholars have aspired to do is to provide a framework for understanding the dynamics of the social interactions that occur as the four cultures compete with each other in daily life. It is important that those scholars and practitioners considering using DCF understand that, in reality, one encounters a combination of different cultures within a social entity. As 6 and Mars (2008) have aptly explained, DCF, correctly understood, requires hybridity and not pure forms of culture because people do not live their lives as members of one cultural type. Discussing the four cultures in their pure forms is only required so that one may be able to produce a consistent set of values and behaviours for each culture.

Finally, some scholars (see Milton 1996) have complained that DCF does not give sufficient importance to human agency. We disagree. In our understanding, DCF conceptualizes human behaviour as the outcome of an ongoing interaction between individuals and their contexts. It attributes human behaviour neither solely to the individual nor solely to the context. Finally, DCF has sometimes been criticized for not clarifying the level of analysis. DCF scholars have defended their stand by explaining that cultural interactions are independent of levels and scales. Since this has been examined in some detail earlier in this chapter, we refrain from repeating this discussion here. While many scholars consider the inherent flexibility of DCF (i.e. the ability that it can be applied across levels and scales) to be an asset, others worry that frameworks (like DCF) that are too widely applicable may have weak predictive powers (Mamadouh 1999).

Concluding remarks

Our discussion in Chapter 8 of this volume showed that DCF scholars have successfully addressed some of the problems with the transactional culture approach. For instance, DCF scholars provided a much richer and varied discussion of rationalities than that provided by Barth. DCF also satisfactorily explained cultural plurality/diversity without relying on dichotomies or on the infinity argument of culture. In the present chapter, we reveal that DCF also overcomes some of the limitations of conventional frameworks of culture. However, we do not claim that DCF is a perfect framework of culture. Making such a claim about any conceptual framework would be erroneous. Indeed, conceptual frameworks are like any other instrument. They are best when used for the specific purpose for which they are designed. A mismatch of tools and objectives will only yield suboptimal results. Therefore, we do not make the mistake of searching for a perfect framework of culture – instead, we are looking for a framework that can be effectively used for cultural sense-making in a specific context when other frameworks of culture are not appropriate. In the present case, the context we have chosen to focus on is that of international business entities. As mentioned in the introductory section of this chapter, Aaron Wildavsky insisted that a theory should be judged not against an impossible standard of perfection but by how well it performs in comparison with rival theories (as cited by Grendstad and Selle 1997). Building on Wildavsky's advice, we suggest that a theory should be judged by how well it performs in comparison with rival theories within a specific context. For instance, using national culture frameworks such as the one proposed by Hofstede (1980) might be sufficient when one is visiting a country for the first time and would like to have a broad and sweeping understanding of how people from said country behave. However, it might be less appropriate when the objective is to understand cultural dynamics in an international strategic alliance where people of different nationalities, different educational back-grounds, different departmental affiliations, different loyalty and interest groups, etc. are brought together to work in a competitive, dynamic and challenging environment. In such a context, one might need frameworks capable of addressing the dynamicity of the context and the plurality of cultures. This is when frameworks such as DCF may be more appropriate than conventional frameworks of culture.

In the next chapter of this book (i.e. Chapter 10), we identify three managerial scenarios where using DCF might be more appropriate than using conventional frameworks of culture. In fact, past scholars have used both conventional frameworks of culture and DCF to explore each of these three scenarios. Through our discussions, we expose how using DCF leads to a richer understanding of the managerial problem at hand and therefore to a better understanding of potential solutions than using conventional frameworks of culture. Another highlight of Chapter 10 is that each of the three studies cited in this chapter offers an illustration of the use of DCF at a different level of application. While managerial scenario 1 illustrates the use of DCF at the inter-organizational level – in this case, in Indo-French alliances – managerial scenario 2 elucidates the use of DCF to make sense of cultural dynamics at the intra-organizational level – in this case, in American hospitals. The last managerial scenario outlined in Chapter 10 shows the use of DCF to understand cultural dynamics between different actors across levels and scales in a study of the British stadia safety industry. These three illustrations come from previously published scholarly work and contribute to a global appreciation of the versatility of DCF as a cultural sense-making tool.

Part IV

Applications of the Douglasian Cultural Framework to resolve a variety of business problems and conclusions

10 Appraising the versatility of the Douglasian Cultural Framework

Illustrations from varied managerial scenarios

Life is the most versatile thing under the sun; and in the pursuit of life and character the author who works in a groove works in blinkers.

Laurence Housman

What you will learn in this chapter:

- commonly observed managerial scenarios that do not lend themselves well to the use of conventional frameworks of culture;
- the usefulness of alternative frameworks of culture such as DCF in the aforementioned managerial scenarios;
- the versatility of DCF.

Introduction

In previous chapters of this book, we have presented several conceptual arguments stressing the limitations of over-relying on conventional frameworks of culture. As explained earlier, such frameworks, while easy to understand and apply, fail to address cultural dynamics in those contexts where the strict boundaries of nations, regions, societies or corporations cannot be specified. In the present chapter, we attempt to provide empirical examples of three studies supporting our arguments. In each of these illustrative studies, we address a specific managerial problem. Each scenario begins with an overview of the managerial problem and exposes why addressing this problem is crucial for managers. Then we present a review of what conventional literature on culture says about the problem at hand and the insights or conclusions it provides. Next, we offer a brief synopsis of one previous study that explores the same managerial problem through the DCF lens. Finally, we compare the insights gleaned from the DCF-based study and those gathered from conventional literature on culture to assess which proves to be more useful for managers. Readers should note that it is not our objective to prove that DCF is superior to other frameworks of culture. Our objective is simply to show that, in certain scenarios that managers may encounter in their professional lives, there is a blurring of the boundaries of nations, societies, regions and corporations. In such scenarios, conventional frameworks of culture, which overly rely on such geographic entities and their boundaries, cannot be used effectively. Hence, in such instances, managers need to be able to identify and use alternative cultural sense-making tools. DCF is one such tool. This chapter, therefore, contributes towards exposing the versatility of DCF as a cultural sense-making tool.

Managerial scenario 1: Making sense of cultural dynamics in international inter-firm relations

Introduction and significance of the study

Cross-border inter-firm cooperations such as ISAs have increased significantly since the 1970s. With growing international competition and the need to succeed across borders, ISAs represent a useful, sometimes necessary tool of global expansion (Fedor and Werther 1996). Notwithstanding, the failure rate of ISAs continues to be high. Many business scholars (see Fedor and Werther 1996) have highlighted that ISAs are complex entities because of legal, political, linguistic and cultural barriers, while others (see Shenkar and Zeira 1992, Schoenberg *et al.* 1995, Barkema and Vermeulen 1997, Steensma *et al.* 2000) pinpoint cultural differences as being particularly problematic for the viability of alliances and mergers and acquisitions (Schneider 1988, Very *et al.* 1993 as quoted by Veiga, Lubatkin, Calori and Very 2000). As crucial as they are, international business collaborations are not immune to the impact of culture, and they experience high failure rates. Therefore, exploring the role of culture in the viability or success of such collaborations becomes important. In the subsequent subsection, we provide an overview of what conventional cultural literature says about the impact of culture on the viability of international inter-firm collaborations.

Conventional wisdom concerning the impact of culture on the viability/ success of international inter-firm collaborations

In Chapter 2 of the present volume, we elaborated in some depth on what conventional literature (e.g. Spekman and Lynn 2000, Li, Lam and Qian 2001) says about the impact of culture on the success of international inter-firm collaborations. Therefore, in the present section, we simply offer a short recap to refresh the memory of the reader. Scholars like Meschi (1997) have recommended carefully controlling cultural differences to ensure the success of cross-border alliances in general. Other scholars (see Woodcock and Geringer 1991, Shenkar and Zeira 1992) have focused more specifically on international joint ventures (IJVs) and identified cultural differences between partners as being a common source of problems. Barkema and Vermeulen (1997) argued that some differences in national culture dimensions (such as uncertainty avoidance and long-term orientation) between partners are more disruptive than others are for IJV survival. While some scholars relate the success or failure of inter-firm alliances to national culture, still others (Haspelasgh and Jemison 1991, Nahavandi and Malekzadeh 1998) have identified differences between organizational cultures as influencing merger outcomes. Differences in organizational cultures have also been associated with outcomes such as lower commitment of acquired employees, increased turnover of acquired executives and lower financial success (see Chapter 2 of this volume for detailed references). Broadly speaking, many scholars from the functionalist epistemological school have agreed that culture clashes are likely to be more pronounced in cross-national mergers than in domestic ones because such mergers bring together firms that not only have different organizational cultures but are also rooted in different national cultures (Schneider 1988, Very *et al.* 1993 as quoted by Veiga, Lubatkin, Calori and Very 2000).

Unlike scholars who rely on conventional frameworks of culture and consequently treat cultural differences as being problematic to international inter-firm collaborations, some scholars assume a much more dynamic perspective on culture. These scholars attempt to understand how new cultures might be generated through international collaborations. In Chapter 2 of this volume, we have offered Rodriguez's (2005) study of American-Mexican alliances as an example of such a dynamic approach. Rodriguez (2005) has explained that, in these alliances, the corporate cultures of both companies converged into a 'third culture'. This third culture combined the task innovation and emotional concern of American managers with the task support and social focus of Mexican managers. Rodriguez (2005) concluded that, by designing an organizational culture that incorporates the cognitive diversity of partners, an intercultural fit in an alliance could be achieved. Culture, according to this study, is dynamic and amenable to change, and cultural differences contribute towards creating a richer and more viable culture as opposed to generating problems. Another recent study that deserves attention was conducted by Ailon-Souday and Kunda (2003). These scholars challenged the functionalist notion that national identity is 'a passive embodiment of a predetermined cultural template' (Ailon-Souday and Kunda 2003: 1074) and contended that this conceptualization fails to take into account the freedom that members exercise in defining what national belonging means to them. Through their ethnographic study of an Israeli-American merger, they showed that members often tailored national identity towards certain socials goals. Acting out certain stereotypes, in fact, served a strategic interest for many Israeli employees, who consciously and systematically reproduced these stereotypes. This, as readers will note, is a far cry from the assumption that individuals are passive recipients of a predetermined national culture. Ailon-Souday and Kunda (2003) surmised that globalized organizational realities cannot be effectively captured by viewing national identity as an objective essence.

This subsection reveals that, although functional frameworks of culture dominate conventional literature on the impact of culture on international business collaborations, many scholars have expressed dissatisfaction with such frameworks and have favoured a more dynamic conceptualization of culture. We took inspiration from this latter group of scholars and decided to use DCF as our conceptual framework to explore cultural dynamics in Indo-French alliances (see Patel 2005, 2007a, 2007b). Although it is beyond the scope of this book to offer a detailed description of our study conducted over a five-year period from 2001 to 2006 (see additional reading section for full references), we offer below a short synopsis of the same.

Using DCF to explore cultural dynamics in Indo-French alliances (Patel 2005, 2007a, 2007b)

In our study, we began with a broad question: How do managers in Indo-French alliances evoke culture? Once we had answered this broad question, we attempted to address another more pertinent question: How can these managers design alliances that are more viable?

In the early part of our study, we learned that the popular notion that culture is a success factor in international alliances does not hold. If anything, most managers considered culture to be a failure factor for their alliances. Although managers provided an extensive list of factors that led to the success of their alliances, 'culture' never appeared on this list. The reason behind this is most managers in these alliances resorted to national culture frameworks to make sense of the complex reality of international alliances. For instance, we often heard remarks like, 'It is difficult to work with the Indians – they never deliver what they promise and never respect deadlines' or 'Working with the French is so difficult – the cultural barriers are just too vast to overcome'. Attributing people's behaviours to their national identity inevitably led these managers to a dead end. Moreover, although this attribution is a popular practice, it does not explain the diversity within and the similarities across nations. Culture thus becomes an 'uncaused cause'. In other words, although managers consider culture problematic for the viability of their alliances, they are unable to explain how culture comes about in the first place. Our study revealed that managers who attempted to explain the differences between their French and Indian colleagues based on commonly known national stereotypes often ended up contradicting themselves. For instance, while one respondent noted that Indians were more collectivistic than the French (which is consistent with Hofstede's national culture framework), he also admitted being confused when he observed the individualistic and mutually competitive behaviours among his Indian colleagues.

While most managers relied on national identity as a cultural sense-making tool, some managers recognized the futility of such tools and resorted to other means. The factors they cited to make sense of people's workplace behaviours included the size of the alliance, the management of the alliance – professional or family run – and the status of the parent companies – privately held or public firms. The fact that some managers offered these variables to explain human behaviour indicates that they are looking beyond national identity. However, these situational variables by themselves were insufficient to explain or predict people's behaviours because these variables were found in different permutations and combinations in alliance partners. For instance, while it was logical to assume that members of a large public sector company are accustomed to bureaucracy, hierarchy and rules, and would therefore have a preference for hierarchical behaviour,[1] it was more difficult to predict behavioural strategies in, say, a large public company that was professionally managed, or in a medium-sized quasi-private company. Hence, although the situational factors cited in this paragraph are interesting, they do not always help managers to predict or understand people's behaviours.

Having recognized that both national identity and situational factors fail to provide a satisfactory understanding of people's behaviours in ISAs, we turned our attention towards corporate culture. We found that most managers perceived that their companies had one overarching corporate culture that served as a guiding principle to all employees. This is very much in line with the standpoint of integration scholars (see Chapter 5 of the present volume). However, further probing and our own observations within these alliances revealed that there are several cultures, and even countercultures, within the same company. This became particularly evident in companies undergoing change. While certain employees supported the proposed change, there were inevitably other groups that resisted the change; while some saw the change as being detrimental to their own well-being, others resisted it with a viewpoint of protecting their more vulnerable colleagues. The notion that organizations have one consistent and commonly shared culture fell apart when viewed from the perspective of the manager in charge of the change. Our field experiences in Indo-French alliances were more consistent with the standpoints of differentiation and fragmentation scholars (see Chapter 6 of the present volume). We concluded that a static conceptualization of corporate culture also proves to be dissatisfactory in the context of ISAs because these organizations are characterized by continually shifting boundaries, constant changes, takeovers, mergers and acquisitions. People from different backgrounds, national origins, educational profiles, professional experiences, and corporate and departmental affiliations are brought together in a dynamic and sometimes mutually competitive environment. Corporate boundaries are constantly redefined, and national, corporate, departmental and other identities are challenged. In such an environment, functionalist frameworks of corporate culture fail to provide the required insight into people's cultural and behavioural preferences.

Some of our respondents who found nationality, corporate culture, and situational variables to be dissatisfactory for cultural sense-making resorted to other explanations; they argued that employees frequently and regularly adapt their workplace behaviour with the environment or the context. As one respondent put it,

> Human behaviour is a lot about the environment. It is also about the personality, but it is more about the environment. After all, I have to feed my family. If I lose my job, it is my family that suffers, not your family! So, it is all about the environment!

The notion that people adapt their behaviours to their contexts is consistent with DCF (see Thompson 1996, Thompson and Ellis 1997). Further, DCF also supports that people's behaviours are subject to different levels of social pressures within a specific context. Our study provided an excellent example of how individuals adapt to the different social contexts in which they find themselves. One of the managers whom we interviewed explained in great detail how the culture of his present employer (an Indo-French alliance) differed from that of his previous employer (a large public sector organization). He also elaborated on how he was required to adapt his behaviour from a hierarchical to a competitive one when he changed jobs. This example offers support to DCF's premise that people can and do change their behaviours to fit with their social context.

Having investigated how managers in Indo-French alliances evoke culture, we next explored whether we may offer them insights regarding designing alliances that are more viable. In order to do this, we used DCF to explore the differences and similarities between the cultural dynamics of viable and failed alliances. In many of the viable Indo-French alliances, we observed a dynamic and mutually rivalrous coexistence of all the four cultures. This is illustrated below through the schematic diagram of one such alliance. As Figure 10.1 shows, people's cultural preferences are not aligned in any way with their national identities.

Our analysis of failed alliances revealed one or more of the following reasons behind the erosion of viability:

1. the inability of members of the hierarchical culture to adapt to the needs/ demands of members of the competitive culture;
2. the preoccupation of members of the competitive group with self-interest, thereby undermining 'rights and wrongs'; or
3. the presence of fatalism and the absence of egalitarian groups.

We also found several examples of interdependence between hierarchical and competitive groups in both failed and viable alliances. Members of hierarchical groups depended on those of the competitive groups because the latter helped them to understand the needs of the customers and adapt the product/ price accordingly. In addition, members of competitive groups were quick in seizing opportunities, taking risks and being creative. Members of hierarchical cultures, left to their own devices, would become overly focused on processes, standards and rules, which would lead to a total paralysis of the system (see 6, 2004). Conversely, members of competitive cultures depended on their hierarchical counterparts to ensure that standards are respected, quality is

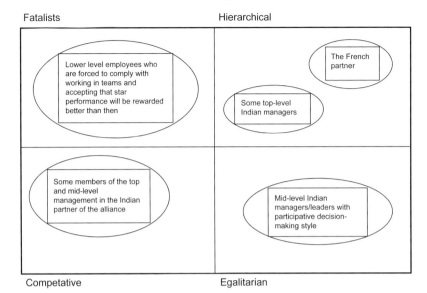

Fatalists   Hierarchical

The French partner

Lower level employees who are forced to comply with working in teams and accepting that star performance will be rewarded better than then

Some top-level Indian managers

Some members of the top and mid-level management in the Indian partner of the alliance

Mid-level Indian managers/leaders with participative decision-making style

Competative   Egalitarian

Figure 10.1 The dynamic coexistence of the four cultures of J.V. Gloconnect
Source: Patel (2005)

maintained, and rules and procedures are followed. Although interesting, this interdependence between the two active cultures was not sufficient for the viability of international alliances – we found such instances of interdependence in both failed and viable alliances.

DCF scholars (see Rayner and Malone 1999, Thompson 1996) have advised that for any complex system to be viable at least three cultures are required. Our analysis of two failed Indo-French alliances suggested that this missing link is not fatalism because fatalist groups were found in both failed alliances (along with the hierarchical and competitive cultures). Therefore, the next logical step for us was to explore whether the egalitarian culture had something to do with the viability of alliances. Our exploration revealed that it was the egalitarian culture that facilitated the formation of cultural coalitions in viable Indo-French alliances by creating an interface between the competitive group and hierarchical groups. The egalitarian culture affected the viability of the alliance by:

1. contributing to sustenance of a dynamic disequilibrium between the four cultural types (requisite variety condition) (Thompson 1996, based on Ashby 1947);
2. reaching out to both the hierarchical and the competitive groups due to the similarity it shares with them;
3. allowing for the accomplishment of complex tasks (Thompson 1996) due to its high level of organization; and
4. averting a 'gridlock' between the two dominant cultures.[2]

Since strategy switching in complex realities requires no fewer than three strategies (Rayner and Malone 1999), we concluded that the active participation of the three active cultures (hierarchical, competitive and egalitarian) is required for viability of ISAs. This led to the realization that managers who wish to design viable alliances need to proactively support this cultural plurality within their organizations. In pursuing the goals of international alliances, managers often promote their own cultural preferences, thus emphasizing their own viewpoint and precluding others. However, doing so might only lead to gridlocks between the dominant cultural groups. What ensures the viability of international alliances is just the opposite. Hence, in designing international alliances, managers should focus more on involving people from different cultural groups rather than focusing on creating one homogenous group. In the next subsection, we compare our findings with past recommendations from conventional literature.

Comparing the knowledge contributions of this study with conventional wisdom

Our ethnographic study of the role of culture in the viability of Indo-French alliances suggests that cultural plurality is the essence of viability for any social system. It states that the vigorous participation of the three active cultures is required for viability of ISAs. Let us now draw our attention towards how this message of cultural plurality compares with insights offered by conventional business literature. Conventional frameworks propagate the idea of one homogeneous culture for an entire nation, society, region or company. While discussing viability of international business collaborations, their attempt has generally been towards reducing or minimizing so-called cultural differences between collaborating parties. Several researchers (e.g. Shenkar and Zeira 1992, Meschi 1997, Barkema and Vermeulen 1997) have suggested that the lesser the cultural difference between collaborating firms, the higher their chances of success. Since cultural similarity is considered a precondition to success, any cultural difference is instinctively perceived as being detrimental to the relationship. In sharp contrast, our study suggests that it is supporting cultural plurality or diversity by encouraging and actively involving different cultural groups that increases the likelihood of the viability of ISAs. Actively supporting the presence and participation of the three active cultures is messy and chaotic, and it is a far cry from the elegance of a single-voice solution, where only one dominant voice is heard. Nevertheless, it is important for policymakers to focus on making the three active voices heard if they want the social system to remain viable. This is what some scholars (Verweij and Thompson 2006) have called a 'clumsy solution'. Even though this clumsy solution lacks the elegance of its single-voice counterpart, it is valuable because it resists the temptation of blocking out the wisdom of different cultural types. Suppressing one or more of the active voices is neither a long-term nor an ideal solution (Thompson *et al.* 2000).

Our study also reveals the significance of the egalitarian group. Although the hierarchical and competitive cultures have received much attention in past literature, the egalitarian group has remained largely neglected. Our study reveals that the egalitarian group serves as the bridge between the other two dominant cultures, thereby contributing towards the viability of ISAs.

Finally, by using DCF, we make it possible to compare across cultures, using a systematic and dynamic tool that does not rely on static representations of culture within artificially imposed national, regional and corporate boundaries. Thus, as compared to conventional literature, our use of DCF to conduct a cultural analysis of ISAs offers different and unique insights to managers regarding the cultural dynamics in such entities.

Managerial scenario 2: Making sense of intra-firm cultural dynamics

Introduction and significance of the study

As discussed in earlier chapters of this book, conventional literature on culture, especially from business studies, tends to conceptualize culture at a variety of different levels: national, regional, societal, corporate and others. As one would expect and as Tsui *et al.* (2007) have pointed out, focusing on different levels of culture has led to the proliferation of a variety of cultural frameworks, each purportedly suited for cultural exploration at a specific level. As explained elsewhere, we do not challenge the need for a rich variety of conceptual frameworks for culture, but we also support Tsui *et al.*'s (2007) call for more commensuration in culture literature. In response to this call, it becomes necessary to demonstrate that there are cultural frameworks that can be effectively applied across a variety of levels. Such frameworks (see Boisot's I-Space model, for instance) do not support a conceptualization of culture as being constrained by specific and previously defined national, regional, societal and/or corporate boundaries. Through the present example, we wish to show that DCF also serves this purpose. In managerial scenario 1 presented earlier, DCF has been applied to study cultural dynamics in international inter-firm collaborations. In managerial scenario 2 we show that the same framework i.e. DCF can also be used to make sense of intra-firm cultural dynamics.

To illustrate scenarios requiring managers to analyse intra-firm cultural dynamics, we offer the example of Steve Rayner's (1986) study of risk perceptions in American hospitals. We explain what conventional literature has to say about the impact of culture on risk perception before presenting a summary of Rayner's (1986) study.

Conventional wisdom regarding culture and risk perception

Conventional literature on the impact of culture on risk perceptions relies largely on national culture frameworks. This comes as no surprise considering that business literature seems to be largely dominated by functionally driven national and corporate culture frameworks. Consider, for example, Gierlach *et al.*'s (2010) study that shows that there are considerable differences among Japanese, Argentinean and North American respondents in the level of perceived risk. Japanese groups have the highest risk perception concerning natural disasters and terrorist attacks, while North Americans and Argentineans have the lowest risk perception for terrorism. Among the different national culture dimensions, uncertainty avoidance (Hofstede 1980) is the most commonly cited as influencing risk-taking. It is believed that there is a strong conceptual link between tolerance of uncertainty and risk-taking (Kreiser *et al.* 2010). Since risk-taking generates a high level of outcome uncertainty, it is believed that managers in uncertainty-accepting societies are comfortable exposing themselves to risk-prone situations (see also Thomas and Mueller 2000). Conversely, people from cultures with high uncertainty avoidance scores try to avoid new situations that are characterized by higher levels of uncertainty regarding the risk involved (Hofstede 1980, Money and Crotts 2003, Chakraborty, Lala and Warren 2003, as cited by Kailani and Kumar 2011). In addition to uncertainty avoidance, Kreiser *et al.* (2010) also identified power distance as having a significant negative influence on risk-taking. Similarly, using data collected in the U.S.A., Jordan and India, Kailani and Kumar (2011) showed that, in cultures where uncertainty avoidance is high, perceived risk with internet buying is high, and this negatively impacts internet buying. These scholars inferred from their findings that countries that exhibit high uncertainty avoidance value security, clear rules and a formal structure to life; their citizens are generally more resistant to change from established patterns and tend to focus on risk avoidance and risk reduction.

As seen in our overview of conventional literature, many scholars use national culture dimensions to make sense of people's risk-taking behaviours at an individual level. In so doing, these scholars transpose national-level generalizations on to individuals, a common error among proponents of national culture frameworks. Further, these scholars offer insights regarding the impact of national culture on risk-taking in specific contexts such as entrepreneurial ventures (Kreiser *et al.* 2010) and internet purchasing (Kailani and Kumar 2011). In making these predictions, these researchers seem to assume that, since risk perception is dictated by a stable and homogenous national culture, this leads to a common risk perception throughout a nation's population. In contrast, Masuda and Garvin (2006) argued that risks are situated within the social experiences and interactions of individuals, groups and institutions (Scherer and Cho 2003). According to them, each cultural group seeks to advocate a view of risk that conforms to its way of seeing the world. They showed that risk perceptions are not isolated within minds of individuals but are manifested as threats to shared ways of life. Additionally, in a circular and reinforcing manner, worldviews influence risk perceptions, and risk perceptions serve to reinforce and legitimate pre-existing worldviews (see also Renn 2003). The approach that Masuda and Garvin (2006) have adopted is evidently very different from the one espoused by conventional scholars of culture. We find that Steve Rayner's (1986) study conducted two decades before that of Masuda and Garvin (2006) also provides a similar message. This study used DCF as its conceptual framework and explored risk perceptions in American hospitals.

Using DCF to explore risk perceptions in American hospitals (Rayner 1986)

In this study, Rayner (1986) examined risk perceptions regarding radiological hazards among medical practitioners, support staff and maintenance staff in American hospitals, which provided a fascinating context for a sociological analysis of risk. Grounding his analysis of perceptions regarding accidental exposure to radioactive substances in DCF, Rayner argued that people's social experiences influence their views towards risks. Individuals will tolerate risks and seek rewards that are consistent with their cultural affiliations. Citing Douglas and Wildavsky (1983) and Thompson (1984), Rayner explained that people in hierarchical, egalitarian competitive, and fatalistic cultures focus on different kinds of risks (technical, societal or environmental) according to what they perceive as most threatening to their own cultures. He identified four groups of people in American hospitals, each with their own unique ways of perceiving risk from accidental exposure to radioactive substances. These four groups coincided with the four cultural types of DCF, and Table 10.1 presents the findings.

Discussing each of the four cultural types in detail, as exposed by Rayner's (1986) study, is beyond the scope of the present chapter. Nevertheless, we now offer a brief summary of the characteristics of each of the four cultures and their perceptions of and attitude towards radiation-related risks. Consider the case of surgeons who had a particularly cavalier attitude to radiation hazards. Their disrespect for rules and procedures regarding experiments with radio-pharmaceuticals made them particularly infamous with Radiation Protection Officers (RPOs). RPOs described these surgeons as 'big ego professionals' and as being 'totally out of control' with respect to procedures. Rayner provided an extreme example of one surgeon who effected the unauthorized removal of a radioisotope from the refrigerator of the RPO in order to carry out experiments. Being a member of the competitive culture, the surgeon simply did not understand why his research programme should be under the control of external agents and their regulations. Only the threat of completely shutting down his laboratory could induce him to return the radioisotope to the office of the RPO. The author also provided other examples of competitive behaviours among physicians and radiologists who would order patients to be exposed to more x-rays than necessary simply to preclude future litigations. Designed solely to protect their own interests, their strategy held little consideration for the rules and regulations governing the use of radioactive material.

Table 10.1 The four cultural types of DCF in American hospitals and their perceptions of radiation-related risks

	Hierarchical	Competitive	Egalitarian	Fatalistic
Personnel	Radio-technicians, hospital administrators	Radio-therapists, radio-diagnostician, specialists in nuclear medicine	Staff of free clinics, coalition for the medical rights for women	Maintenance staff, junior nurses, cleaners and porters
Transactional arena	Organic groups	Ego-based networks	Mechanical groups	Atomized niches
Transactional mode	Routine procedures	Competition	Collaboration	Control
Decision making	Committee	Individual	Consensus	Limited by others
Driving values	System maintenance	Expansion	Equality	Survival
Focus of attention	Routinization of procedures (standardization)	Professional career (cure)	Health maintenance (prevention)	Diverse
Concern for radiation risk	Low concern for own radiation risks	Low concern for own radiation risks	High concern for own radiation risks	High concern for own radiation risks
Satisfaction with safety measures	High satisfaction with safety measures	High satisfaction with safety measures	Low satisfaction with safety measures	Low satisfaction with safety measures

Source: Rayner (1986)

On the other hand, RPOs (characterized by their strict adherence to radiation-related rules, regulations and procedures), hospital administrators and clinical technicians demonstrated hierarchical preferences. Clinical technicians, for example, scrupulously carried out regular wipe tests for radioactive contamination of work surfaces, telephone handsets, etc. Rayner (1986) explained that, while members of the competitive culture were more comfortable with individual judgement and the sense of personal control, members of the hierarchical culture were more at ease following rules and regulations to the letter. 'It is only through adherence to rules and regulations that hazards can be avoided' was their way of rationalizing their preferences. For them, the governing bodies decided where the risks lie, and how to avoid these risks. In case of accidents, members of hierarchical groups would follow clear procedures for fact finding and problem solving. Despite their strengths, members of the hierarchical culture also had some 'blind spots'. For instance, they suffered from a propensity to undermine risk by engaging in time-consuming routines, which sometimes resulted in aggravating the risk. Another common problem with members of hierarchical groups was their blind adherence to standards, which led to the assumption that exposure to radiation below the set standards was safe and did not need to be monitored. Members of the competitive culture also had their weaknesses; they sometimes overestimated the extent of their own control on the risk in question, inadvertently augmenting the risk for all concerned.

Unlike members of the competitive culture who underplayed risks and members of the hierarchical culture who prioritized following rules, regulations and procedures over addressing the risk at hand, members of the egalitarian culture were very conscious and careful concerning radiation hazards. For these individuals, a risk to any one member of their group was perceived as a risk for all members. Rayner (1986) offered the Coalition for Medical Rights of Women and small not-for-profit cooperative clinics as examples of egalitarian culture. Conversely, he offered junior nursing and auxiliary staff (such as janitors, plumbers and cleaners) as examples of fatalistic groups. This last group of employees had both less protection against and less information regarding radiation hazards. The plethora of regulations and precautions regarding radiation-related risks confused members of fatalist groups. They had little confidence in experts charged with their safety. They were also sceptical of the regulations governing the disposal of radioactive waste in these hospitals. Notwithstanding their concerns, members of the fatalistic groups did not object to working in risk-prone areas. They only sought more information regarding and more control over their working environment and the risks this environment presented. In fact, in one particular hospital, when these employees were offered more control over handling radioactive substances, they readily discarded their fatalistic mind-set and became more engaged and involved in the discussion.

As a final point, Rayner (1986) explained that, compared to members of hierarchical and competitive groups, those of fatalist and egalitarian groups shared a higher level of dissatisfaction with safety measures and a higher concern about their own exposure to radiation hazards. Despite these apparent similarities, the underlying rationalities of members of the four cultures are very different. While competitive individuals are risk-takers who view radiation hazards as the legitimate costs of individual choices, hierarchical individuals use rules, regulations, procedures and standards as ways of avoiding risks. Members of both fatalist and egalitarian groups are risk-averse, but for different reasons. Fatalists resent not having a choice in deciding whether or not to work in a risky environment. On the other hand, egalitarians avoid risks because they consider the threat to one of their members as an equal threat to all members. Rayner (1986) elaborated that not only are the four cultures opposite and contradictory in their perceptions of risk, but they also recognize each other's merits and overcome each other's blind spots. There is a certain amount of tension as well as a degree of give and take between them. For example, although RPOs have a penchant for rules, regulations and procedures, they acknowledge that there are times when rules need to be bent. Similarly, although most surgeons have a distinct disrespect for procedures, many of them acknowledged that routines offer protection to ill-informed individuals. Thus, there are few purely competitive or purely hierarchical individuals.

Comparing the knowledge contributions of this study with conventional wisdom

Rayner (1986) made three distinctive contributions as compared to past literature on culture and risk perception. First, he showed that different cultures coexist in the same hospital. Members of each culture have different appreciations of the same risk and try to protect themselves from what they consider risky (see also Masuda and Garvin 2006). Second, Rayner's (1986) findings show that people within the same entity (nation or hospital) display varied propensities for risk, thereby challenging the tendency to simplistically categorize entire nations as being high or low on risk-taking (Hofstede 1980). Rayner's (1986) explanation of how cultures influence risk perceptions offers more conceptual richness than the commonly cited conventional dichotomy of risk-takers versus risk-avoiders. In other words, by using DCF to explore intra-firm dynamics, Rayner (1986) went beyond the simple exercise of classifying people based on national origin and focused instead on explaining why people behave as risk-takers or risk-averse in certain situations. The underlying differences in the way people rationalize risk offers several valuable insights regarding methods of promoting increased vigilance against safety hazards. Considering that people choose to be risk-takers or risk-averse for different reasons, we reckon that methods of promoting vigilance against safety hazards will also differ for members with different cultural affiliations. Third, past studies usually relate risk perceptions to specific national cultural dimensions, such as uncertainty avoidance and power distance (Kailani and Kumar 2011). Such scholars inadvertently transpose national culture dimensions on to the individual level (Leung *et al.* 2005). In contrast, Rayner (1986a) showed that people's risk perceptions are informed by their underlying values and behavioural preferences rather than their national origin and/or corporate affiliations. Understanding the plural rationalities and perceptions of risk that coexist in social entities is necessary if policymakers and managers wish to address risk and safety issues more effectively.

Managerial scenario 3: Making sense of cultural dynamics in a firm–community nexus

Introduction and significance of the study

As seen in earlier chapters, one of the major concerns of conventional frameworks of culture, and studies grounded in such frameworks, is the tendency to equate culture with an entity – usually a nation or a company. In other words, for these scholars, a culture exists within predetermined boundaries of a nation or a company. Additionally, within these boundaries, culture is homogenous, uniform and stable. Guided by such notions, past discussions of culture, at least in business literature, have focused excessively on boundaries and on their supposed stability and durability. However, managers are often faced with scenarios wherein the notion of stable and durable boundaries does not apply and is instead replaced with the notion of porous, changing and flexible boundaries. In such scenarios, applying the notion of culture as a mosaic (colourful tiles isolated from one another and with clearly defined boundaries) is unsuitable and needs to be replaced by the idea of culture being more like impressionist portraits of nested, overlapping cultures that interpenetrate and blur boundaries between them (Martin 2002). Following this idea, Martin (2002) called for what she refers to as 'a nexus view of culture'.

According to the nexus view of culture, a cultural entity is engrained in the society where it is found. The nexus approach avoids juxtaposing culture with a specific social entity, and it posits instead that a social entity, such as an organization, is a nexus in which a variety of internal and external influences come together. What makes a culture unique in such a scenario is its own blend of external and internal cultural influences. Within the nexus approach, boundaries of a culture are conceptualized as being permeable, moveable and fluctuating, thereby allowing for intercultural penetration and cultural change. Martin (2002) explained that the nexus approach is the most appropriate for many contemporary organizations including multinational entities where people from varied racial, ethnic, national and other backgrounds are brought together to work in mutually collaborative or conflicting relationships.

Another managerial scenario where the nexus approach to culture could be useful is illustrated by Steve Frosdick's (1995a, 1995b) study of hooliganism in the British Stadia Safety Industry (BSSI). In this study, Frosdick explored interactions between varied stakeholders who collectively influence the safety culture in British football stadia. We have chosen to include Frosdick's study as an example in the present chapter for three reasons: (1) it illustrates how DCF can be used as a tool of the nexus approach to culture, (2) it shows how DCF can be used to explore cultural interactions between different kinds of social entities across levels and scales, and (3) it shows that, in addition to being used effectively for exploring inter-firm and intra-firm cultural dynamics, DCF can also be used to study firm–community interactions.

Conventional wisdom regarding cultural perspectives on safety

Safety culture and climate are key predictors of safety behaviour and performance (Cox and Cheyne 2000, Glendon and Litherland 2001). Yet, past literature on safety culture and climate remains confusing and inconclusive (Havold 2007). Helmreich and Merritt (1998) have shown a link between national culture, organizational culture, and stress and safety. They explained that, in situations where national culture and organizational cultures are in harmony, stress factors do not influence safety, but, in situations where national culture and organizational culture are in discord, stress leads towards compromising safety. Merritt's (2000) subsequent study also concluded that national culture, and more precisely the national culture dimensions of power distance and uncertainty avoidance, influence concerns regarding safety. Similarly, Havold (2007) showed that national culture is related to safety culture, such that high power distance, high uncertainty avoidance and high individualism are positively related to safety.

As is evident from conventional literature, many safety researchers treat the concept of culture in an instrumental and technical manner, a practice that other scholars such as Tharaldsen and Haukelid (2009) have found dissatisfactory. They complained that, in conventional literature, the scientific roots of the culture concept are often superficially treated and much of the organizational safety culture research is dominated by functional safety management approaches. Also in the field of safety research, there is an ongoing debate about the difference between behavioural and cultural approaches to safety and how to perform effective interventions in order to improve safety in organizations. In recent years, safety researchers (e.g. DeJoy 2005) have treated cultural approaches as top-down strategies and behavioural approaches as bottom-up. Tharaldsen and Haukelid (2009) proposed a more balanced model by integrating the tacit and explicit sides of culture with the behavioural aspects of safety. They also incorporated time, stability and change in their model. In so doing, we believe that they supported ongoing efforts towards developing a more dynamic and comprehensive understanding of safety. Frosdick (1995a, 1995b) also advocated this recent trend. However, there is one major difference between the works of Tharaldsen and Haukelid (2009) and Frosdick (1995a, 1995b). In line with DCF, Frosdick (1995a, 1995b) did not consider cultural values and behaviours as being separate from one another. In fact, he argued that risk is a socially constructed phenomenon. How people perceive risk, behave in the face of risk and react to safety measures is a function of their underlying cultural preferences. According to Frosdick (1995a, 1995b), culture and behaviour are not as disconnected from one another as Tharaldsen and Haukelid (2009) have professed.

Using DCF to make sense of safety cultures in the BSSI (Frosdick, 1995a, 1995b)

Steve Frosdick (1995a, 1995b) conducted a two-part study to explore hooliganism in football stadia in UK. He explained that the 'regulation by crisis' method has failed to prevent successive disasters in football stadia. Not only does hooliganism during sporting events continue to cause deaths and injuries (for example, the incident that killed 96 and injured over 400 in Hillsborough, Sheffield, in 1989), but it also appears that concerned parties have learned very little from such recurring tragedies. Using the earlier work of Schwarz and Thompson (1990), Frosdick (1995a) first outlined four different worldviews with four different attitudes towards nature and disasters (in a broad and large sense).

1. Nature benign: This worldview emphasizes global equilibrium. Members adhering to this worldview are forgiving and believe that no matter how you treat nature, it will always come back to its original state of equilibrium.
2. Nature perverse/tolerant: Members of this worldview see nature as forgiving of most events, but they also believe that nature is vulnerable because a single incident is enough to destroy its balance. Regulations, therefore, are required to protect nature against such unusual occurrences. However, once the minimum standards have been met, people should be left alone to make their own decisions.
3. Nature ephemeral: This worldview is almost the exact opposite of the nature benign attitude. Members of this worldview believe that the world is an unforgiving place, and the smallest error will lead to a catastrophic collapse of the world. Hence, the ecosystem needs to be treated with extreme care.
4. Nature capricious: People adhering to this worldview believe that the world is a random place. Therefore, there is little that they can do, other than cope with whatever cards are dealt out to them.

Having followed Schwarz and Thompson's (1990) understanding of the four worldviews and their respective attitudes towards nature and disasters, Frosdick (1995a) combined this understanding with the four cultures of DCF to show that the different groups of stakeholders involved in BSSI exhibit preferences of members of the four cultures – each with its own attitude towards nature, risk and safety. Football organizations, match officials, television companies, football-licensing authorities, certifying authorities, the local and national government, and the police department exhibit behavioural preferences of the hierarchical culture. In fact, BSSI seems to be largely dominated by a hierarchal outlook towards disasters and safety. Since members of the hierarchical culture blame disasters on deviance and rule breaking, their understanding of safety focuses on rules, history, tradition and deference to authority.

Frosdick (1995a) classified football players, managers, football clubs, stadium owners and those concerned with stadia development and design as being competitive in their cultural orientation. These members are more interested in the bottom line than in safety issues. For members of competitive groups, rule breaking is justified if it leads to short-term advantages. These individuals see disasters as random events and choose to minimize expenditure on security and insurance. Risk management for them is about revenue protection.

Next, Frosdick (1995a) identified stadium communities and supporter groups as egalitarians. One example of such an egalitarian group is the Federation of Stadium Communities, which aims to improve relationships between clubs and their local communities. Egalitarian members are conscious of the need for precautions against disasters, which they blame on 'the system' and on the intrusion of authorities beyond their defined boundaries. On the other hand, individual fans and supporters who do not belong to any of the groups cited earlier in this subsection are categorized as fatalists. We quote from one of Frosdick's later works:

> Notwithstanding poor facilities the threat of hooliganism or crushing and the [...] territorialisation of football, these low group individual supporters come to football because ... [the] stadium represents a focus of local pride and collective identification: a sacred place, 'home', an attractive scenic space and source of local heritage.
>
> (Frosdick 2006: 117)

For these passive local residents or long-suffering spectators, disasters on football fields are 'acts of God'. There isn't anything they can do about it except endure the annoyance and the indignities.

In another related study published in the same year, Frosdick (1995b) explored how members of the four cultures interact with each other within the BSSI, thereby creating distinct safety cultures in each stadium. More precisely, he exposed the weakness of the four cultures, each of which makes the system susceptible to disasters in a different way. Since members of the competitive culture attach less importance to the group dimension, they pay less attention to coordinating routine situations and communicating with other agencies. Members of the hierarchical culture, being overly attached to ranks and rules, may stifle the reactivity of lower-level members. Reactions to emergencies may be slow since superiors are required to 'assess the situation' first. Senior managers may make decisions without consulting junior staff who might know more about the problem at hand. In addition, the ethnocentrism of members of the hierarchical culture could lead to risk blindness by inhibiting awareness of equally valid risk perceptions of the other cultures. Members of egalitarian groups put considerable emphasis on consensus, thereby losing valuable time in the consultative process. Considerable tolerance may be shown towards misbehaving members, with expulsion being the solution of last resort. Those with a fatalistic orientation perceive one agency as being in charge of safety, thereby adopting a 'laissez-faire' attitude during a crisis. Within this culture, communication is reserved only for those with high status, and those at lower levels function in isolation. Since members of each culture have different weaknesses, they play different roles in making the system vulnerable to disasters.

Having looked closely at the cultural dynamics between different agencies involved in ensuring safety during football matches, Frosdick extended the same understanding to other public events such as pop concerts, New Year festivities, etc. He stated that DCF offers the possibility of disintegrating the context for deeper analysis. By understanding why different agencies behave in such diverse ways in terms of their attitude towards safety and how they make the system vulnerable to disasters, a better awareness and appreciation of each other's points of views can be established.

Comparing the knowledge contributions of this study with conventional wisdom

Frosdick's (1995a, 1995b) study made three unique knowledge contributions. First, it revealed that, although different agencies have different attitudes towards safety and different sets of weaknesses, traditional safety measures have focused selectively on one specific measure – creating and applying rules that are more stringent than the rules that existed before. Such measures have a limited impact on members other than those of the hierarchical culture. Exposure by Frosdick (1995a, 1995b) of the distinct attitudes that members of different cultures have towards safety facilitates better policy decisions for preventing sports-related disasters. Second, while some previous scholars have shown that national culture and, in particular, dimensions such as high power distance, high uncertainty avoidance and high individualism have a positive impact on safety (see Merritt 2000), others (Tharaldsen and Haukelid 2009) have criticized such studies for their superficial treatment of culture. Taking his cue from the latter group of scholars, Frosdick (1995a, 1995b) showed that people's attitude to safety is a function of their underlying values and behavioural preferences, rather than their national origin. Third, the field of safety research is plagued by an ongoing debate about the difference between behavioural and cultural approaches to safety (DeJoy 2005), with some recent scholars (Tharaldsen and Haukelid 2009) attempting to combine the two approaches. Frosdick (1995a, 1995b) has shown that people's risk perceptions, their risk-related behaviour and their reactions to safety measures are a function of their underlying cultural preferences. Therefore, culture and safety-related behaviour are not as disconnected as some would think.

As a final remark, Frosdick's (1995a, 1995b) study shows that DCF can be used as an instrument of the nexus approach to culture, which Martin (2002) (see Chapter 11 for details) propagated as one of the potential areas of focus for future culture scholars. This study also demonstrates that DCF can be successfully used as a conceptual framework to explore culture across a variety of levels and scales. By way of an example, this study explores cultural dynamics between national-level agencies (for instance, the national government), industry-level agencies (BSSI, for example) and local-level agencies (such as local football clubs, the local community, etc.). Finally, while the two examples cited earlier in this chapter, i.e. our study of the viability of Indo-French alliances (Patel 2005, 2007a, 2007b) and Rayner's (1986) study of risk perceptions in American hospitals, show that DCF can be used to explore cultural dynamics in inter-firm and intra-firm relations, this last example shows that DCF can also be implemented to study cultural dynamics in firm–community networks. This further consolidates our arguments in favour of the versatility of DCF as a cultural sense-making tool.

Concluding remarks

In this chapter, we attempt to demonstrate that there are certain managerial scenarios, where using conventional frameworks of culture is not appropriate. We identify three such scenarios:

1. in international inter-firm collaborations when national and corporate identities become blurred as seen in our (Patel 2005, 2007a, 2007b) study of the viability of Indo-French alliances;
2. in intra-firm studies where the focus is on the cultural diversity within the firm, as seen in Rayner's (1986) study of risk perceptions in American hospitals; and
3. in cultural interactions studies between different kinds of social entities across levels and scales, as illustrated by Frosdick's (1995a, 1995b) study of safety cultures in the BSSI.

The three examples offered in this chapter show that, although one may choose to use conventional frameworks of culture grounded in the function-alist tradition for making sense of culture in such scenarios, the insights they provide are fairly superficial and self-limiting. If people's behaviours with one another, their perceptions of risk and their attitudes towards safety are the non-negotiable outcomes of their predetermined cultural template, then managers can do little to alter these preferences. Fortunately for the culture scholar, there are frameworks such as DCF that serve as valid alternatives for cultural analysis in each of these scenarios. As readers will note, using DCF for cultural sense-making in each of the aforementioned managerial scenarios offers a richer conceptual understanding than that offered by conventional frameworks of culture. For instance, while conventional frameworks of culture stop short of classifying Americans as high on risk-taking and low on uncertainty avoidance, DCF shows that different groups of people in American hospitals have different perceptions of risk. There is an ongoing tension but also a continuous give and take between members of these different cultural groups. Thus, the use of DCF allows us to go much beyond the traditionally accepted dichotomy of risk-takers and risk-avoiders and explains that underlying values and preferences rather than people's national origin and/or corporate affiliations inform their risk perceptions. Therefore, DCF allows a better under-standing of the plural rationalities regarding risk that coexist in social entities than those offered by conventional frameworks of culture.

Conceptually speaking, DCF allows us to study the configural property of culture, i.e. it allows us to explore variations within social entities by evoking different rationalities. Thus, we partially meet Tsui *et al.*'s (2007) call for more theoretical development regarding the configural property of culture. Second, as explained earlier, cultural literature embraces a wide variety of theoretical approaches and frameworks. Although theoretical pluralism is important and deserves to be encouraged, excessive pluralism leads to unnecessary theoretical compartmentalization (Astley and Van de Ven 1983: 245) and obscures the connection between different schools of thought (Glynn and Raffaeli 2010). Therefore, a certain degree of consolidation in culture literature is desired (Tsui *et al.* 2007). This consolidation is difficult to achieve as long as one continues to use different frameworks to study culture at different levels and scales and within different geo-ethnic boundaries. As this chapter shows, the application of DCF across levels, scales and boundaries has the potential to produce some degree of consolidation in cultural literature. In addition, DCF is capable of serving as a transactional tool for the nexus approach to culture (Martin 2002). To conclude, the varied applications of DCF as demonstrated in this chapter coupled with DCF's use to explore a wide variety of managerial concerns in past years[3] affords evidence of its versatility.

Notes

1 Or that employees of small private and professionally managed companies are habituated to a more competitive and flexible environment and may behave accordingly.
2 As Rayner and Malone (1999) stated, the best the two dominant cultures (i.e. hierarchical and competitive cultures) can do by themselves is to flip back and forth from one state of affairs to the other. The egalitarian group prevents this by acting as a buffer.
3 DCF has been used to study environmental issues (Rayner 1991), consumption patterns (Douglas 1996), ethical decision making (Patel and Schaefer 2009) and many more managerial concerns.

Additional reading

T. Patel, (2007a) 'Using Cultural Theory to explain the viability of international strategic alliances: A focus on Indo-French alliances', *Management Decisions*, 45(10): 1532–59.
T. Patel, (2007b) *Stereotypes of Intercultural Management*, Delft: Eburon Academic Publishers.

11 Culture in business

Drawing the big picture

In order to properly understand the big picture, everyone should fear becoming mentally clouded and obsessed with one small section of truth.

Xun Zi

What you will learn in this chapter:

- a summary of the key points from chapters 1 through 10 of this book;
- key knowledge contributions of this book;
- avenues for future studies regarding the role of culture in business.

Introduction

In the present chapter, we attempt to draw a big-picture perspective of our understanding of culture based on the discussions evoked in the previous ten chapters of this book. This closing chapter is divided into three main sections. In the first section, we summarize the key points from the preceding ten chapters. In the next section, we draw readers' attention to the key knowledge contributions of this book. In the third and final section, we offer certain directions for future studies regarding the role that culture plays in business.

Summary of key points from preceding chapters

This book is divided into four parts. In Part I of this book (Chapters 1 and 2), we introduced the concept of culture in the context of business studies. Culture is a complex construct of many layers, and both in business and anthropology literature, scholars define it in many different ways. Culture is also a subject that has provoked much debate among scholars and practitioners. Many scholars have challenged the conventional belief that culture is shared, stable, unique and homogenous within a geographic entity. Some scholars have offered alternative terms such as 'ideology', 'frames of reference' and 'cognitive schemas' to allow for an evolving and dynamic conceptualization of culture, as opposed to a more conventional and static conceptualization. In part, many debates regarding the nature of culture are grounded in varied epistemological approaches (such as functionalism, interpretivism, and postmodernism). In Chapter 1 of this book, we argued that, while each epistemological approach has its strengths, excessive focus on any one approach could lead to compromising our overall understanding about culture. Each epistemological approach has its 'blind spots', and it is only by appreciating what different epistemological approaches have to offer that we will cultivate a more complete understanding of culture. Hence, in this book, we embark upon a quest to expose cultural frameworks adhering to different epistemological viewpoints. It is also our objective to move away from frameworks that treat culture as an explanation of the last resort and as an uncaused cause. In addition, we make a conscious attempt to shift our focus away from the 'difference-oriented lens', which many past scholars have used in studying culture, towards an approach that allows for a focus on similarities between and differences within entities.

In Chapter 2 of this book, we offered an overview of what past literature has to say about the impact of culture on various aspects of organizational behaviour (e.g. motives, rewards, feedback, job satisfaction, learning, negotiations, and others). We also presented a brief synopsis of the impact of culture on specific aspects of international business (for instance, trust-building among partners in international business collaborations, perceived alliance performance, the success or failure of international strategic alliances, etc.). Most of this literature is grounded in conventional frameworks of culture that conceptualize culture as being static at a point in time and focus on the national/societal/regional levels of its manifestation. Although such a conceptualization of culture contributes to making conventional frameworks of culture popular both with scholars and with practitioners, it also has many disadvantages, which we discussed in subsequent chapters.

In Part II (more precisely, Chapters 3 and 4) of this book, we exposed some of the conventional frameworks of culture. The discussion of each framework was accompanied by an overview of its strengths and weaknesses. Many frameworks discussed in this chapter, namely, Hofstede's (1980) national culture framework, Hall's (1960) high- versus low-context framework, Hall and Hall's (1990) framework of different perceptions of time, Trompenaars and Hampden-Turner's (1997) societal culture framework and the GLOBE study's regional culture framework simplify the otherwise intricate and complex task of making sense of human behaviour by attributing it to the individual's national, societal and/or regional origin. While this contributes to the popularity of these frameworks, this also opens them up to criticism for generating and encouraging stereotypes at the national, societal or regional levels and for propagating the idea of geographically bounded cultural entities that are internally coherent, culturally homogenous and stable. In contrast, Shalom Schwartz's (2004, 2006) framework conceptualizes cultural orientations as an integrated system. According to this framework, mutually congruent, conflicting and, sometimes, antagonistic cultural orientations can and do coexist within the same society. This raises questions about the assumption that other scholars have made regarding cultural homogeneity within entities (nations, societies, regions, etc.). Schwartz's cultural orientations framework draws our attention to in-group cultural differences as well as towards potential intergroup cultural similarities. Additionally, his values theory conceptualizes in a dynamic way which values will be manifested by individuals in light of their past socialization and the particularities of their present circumstances. Chapter 3 closed by highlighting that cultural frameworks are like any other tool – users need to know how and when to use them if they wish to be effective.

In Chapter 4, we delved further into comparing and critiquing the different conventional culture frameworks presented in Chapter 3. This critique was configured around six reflection points: (1) Have the conventional frameworks of culture satisfactorily conceptualized and operationalized culture? (2) Is national identity a passive embodiment of a predetermined cultural template as conventional frameworks of culture dictate? (3) Are the terms 'intercultural' and 'international' interchangeable? (4) Do we need to address culture at different levels (for instance, national, societal, regional, etc.) for optimal cultural sense-making? (5) Do conventional frameworks of culture explain social change? (6) Is culture simply an 'uncaused cause' as conventional frameworks of culture posit? Our reflection on these six questions led us to conclude that, despite their popularity, conventional frameworks of culture suffer from many limitations. Recently, scholars who have recognized these limitations have set out to address and, where possible, overcome the same. For instance, Taras *et al.* (2010) have shown that there are specific boundary conditions within which frameworks such as the one offered by Hofstede (1980) may be effectively used. Recent works in this area (see Tinsley and Brodt 2004, Hong *et al.* 2000) have signalled a gradual shift from a static to a dynamic conceptualization of culture. In addition, more recently, scholars have supported a multilayered, multifaceted, contextual and systems view of culture (Leung *et al.* 2005) as opposed to the static conceptualization of culture popular in the 1970s and 1980s.

In the remaining chapters of Part II of this book (i.e. Chapters 5 and 6), we exposed a different set of frameworks by addressing culture at the corporate level. In Chapter 5, we outlined corporate culture frameworks that follow the integration perspective (such as those offered by Hofstede *et al.* 1990 and Trompenaars and Hampden-Turner 1997). In other words, these frameworks address culture as being static and homogenous within a company and assume that consistency, organization-wide consensus and clarity characterize a company's culture. This simplistic viewpoint was contrasted in Chapter 6 where we exposed corporate culture frameworks adhering to differentiation and fragmentation perspectives. Differentiation studies question the oversimplified coherence of the integration view. However, they still continue to emphasize consistency, consensus and clarity, this time at the subculture level. In comparison, scholars adhering to the fragmentation perspective go much further in supporting cultural plurality, cultural change and ambiguity. They treat culture as a constantly evolving web of interpersonal relations. Some of the frameworks adhering to the fragmentation perspective have another added advantage – they can be applied to study culture not only at the corporate level but also at the departmental, industry, national and international levels. This observation supports our argument that the availability of an innovative and insightful cultural framework would preclude the need to rely on a plethora of cultural frameworks, each supposedly addressing culture at one of its many levels. We concluded Chapter 6 by pointing out that, despite the many advances made in understanding how culture plays out in companies, the field remains rife with unresolved debates regarding whether it is fair to juxtapose culture and organization and whether or not corporate culture is amenable to managerial control. Nevertheless, scholars of corporate culture have also observed the shift from a static to dynamic conceptualization of culture that we have noted among proponents of national/regional/societal culture. In other words, the overall field of culture studies seems to be experiencing a shift from a functionalist to a postmodernist standpoint, although, ideally speaking, most dynamic frameworks of culture would be located somewhere along a continuum connecting the interpretivist and postmodern traditions.

In Part III of this book (Chapters 7, 8, and 9), we moved away from business literature towards anthropological literature on culture. The fact that most anthropologists have long since abandoned the idea that national cultures are unique and that individuals are passive recipients of culture (McSweeney 2009) guides our choice. Therefore, we believe that advances made in anthropology in the past fifty years might help us in our search for dynamic frameworks of culture. As noted elsewhere in this volume, some scholars have resorted to disciplines like cognitive psychology (see, for instance, Leung *et al.*'s 2005 work) in search of alternative explanations of human behaviour. Irrespective of these differences in disciplinary affiliations, we have a common objective: to seek more credible explanations of human behaviour in the workplace than has been afforded so far by conventional frameworks of culture. Hence, all such efforts to expand the horizon of culture studies deserve to be encouraged.

In Chapter 7, we focused our attention on the anthropology-based trans-actional culture approach. We reviewed the work of Fredrik Barth, one of the most acclaimed transactional scholars, who made many significant contributions towards our understanding of human behaviour. Not only did he challenge the dominance of normative and structural-functional approaches popular in his time, he also offered an alternative way of making sense of human behaviour through his transactional approach and his concept of 'rationality'. He advanced our understanding of social change and called for generative models capable of explaining why and how certain behavioural patterns emerge. Despite these significant contributions, Barth's work has its limitations, prominent among these are his excessive focus on 'self-interest' as the preferred form of rationality and his inability to explain social change as a non-linear, never-ending phenomenon. Other transactional scholars (such as Geertz 1980, Kapferer 1972, Leach 1954, 1961, Marriott 1976) also inspired criticism by inadvertently replacing the notion of 'cultural unity' with that of 'cultural infinity', thereby rendering cultural comparisons impossible. Having reviewed the transactional culture literature and having recognized both its strengths and weaknesses, we propose that there is a need for a cultural framework, which, while being grounded in Barth's transactional framework, also overcomes some of its weaknesses.[1] Mary Douglas's Cultural Framework (DCF) promises to meet some of these criteria, and it was presented in Chapter 8 of this volume.

In Chapter 8, we presented a detailed overview of DCF. The overall aim of DCF is to serve as a transactional tool that cultural analysts may use in order to relate differences in organizational structures to the strength of values that sustain them (Gross and Rayner 1985). DCF offers two social dimensions that influence human transactions: (1) the horizontal group axis, which represents the extent to which people are restricted in thought and action by their commitment to a social unit larger than an individual, and (2) the vertical grid axis that indicates the extent of explicit public social classification based on criteria such as gender, colour, position in the hierarchy, holding a bureaucratic office, belonging to a clan or lineage, or progression through an age-grade system (Gross and Rayner 1985). Plotting high and low strengths of grid and group against one another gives rise to four cultures: (1) competitive, (2) hierarchical, (3) egalitarian and (4) fatalistic. Some DCF scholars also mention a fifth type of culture – the hermit – which is located in the centre of the grid–group matrix and has unfortunately not received much attention in past literature. In Chapter 8, we described each of these four cultures of DCF and explained how scholars such as Thompson (1996) have converted this seemingly static model of culture into a dynamic one. Unlike conventional frameworks of culture, DCF conceptualizes people's behaviours to be a function of their grid–group preferences. The four cultures are not rigid categories (Mars 2001) but rather are shifting patterns of behavioural preferences because people arrange themselves along different grid–group configurations at different times and in different contexts. The latter half of Chapter 8 focused on demonstrating how DCF overcomes some of the limitations of Barth's transactional culture approach. For instance, DCF is capable of explaining changes in people's behaviours as a function of the different levels of social pressures they encounter in their environment, ongoing internal competition among cultural groups and external stimuli (Thompson 1996). DCF is also capable of explaining how members of the four cultures, despite their differences and ongoing rivalry, continue to interact with one another due to their mutual interdependence. When forced to work with one another, members of different cultures temporarily foreground their similarities and underplay their differences. In so doing, they create temporary but workable coalitions with one another. Finally, DCF offers four different kinds of rationalities: (1) the pragmatic and substantive rationality of members of the competitive culture, (2) the rules and process-oriented rationality of members of the hierarchical culture, (3) the internally egalitarian and externally critical rationality of members of the egalitarian culture, and, finally, (4) the resigned and passive rationality of members of the fatalistic culture. By elaborating on four kinds of rationalities, DCF scholars overcome Barth's excessive focus on 'self-interest' as the preferred form of rationality. With regards to social change, the four-fold DCF model outshines conventional dichotomous models of culture, by allowing for twelve possible transitions (three for members of each culture), thereby making social change a non-linear, never-ending and non-predictable phenomenon. Finally, through their discussion of DCF's impossibility theorem, requisite variety condition and constrained relativism, DCF scholars support the plurality of cultures without resorting to popular dualistic cultural frameworks and without falling prey to the unity versus infinity debate. To recapitulate, Chapter 8 exposed that DCF overcomes many of the limitations of the transactional school, while it retains many of its key strengths.

In Chapter 9, we engaged in a final comparison between DCF and the conventional frameworks of culture as discussed in Part II (Chapters 3 through 6) of this volume. Rather than engaging in an ideological or decontextualized comparison between the two, we chose to assess which of them is more useful within the precise context of international business entities, which, as discussed elsewhere in this volume, are characterized by continuously changing boundaries, roles, structures and relations. We structured our arguments along the same six reflection points that we had evoked earlier in Chapter 4. To begin with, we showed that, as compared to conventional frameworks, DCF with its dynamic and pluralistic conceptualization of culture proves to be a better sense-making tool in the context of international business entities. Second, we argued that, in the context of international business collaborations, national identity is just one of the many influences being exercised on the individual. Therefore, a more dynamic and multifaceted approach to individual identity as propagated by DCF scholars makes more sense that conventional culture frameworks, which treat national identity as a passive embodiment of a predetermined cultural template. Third, through examples of various past studies grounded in DCF, we argue that proponents of DCF do not make the mistake of equating 'nation' with 'culture'. Instead, they acknowledge and emphasize intra-group cultural diversity and inter-group cultural similarities. Fourth, we showed that, by allowing for exploration of cultural dynamics beyond and across specific levels, DCF scholars contribute towards generating a certain degree of commensurability and consensus in culture literature. The fifth reflection point exposed how DCF scholars offer a richer insight into social change as a non-linear, never-ending phenomenon as compared to conventional culture frameworks (see also

Chapter 8 for a similar discussion). Finally, as a last reflection point, we showed that proponents of DCF provide us with a link between sense-making and action bias. This implies that, unlike proponents of conventional culture frameworks, DCF scholars do not treat culture as an uncaused cause. Having exposed how DCF overcomes some of the limitations of conventional culture frameworks, we also recognized the former's limitations and presented these in the concluding section of Chapter 9.

Part IV (Chapters 10 and 11) formed the concluding section of this book. In Chapter 10, we offered three examples of managerial scenarios where using conventional frameworks of culture is not appropriate. These are scenarios involving (1) international inter-firm collaborations where national and corporate identities become blurred as seen in our (Patel 2005, 2007a, 2007b) study of the viability of Indo-French alliances; (2) a focus on intra-firm cultural dynamics, as seen in Rayner's (1986) study of risk perceptions in American hospitals; and (3) the aim to understand cultural interactions between different kinds of social entities across levels and scales, as illustrated by Frosdick's (1995a, 1995b) study of safety cultures in the BSSI. The three illustrative studies show that, although one may choose to use conventional frameworks of culture grounded in the functionalist tradition for making sense of culture in such scenarios, the insights they provide will remain superficial and self-limiting. Conversely, frameworks such as DCF serve as valid alternatives for cultural analysis in each of these scenarios. Moreover, using DCF for cultural sense-making in such scenarios offers a richer conceptual understanding than that offered by conventional frameworks of culture. The discussions presented in this chapter also show that DCF exposes the configural property of culture, thereby meeting Tsui *et al.*'s (2007) call for more theoretical developments in this area of research. Also, our exposition of DCF as a tool useful for cultural sense-making at and across different levels and scales offers a much-desired consolidation to cultural literature. Finally, our last example shows that DCF can be used as a tool for what Martin (2002) referred to as the nexus approach to culture, and which she considers as an important avenue for future theoretical development. These varied applications of DCF to explore cultural dynamics in the context of inter-firm, intra-firm and firm-community relations are evidence of its versatility.

Key knowledge contributions of this book

Our study offers some useful insights both for students of culture and for current and future managers. In this section, we outline first the conceptual strengths of our work, followed by some managerial implications of the same.

Conceptual strengths

One of the major conceptual strengths of this volume is that, unlike past business scholars who have focused largely on conventional culture frameworks guided by the functionalist tradition, we offer a variety of dynamic cultural frameworks both from business studies (for example, Boisot's I-Space Model and Quinn and Rohrbaugh's Competing Values Framework) and from anthropology (Barth's transactional culture framework and Mary Douglas's Cultural Framework). In so doing, we offer the reader a richer and broader perspective on culture from two different disciplines. Business scholars have largely neglected anthropological studies of culture, despite their immense richness. By incorporating anthropology-based literature on culture in this volume, we expand the business students' scope of cultural understanding. Also, we steer away from discussions of frameworks based on a 'difference-oriented lens' towards frameworks that focus on intra-group diversity and inter-group similarity. Although we expose readers to a variety of cultural frameworks and epistemological viewpoints, we do not impose a specific viewpoint or ideology on them. Instead, we lay out the strengths and weaknesses of each framework as grounded within a specific epistemological tradition to furnish readers the opportunity to make their own informed decisions about the most appropriate frameworks in their specific contexts. Also, rather than offer our students simplistic 'how to' guidelines (for instance, how to negotiate with the Indians or how to do business with the Germans), we offer a much more critical perspective to culture. Rather than presume to tell students how to manage cultural differences, we offer them a variety of frameworks that will help them make their own decisions regarding how to address cultural dynamics as they navigate their ways through their personal, social and professional relations.

Another key theoretical contribution of the present volume is that, while past scholars mainly focus on the role of culture in inter-firm (usually international) collaborations, through the illustrative studies presented in Chapter 10, we focus on the role of culture in inter-firm, intra-firm and firm – community relations. In particular, in the third illustrative study, we expose how the use of an innovative framework such as DCF allows us to explore phenomena spanning across a variety of levels and scales. Each of the illustrative studies presented in Chapter 10 reveals that the use of frameworks, such as DCF, provides a deeper and richer insight into specific managerial scenarios as compared to conventional cultural frameworks. We reiterate that our objective in evoking precise managerial scenarios and offering three corresponding illustrative studies is not to present DCF as the ultimate tool for cultural sense-making for managers. Our objective is simply to expose that, in certain managerial scenarios, an over-reliance on simplistic and categorical cultural frameworks might not be the most effective. While functionalist frameworks offer clarity, consensus and simplicity, they are ill equipped to explain the dynamic complexity of certain scenarios that managers encounter in their professional lives.

Another theoretical merit of the present volume is that we meet Fredrik Barth's call for a generative model of culture. A generative model seeks to identify a set of factors that, through specified operations will produce a determined output ... The structural-functional model seeks to generalize the overt form of a society and show its coherence with people's own cultural representations. A generative model tries to identify sets of regular events, processes that lend toward the emergence of such an observed form in a local or regional social system.

(Barth 2007: 8)

In the present volume, we offer DCF as a generative model of culture. Through its discussion of people's values and rationalities, as well as the ongoing interaction between individuals and their social contexts, DCF helps explain how patterns of behaviours emerge and how these evolve over time and with changing circumstances. Additionally, in offering DCF as an alternative framework of culture, we bridge the gap between different epistemological approaches. As discussed earlier, each epistemological approach has its 'blind spots'. Although studies grounded in each of these approaches have contributed towards advancing our understanding of culture in some ways, the larger field of cultural studies may have suffered because the functionalist tradition has continued to dominate business literature since the 1970s. Also, since proponents of different epistemological approaches are divided by intellectual and philosophical barriers, they may have inadvertently thwarted the possibility of synergies between different approaches. In our present work, we offer a partial solution to this dilemma. By offering DCF as a cultural framework, we shift attention away from the excessive functionalist orientation of business scholars and towards the interpretivist and postmodernist schools. Since DCF is positioned midway between the interpretive and postmodernist traditions, it overcomes, at least in part, the limitations of each of these approaches. In line with the interpretive tradition, DCF scholars expose the interrelated cyclic processes of interpretation, sense-making, understanding and action. Conversely, in line with the postmodernist tradition, DCF scholars focus on the processual character of human institutions. Yet these scholars do not treat culture as being absolutely volatile and chaotic (as extreme postmodernists would do). Without claiming that any one epistemological approach or cultural framework is better than the other is, this volume offers the readers an alternative and, hopefully, more comprehensive understanding of culture.

Finally, while past years have seen the development of many cultural frameworks, thereby offering more choices to the cultural researcher, this proliferation of cultural frameworks has also led to certain drawbacks. For instance, the plethora of frameworks available to culture scholars today supposedly helps them to make sense of culture at a variety of different levels, but it also perpetuates a lack of a dominant paradigm. While we do not question the need for variety in cultural frameworks, we are not convinced that these varied frameworks allow for better cultural understanding. Through our illustrations in Chapter 10 of the use of DCF, we show that the same framework can be used to study culture at and across different levels. Thus, by offering a framework that can be applied across levels and scales and across varied disciplines, we contribute to a certain extent towards generating a degree of commensurability in culture literature.

Managerial implications

Our present volume also offers certain managerial implications. Our critique of the conventional frameworks of culture opens up avenues for further reflection concerning the usefulness (or lack thereof) of the variety of cross-cultural training programmes popular today, both in the corporate world and in business schools. Admittedly, such training programmes are designed to increase people's awareness of their own culture and those of others, and they are believed to positively influence skill development, adjustment and perfor-mance (see Black and Mendenhall 1990). The kind of questions evoked in such training programmes are: Considering that the Chinese are highly collectivistic and the Germans are highly individualistic, how should German expatriates modify their behaviour when working in China? The objective of such training programmes is to impress upon trainees (business students and current or future expatriates) the need to 'adapt' to the new and inherently different national culture that they are about to encounter. Such training programmes are inherently grounded in functionalist and static conceptualiza-tions of culture – they take a static picture of two (or more) cultures and compare them on specific isolated behaviours grounded in supposedly stable and static cultural dimensions. Since these kinds of training programs are based on comparisons of supposedly objective, stable, and resolute attributes of national cultures, they might indirectly endorse a stereotypical notion of national identity (Osland and Bird 2000) and inadvertently encourage a distinction between 'us' and 'them' (Ailon-Souday and Kunda 2003, Patel 2007a, 2007b). In other words, rather than helping people to overcome cultural biases, these training programmes may indirectly 'help preserve and even sanction the symbolic production of a sense of difference' (Ailon-Souday and Kunda 2003: 1090). What these training programmes ignore is the fact that people across different companies, countries, regions, nations and societies are dynamic entities. People share certain common features with one another across borders, and they also manifest considerable diversity within the group (based on differences in age, religious beliefs, sexual orientations, economic class, educational backgrounds or simply on different personalities, motivations and life experiences). Therefore, such training programmes grounded in a conventional and static understanding of culture fail to provide a realistic perspective of cultural dynamics in social entities. At best, they prepare trainees to anticipate certain kinds of behaviours from foreign collaborators and bias their subsequent behaviours accordingly.

Consider, as an example, the case of a German manager being expatriated to China. Conventional culture frameworks would dictate that Chinese employees are more collectivist in their behaviour as compared to German employees. Training programmes grounded in such conventional frameworks would dictate that the German manager acknowledge this difference and adapt to the collectivistic behaviour of the Chinese colleagues (assuming the German manager's behaviour can be adapted at will). Consequently, the German manager's behaviour with respect to the Chinese collaborators will be such that it will reinforce their supposedly 'collective' identity. This may inadvertently send out behavioural cues to the Chinese counterparts, and they might align their behaviours to what they assume are the expectations of their expatriate manager. Both parties in this interaction are thus acting based on their expectations. Therefore, it follows that both parties will experience a surprise or a shock when these expectations are challenged. For instance, the German expatriate may be taken aback when some of the Chinese colleagues behave in individualistic and/or competitive ways with one another. Thus, the broad generalizations offered by conventional frameworks of culture not only prove to be ineffective, but they also impede the understanding of cultural dynamics. The logical question then is the following: What kind of cross-cultural training programmes should companies and business schools put into place to prepare current or future managers for the cultural dynamics they will encounter in the workplace?

We reckon that training programmes grounded in conventional frameworks of culture should be replaced with ones that offer a more realistic, dynamic and pluralistic perspective of cultural realities in business entities. Managers should be trained to handle the inevitable dynamicity and plurality of business entities, to identify the diverse cultural groups in their professional and social environments, and to converse and collaborate with these groups, despite their mutual differences. This ability to collaborate with inherently different groups is what ensures success, both organizational and individual.

In the final section of this volume, we presented some ideas about future direction for cultural studies in business literature. For this discussion, we draw on reflections of scholars like Gelfand *et al.* (2007), Tsui *et al.* (2007), Martin (2002)/cite>, and Usunier (1998).

Future directions for cultural studies in business literature

In recent years, many questions have been raised about the usefulness and applicability of conventional culture frameworks. For instance, some researchers (Patel 2007a and 2007b, Patel and Rayner 2012, Tung 2008, Bird, Osland, Mendenhall and Schneider 1999) have questioned the national culture approach, and others have refined it (Taras *et al.* 2010). Recent developments also indicate a distinct move towards conceptualizing culture as dynamic (Hong *et al.* 2000) and paying more attention to organizational context factors (Aycan *et al.* 2000), new taxonomies of cultural values (House *et al.* 2004, Schwartz 1994), beliefs (Bond *et al.* 2004), norms (Gelfand *et al.* 2006b) and sophisticated ways of combining culture-specific and universal perspectives on cultural differences (Morris *et al.* 1999) (scc Gelfand *et al.* 2007 for details). We suggest that more studies identifying boundary conditions to the effective use and application of conventional frameworks of culture be conducted. Although these frameworks have formed the basis of cultural reflections among business scholars for the past half century, they are less appropriate for the study of modern and complex business scenarios. It is by challenging the limits of these frameworks that we will acquire a more meaningful handle on culture and its role in contemporary business entities.

Tsui *et al.* (2007) have reviewed literature on cross-cultural organizational behaviour from 16 leading management journals over a period of 10 years. Based on this review, they offered a number of recommendations for future culture scholars. First, they encouraged culture scholars to focus more on the configural nature of culture. As we know, culture is commonly acknowledged as a group-level construct. However, what is less commonly understood is that a group-level construct can be global, shared or configural[2] (Klein and Kozlowski 2000). Although the global and shared properties of culture are commonly explored, the configural property is often neglected (see Early 1993, Triandis 1989 for exceptions). Tsui *et al.* (2007) pointed out that focusing on the configural property of culture would allow for much theoretical advancement in the field. Although we have made a modest effort in this direction in the present volume, more work in this area is desired.

Tsui *et al.* (2007) also offered the concept of looseness or tightness of culture (as initially proposed by Pelto (1968) and further elaborated by Triandis in 1989) as one interesting developmental axis for future culture studies. Tightness versus looseness of culture is defined as the strength of social norms and degree of sanctioning when a member's behaviour deviates from the social norms of the society (Gelfand, Nishii and Raver 2007). In a context with loose norms, there is more tolerance for variations in behaviours. Therefore, one might argue that the same cultural value would have a shared property in nations with tight norms and a configural property in nations with loose norms. This is another promising area of research for future culture scholars. Next, and very much in line with our own reflections presented earlier in this book, Tsui *et al.* (2007) advised future scholars to work towards developing cross-level models and to avoid theorizing at only the individual and/or national levels. They also called for a focus on developing poly-contextual approaches to culture studies (i.e. approaches that incorporate multiple contexts for a holistic and valid understanding of any phenomenon[3]). They also suggested that future scholars should focus on the development of dynamic models of culture by tracking changes in culture over time and the effect of these cultural changes (see Ralston, Terpstra-Tong, Terpstra, Wang and Egri 2006 as an example).

Finally, Tsui *et al.* (2007) noted that many cross-cultural researchers use existing models (most of which have originated in the United States) to draw cross-country comparisons. In so doing, these researchers draw on an existing body of literature and join an ongoing intellectual dialogue, and they inform

U.S. multinational corporations about conducting business in other countries. However, these scholars pose questions and get responses in line with a difference-oriented lens (Tsui *et al.* 2007, Ofori-Dankwa and Ricks 2000). Instead, they should be focusing on more country-specific research, especially in Asia, South America and other developing regions of the world (Tsui *et al.* 2007). Tsui *et al.* (2007) also encouraged cross-national collaborations between researchers. Such collaborations should bring together Western researchers with local researchers or those who already have an in-depth knowledge of and exposure to the cultures in question. Such long-term collaborations among scholars from different parts of the world are one way of facilitating the development of such 'indigenous' studies (Tsui *et al.* 2007).

In addition to the work of Anne Tsui, we have drawn much inspiration from the work of Joanne Martin in writing the present volume. Therefore, it is natural that in ending our present work we revert to her reflections regarding future directions for culture studies. In *Organizational Culture: Mapping the Terrain*, Martin (2002: 316–18, following Ozick 1996) raised some very pertinent questions: How do we draw a boundary around a culture? How do I know who is inside the boundary and who is not? Are there multiple ways to define the boundary of a culture? In modern industrialized societies, where people belong to many and sometimes overlapping cultural collectivities, what does being the member of a culture imply? Following these axes of reflection, Martin (2002: 316) proposed that it is time to move away from viewing cultural boundaries as being fixed, impermeable and clearly defined and to move towards viewing them as fluctuating, permeable and blurred. She explained that, although there was a time when cultural ethnographies were written as if they were snapshots frozen in time or as delineated tiles in a mosaic (isolated from one another and with clearly defined boundaries), today ethnographies are more like impressionist portraits of nested, overlapping cultures that interpenetrate and blur boundaries between them. Any cultural snapshot that presents a version of reality frozen in time is misleading. A cultural study is more like a collection of rarely ending videos, with each video camera aimed at different events. While researchers control some of these cameras, cultural participants control others, and both are being filmed as they interact with one another (Martin 2002: 334). In addition, Martin (2002) suggested that culture studies need to keep pace with the environmental changes (for instance, ongoing inter-organizational alliances, creation of international markets, facilitation of air travel, evolutions in information technology, etc.). Organizational theories of culture that reflect this rapidly evolving environment deserve to be developed in contemporary research. As the illustrative studies presented in Chapter 10 of this volume reveal, we have (at least partially) addressed both the notion of porous and changing boundaries and of ongoing environmental changes that influence business entities. Having said this, much remains to be done in this direction.

Martin (2002) also encouraged us to question the past practice of juxtaposing organizations with culture, which goes hand in hand with the assumption that every person in a specific context is a participant of the commonly shared culture in that context. This assumption is probably grounded in the understanding that close proximity allows for more frequent interactions and therefore the opportunity to cultivate a shared culture. Instead, Martin (2002) argued that the boundaries of an organization and those of a culture are not necessarily identical, either conceptually or empirically. Besides, today, culture may not be embodied in a straightforward way. She offered the example of EUREKA, a pan-European programme for the promotion of cross-border and cross-institutional collaboration on technological development. In this programme, participants were geographically dispersed and rarely ever saw each other. Yet, over time, a soft culture evolved with its own symbols and language, which were partly shared by some (but not all) members. Martin (2002) also offered the example of The Well, an online community that was originally created as a chat room. Initially, there was one person in charge of maintaining membership and controlling online behavior. Over time, however, a complex organization emerged, which outlined clear rules for behavior and communication in this virtual community. This change was also accompanied by certain participants accepting the rules and others resisting them. This was not a superficial community but one in which members interacted with one another with different levels of intimacy. Although face-to-face encounters between members were rare, The Well generated and sustained its own culture over time. Martin (2002) suggested that, since such organizations are expected to proliferate in the future, such instances of disembodied cultures deserve our special attention. There are interesting questions to be explored in the context of such virtual communities: What does it mean to say that The Well has a culture? Is such a culture really disembodied or do bodily images affect what is said and done? At what time does an online community become a culture? We reckon that the same kinds of questions can also be raised regarding geographically dispersed business entities such as multinational organizations. What kind of cultural dynamics can one expect in such organizations? How do these different cultural groups interact with one another? Which cultural preference will prevail under which conditions? While some of these questions have been addressed in the present volume through illustrative studies offered in Chapter 10, other questions can be taken up by future culture scholars.

Martin (2002: 326) also challenged the dominance of the functionalist tradition in conventional frameworks of culture. In this regard, she raised a range of questions: What is the cultural participation of an employee who is from one country and works in another? Are participants in minority groups or residents of outlying parts of a country, perhaps from island colonies, full participants in a national culture? Can a cultural member be an immigrant? If so, does that immigrant status have to be legal? Once that status is legal, does cultural participation ensue instantly, or does it take time to develop? What about mixed ethnicity, racial or religious identities that cross national borders? What does it mean to speak of national cultures in the context of cross-national entities, such as a multinational corporation or the common markets in Europe? Each of these questions implies that juxtaposing culture with a nation-state or a company is neither a convincing nor a credible exercise. Our discussion of DCF and our study of Indo-French alliances (see Chapter 10) address this problem to a certain extent. Since DCF does not conceptualize culture within fault lines of nations, countries or any other social entity, it allows us to evade the practice of juxtaposing culture with specific national or corporate boundaries. We suggest that future studies of culture should follow this same line of reflection.

Martin (2002) also has drawn our attention towards those individuals who, to varying degrees, are members of several partially overlapping or nested cultures. She offered the example of Anzaldua women who by virtue of their mixed ancestry are holders of multiple cultural identities. These women choose to display their Indian side in some Mexican contexts and their Mexican side in some Anglo contexts. This reminds us of Ailon-Souday and Kunda's (2003) argument about how individuals choose to emphasize one identity while suppressing another in a specific context when this suits their strategic interests. Such questions deserve further exploration in the future. Similarly, Martin (2002) has pointed our attention to the fact that the intensity of members' participation in a culture also varies with time. As new members are socialized into a culture, others are alienated. Consider Van Maanen's (1991) description of his increasing alienation as an employee of Disneyland. It is important to study such cases because such examples signify what it means to be 'in' a culture or 'out' of it. This phenomenon of moving 'in' and 'out' of a culture deserves further exploration since it raises questions about the implicit assumption that culture is a unitary phenomenon, shared equally and similarly by all people in a particular context.

Further, unlike past scholars who have often relied on a mosaic view of culture, Martin (2002) has called for a nexus view of culture. According to this view, a cultural entity is engrained in the society where it is found. The nexus approach avoids juxtaposing culture with the social entity and posits instead that a social entity such as an organization is a nexus in which a variety of internal and external influences come together. What makes a culture unique is its own blend of external and internal cultural influences and its ever-changing boundaries. Martin (2002) explained that the nexus approach is the most appropriate for contemporary organizations in which buzz words such as 'multinational' and 'global' abound. The nexus approach is also suitable for organizations with multicultural workforces composed of people from varied racial, ethnic, national and other backgrounds. Within the nexus approach, boundaries of a culture are conceptualized as being permeable, moveable and fluctuating, thereby allowing for intercultural penetration and cultural change. Within this approach, cultures and subcultures could be nested, overlapping and multiple, and could have blurred edges. Martin (2002) concluded that conceptualizing culture in line with the nexus approach allows for new avenues of cultural exploration. With regards to the present volume, readers will see parallels between the nexus approach and the third illustrative study presented in Chapter 10. We encourage culture scholars to pursue this developmental axis in their future research.

In addition to the various conceptual developments discussed above, it is also likely that culture scholars will need to use more innovative techniques and methods in conducting cultural studies in the future (Martin 2002). For instance, scholars may need to surpass the historically observed over-reliance on the spoken word and use alternative tools such as videos (Martin 2002). Martin (2002) argued that using videos would allow researchers to focus not only on the voice but also on non-verbal communication patterns, the face and dress of cultural members, and the details of their physical surroundings. Other tools such as CD-ROMs, web pages, photos, hyperlinks, etc. could be equally useful. We support this argument in favour of innovative tools of research, especially in light of increasing interest in the cultural dynamics of online communities. Additionally, we argue that culture researchers will also need to develop new research methodologies and designs to allow for a more effective exploration of newly emerging cultural realities. Consider, for instance, the use of netnography for the cultural exploration of online communities (Kozinets 2006). Netnography is defined as 'a qualitative, interpretive research methodology that adapts the traditional, in-person ethnographic research techniques of anthropology to the study of the online cultures and communities formed through computer-mediated communications' (Jupp 2006: 193). The use of such alternative methodologies may also raise new ethical issues. For instance, for the study of cultural dynamics in online communities, one may need to obtain records of saved email conversations, bulletin boards and other communication. Obtaining such data may require permission of those involved in generating such communication, which might prove to be challenging considering that one of the main motivations behind people joining online communities is the anonymity that such communities offer (Martin 2002). Notwithstanding these challenges, it is likely that the search for alternative and more meaningful methodologies will accelerate in coming years.

Finally, we turn to the work of Jean-Claude Usunier (1998), who recommended that culture scholars learn to deconstruct their own cultural identities when they study culture. He defined deconstruction as the critical introspection of one's own research approach. Second, he called for future scholars to pay more attention to the role of language and how it does or does not indicate the context-laden nature of inquiry. He also suggested that future scholars should overcome the artificial divide between those who engage in qualitative and quantitative methods of research. Both words and numbers, he explained, are carriers of meaning and, in that sense, they complement one another. Like Tsui *et al.* (2007) and Martin (2002), Usunier (1998) also advised against the tendency of equating nation with culture and the tendency of excessively focusing on in-group similarities at the expense of in-group diversity. Additionally, he warned culture scholars against applying what works in one context to another context. For instance, he pointed out that French-speaking Canadians demonstrate more willingness to use a problem-solving orientation when dealing with their Anglophone counterparts than when dealing with one another. Therefore, if one draws conclusions based purely on observations made in intra-group settings, these would be misleading. In order to avoid the excessive dominance of what he called the 3A (Anglo-American Assumptions) worldview, he suggested that culture scholars should state their basic assumptions clearly upfront, and they should cooperate with research colleagues from different cultures (see also Tsui *et al.* 2007). Usunier (1998) concluded that cross-cultural research should include a strong critical component and should offer a better coverage of topics such as cross-cultural interactions, cultural inter-mediations, cultural mediators, intercultural competence, etc. Culture studies should emphasize both cultural learning and unlearning because new skills cannot be superimposed on existing ones. Finally, Usunier (1998) suggested that culture scholars should not focus solely on the average behaviors, linearity and continuity of patterns. Instead, focusing on discontinuity and failures in relationships and in business ventures will offer equally meaningful insights.

Concluding remarks

One of the many stated objectives of this book, as mentioned in the opening chapter, is to encourage business students to think of culture in a critical way. Although easy to understand, the frameworks of culture grounded in national/societal/regional origins and corporate affiliations prove to be less meaningful in discerning cultural dynamics in modern business entities. Perhaps these conventional frameworks of culture served a purpose when they first emerged in business literature – they offered preliminary guidelines to managers regarding how to behave with members of 'another culture' at a time when business entities were still opening up to a larger world and when interacting with people from different backgrounds was a new and infrequent event. It made sense to think of Indians as a distinct and unique cultural group and to compare their behaviours, values and preferences with those of the Americans when a company was considering setting up its operations in India for the very first time. This exercise is qualitatively no different from that of anthropologists who ventured into the remote and less-known territories to study the so-called primitive tribes inhabiting these regions and subsequently described in their travel records. However, the business community has come a long way since then.

Business entities today conduct business with a variety of stakeholders (customers, suppliers, distributors and outsourcing agencies) from different parts of the world, and their own domestic markets have become extremely diverse. Therefore, one need not cross national boundaries to encounter new cultures. Simultaneously, cultural boundaries are becoming more blurred, permeable and volatile. Concurrently, the role of the manager has also evolved. The manager is no longer solely in charge of the production of goods and services. The manager is involved in frequent and ongoing interactions with a variety of stakeholders, each with their own distinct and evolving sets of cultural preferences. Today, an effective manager is someone who understands and appreciates diverse ways of being and can intervene when required to resolve conflicts among groups with diverse viewpoints. The manager's skill lies in getting these groups with diverse viewpoints to collaborate effectively with one another, despite their inherent differences, while simultaneously nurturing this diversity. In light of these changes, using a dynamic conceptualization of culture seems to be a more appropriate practice for contemporary managers as opposed to relying on passive and static frameworks.

While we have made every attempt to offer the readers a balanced overview of different cultural frameworks from different epistemological traditions, it is inevitable that our own cultural background has inadvertently introduced certain biases. Writing is essentially a means for the author to interact with readers. Since an interaction cannot be separated from the interactor, it is inevitable that our own identity (or identities), our past experiences and our own cultural and educational heritage will have influenced the way we perceive different cultural frameworks and how we present these in this volume. Therefore, deconstructing our own cultural approach might be a worthwhile exercise. Having been born and brought up in India and having spent a considerable number of years in Europe (UK, Finland, Spain and France), we have been exposed to a rich variety of so-called national cultures. We have experienced people shifting and changing behavioural preferences to keep up with environmental changes. Having interacted closely with people from different professional, religious, educational and national backgrounds, we have had the opportunity to observe both the similarities and differences among them. Also, having studied natural sciences in our early years, man-agement in later years and business anthropology during our doctoral years, we have had the opportunity to experience different ways of thinking engrained in various discipline-based traditions. This has inspired us to seek synergies between the predominantly positivist tradition in business studies and the more interpretive and postmodernistic tradition in anthropology. Further, the multiple roles that we (and others) play in day-to-day life (researcher, academic, wife, sister, mother, daughter, etc.) have compelled us to reflect on why some of these identities become more prominent under certain circumstances than others. Like everyone else, we are subject to the biases emanating from our own past experiences and intellectual training. While some of these biases are sure to have infiltrated our thinking and our writing as we worked through the eleven chapters of this book, these are inherently a part of our identity and may have contributed to making our work unique. While we do not regret these biases, we simply underline that these biases explain, in part, our standpoint on culture and how it came to be.

Notes

1 In other words, we seek a cultural framework that (1) explains social change as a never-ending process, (2) offers a feedback mechanism to explain the continuity of

a social relationships, (3) offers a richer explanation of rationality and the social contexts that stimulate them, (4) explains the diversity of human behaviour without resorting to dualistic categories found in Western literature, and (5) supports the plurality of cultures without relying on the 'infinity' argument of culture.

2 A global property is objective, easily observable and independent of the perception of individual group members (for example, GDP, population, etc.) A shared property originates in the common experiences, perceptions or behaviours of the members of a group and represents a consensual aspect of culture. Finally, a configural property captures variations in individual characteristics within a group, and, although they emerge from characteristics of individual group members, they are not expected to be consensual.

3 Tsui *et al.* (2007) criticized the conventional national culture approach for not identifying any factor other than national culture that may account for differences in workplace behaviour across nations. There could in fact be many explanations for why people behave the way they do other than their national culture. Consider, for example, the work of Cullen (2004), which showed variations in cultural values in accordance with objective indicators such as economy, welfare socialism, family strength and educational attainment. Following a similar argument, Tsui *et al.* (2007) encouraged exploring work behaviour outcomes from poly-contextual approaches.

Bibliography

Ackerman, L. S. (1984) 'Development, transition or transformation: The question of change in organizations', *Organizational Development Practitioner*, December: 1–8.

Adair, W. L. and Brett, J. M. (2005) 'The negotiation dance: Time, culture, and behavioral sequences in negotiation', *Organization Science*, 16(1): 33–51.

Adigun, I. (1997). 'Orientations to work: A cross-cultural approach', *Journal of Cross-Cultural Psychology*, 28(3): 352–55.

Adler, N. and Doktor, R. (1986) 'From the Atlantic to the Pacific century: Cross-cultural management reviewed', *Yearly Review of Management of the Journal of Management*, 12(2): 295–318.

Ailon, G. and Kunda, G. (2009) 'The one-company approach: Transnationalism in an Israeli–Palestinian subsidiary of an MNC', *Organization Studies*, 30(7): 693–712.

Ailon-Souday, G. and Kunda, G. (2003) 'The local selves of global workers: The social construction of national identity in the face of organizational globalization', *Organization Studies*, 24(7): 1073–96.

Alkailani, M., Azzam, I. and Athamneh, A. (2012) 'Replicating Hofstede in Jordan: Ungeneralized, reevaluating the Jordanian Culture', *International Business Research*, 5(4): 71–80.

Al–Nashmi, M. M. and Syd Zin, S. A. R. (2011) 'Variation in communication satisfaction of academic staff in universities in Yemen depending on national culture', *Cross Cultural Management: An International Journal*, 18(1): 87–105.

Alvesson, M. (1987) 'Organizations, culture, and ideology', *International Studies of Management and Organizations*, 17(3): 4–18.

——(1990) 'Organization: From substance to image?', *Organization Studies*, 11(3): 373–94.

——(2002) *Understanding Organizational Culture*, London: Sage Publications.

Anderson, E. and Gatignon, H. (1986) 'Modes of foreign entry: a transaction cost analysis and propositions', *Journal of International Business Studies*, 17(3): 1–26.

Angwin, D. and Vaara, E. (2005) Introduction to the special issue: 'Connectivity in merging organizations: beyond traditional cultural perspectives', *Organization Studies*, 26 (10): 1445–53.

Asad, T. (1972) 'Market model, class structure and consent: A reconsideration of Swat political organization', *Man*, (n.s.), 7(1): 74–94.

Ashby, W. (1947) 'Principles of the self-organising dynamic system', *Journal of General Psychology*, 37: 125–28.

Astley, W. G. and Van de Ven, A. H. (1983) 'Central perspectives and debates in organization theory', *Administrative Science Quarterly*, 28(2): 245–73.

Aycan, Z. Kanungo, R.N., Mendonca, M., Yu, K., Deller, J. *et al.* (2000) 'Impact of culture on human resource management practices: A ten country comparison' *Appl. Psychol. Int. Rev*, 49: 192–220.

Bandura, A. (2002) 'Social cognitive theory in cultural context', *Applied Psychology*, 51(2): 269–90

Barkema, H. and Vermeulen, F. (1997) 'What differences in the cultural backgrounds of partners are detrimental for international joint ventures?', *Journal of International Business Studies*, 28(4): 845–65.

Barth, F. (1956) 'Ecologic relationships of ethnic groups in Swat, North Pakistan', *American Anthropologist*, 58: 1079–89.

——(1959a) 'Political Leadership Among Swat Pathans', *London School of Economics Monographs on Social Anthropology*, 19, London: Athlone.

——(1959b) 'Segmentary opposition and the theory of games', *Journal of the Royal Anthropological Institute*, 89(1): 5–22.

——(1966a) 'Anthropological models and social reality', *Proceedings of the Royal Society of London,* The Second Royal Society Nuffield Lecture, 165(998): 20–34.

——(1966b) 'Models of social organization', *Royal Anthropological Institute of Great Britain and Ireland*, Occasional paper, 23, London.

——(1967) 'On the study of social change', *American Anthropologist*, 69: 661–69.

——(1978) (Ed.) *Scale and Social Organization*, Oslo: Universitetsforlaget, 163–83.

——(1992) 'Towards greater naturalism in conceptualizing societies', in A. Kuper (Ed.) *Conceptualizing Society*, London: Routledge, 17–33.

——(2007) 'Overview: Sixty years in anthropology', *Annual Review of Anthropology*, 36: 1–16.

Bartunek, J. and Moch, M. (1991) 'Multiple constituencies and the quality of working life intervention at Foodcom' in P. Frost, L. Moore, M. Louis, C. Lundberg and J.Martin (Eds) *Reframing Organizational Culture*, Newbury Park, CA: Sage, 104–14.

Bate, P. (1984) 'The impact of organizational culture on approaches to organizational problem-solving', *Organization Studies*, 5: 43–66.

Baudrillard, J. (1988) *Selected Writings*, Stanford, CA: Stanford University Press.

Bell, S. T. and Arthur, W. Jr. (2008) 'Feedback acceptance in developmental assessment centers: the role of feedback message, participant personality, and affective response to the feedback session', *Journal of Organizational Behavior*, 29: 681–703.

Berry, P. M., Dawson, T. P., Harrison, P. A. and Pearson, R. G. (2002) 'Modelling potential impacts of climate change on the bioclimatic envelope of species in Britain and Ireland', *Global Ecology and Biogeography*, 11: 453–62.

Bhagat, R. S. and McQuaid, S. J. (1982) 'Role of subjective culture in organizations: A review and directions for future research', *Journal of Applied Psychology*, 67(5): 653 85.

Black, S. and Mendenhall, M. (1990) 'Cross-cultural training effectiveness: A review and a theoretical framework for future research' *Academy of Management Review*, 15(1): 113–136.

Boisot, M. (1998) *Knowledge Assets: Securing competitive advantage in the information economy*, Oxford: Oxford University Press.

——(2000) 'Is there a complexity beyond the reach of strategy?', *Emergence*, 2(1): 114–34.

Boisot, M. and Cohen, J. (2000) 'Shall I compare thee to … an organization?', *Emergence*, 2(4): 113–35.

Boje, D. M., Fedor, D. B. and Rowland, K. M. (1982) 'Myth making: A qualitative step in OD interventions', *Journal of Applied Behavioral Science*, 18: 17–28.

Bond, M. and Mai, K. (1989) *Trusting to the Tao: Chinese values and the re-centering of psychology*, Paper presented at the conference on moral reasoning in Chinese societies, Taipei, Taiwan.

Bond, M. H. and 68 co-authors (2004) 'Culture-level dimensions of social axioms and their correlates across 41 cultures', *Journal of Cross-Cultural Psychology*, 35: 548–570.

Bosland, N. (1985a) *An Evaluation of Replication Studies Using the Values Survey Module*, working paper 85–2, Maastricht: Institute for Research on Intercultural Cooperation, Rijks–universiteit Limburg.

Boswell, D. (1975) 'Review of Bruce Kapferer's strategy and transaction in an African factory: African workers and Indian management in a Zambian town', *Economic Development and Cultural Change*, 23(4): 786–93.

Brahy, S. (2006) 'Six solution pillars for successful cultural integration of international M&As', *Journal of Organizational Excellence*, Autumn (Fall), 25(4): 53–63.

Braunscheidel, M. J., Nallan, S. C. and Boisnier, A. D. (2010) An empirical investigation of the impact of organizational culture on supply chain integration, *Human Resource Management*, 49(5): 883–911.

Brockner, J. and Chen, Y. (1996) 'The moderating roles of self-esteem and self-construal in reaction to a threat to the self: Evidence from the People's Republic of China and the United States', *Journal of Personality and Social Psychology*, 71(3): 603–15.

Brown, C. and Reich, M. (1997) 'Micro-Macro linkages in high-performance employment systems', *Organizational Studies*, 18(5): 765–81.

Buckley, W. (1960) *Sociology and Modern Systems Theory*, Englewood Cliffs, NJ: Prentice Hall.

Buono, A. F., Bowditch, J. L. and Lewis, J. W. III (1985) 'When cultures collide: The anatomy of a merger', *Human Relations*, 38(5): 477–500.

Cameron, K. S. and Quinn, R. E. (1999) *Diagnosing and Changing Organizational Culture: Based on the competing values framework*, Reading, MA: Addison-Wesley.

——(2006) *Diagnosing and Changing Organizational Culture: Based on the competing values framework*, New York, NY: John Wiley and Sons.

Cardon, P. W. (2008) 'A critique of Hall's contexting model: A meta-analysis of literature on intercultural business and technical communication', *Journal of Business and Technical Communication*, 22(4): 399–428.

Chakraborty, G., Lala, V. and Warren, D. (2003) 'What do customers consider important in B2B websites?', *Journal of Advertising Research*, 43: 50–61.

Chatterjee, S., Lubatkin, M. Schweiger, D. M. and Y. Weber (1992) 'Cultural differences and shareholder value in related mergers: Linking equity and human capital', *Strategic Management Journal*, 13(5): 319–34.

Chen, Y-R., Brockner, J. and Katz, T. (1997) '*Individual-Primacy and Collective-Primacy as Bases for Ingroup Bias: Evidence from the United States and the People's Republic of China*', Paper presented at the annual meeting of the Academy of Management, Boston.

Chhokar, J.S. *et al.* (Eds) (2007) *Culture and Leadership across the World: The GLOBE Book of in-depth studies of 25 societies*, Mahwah, NJ: Lawrence Erlbaum.

Child, J. and Tayeb, M. (1983) 'Theoretical perspectives in cross-national organizational research', *International Studies of Management and Organization*, 12(4): 23–70.

Clark, B. (1972) 'The organizational saga in higher education', *Administrative Science Quarterly*, 17(2): 178–84.

Clifford, J. (1986) 'Partial Truths', in J. Clifford and G. E. Marcus (Eds) *Writing Culture: The poetics and politics of ethnography*, Berkeley, CA: University of California Press, 1–26.

Clifford, J. and Marcus, G. (1986) *Writing Culture: the poetics and politics of ethnography*, Berkeley, CA: University of California Press.

Collins, J. and Porras, J. (2002) *Built to Last: Successful habits of visionary companies*, New York, NY: Harper Business.

Cooper, R. and Burrell, G. (1988) 'Modernism, postmodernism and organizational analysis: An introduction', *Organization Studies*, 9(1): 91–113.

Corney, W. J. and Richards, C. H. (2005) 'A comparative analysis of the desirability of work characteristics: Chile versus the United States', *International Journal of Management*, 22. 159–65.

Cox, S. and Cheyne, A. (2000) 'Assessing safety culture in offshore environments'. *Safety Science*, 34(1–3): 111–129.

Coyle, D. (1997) 'A cultural theory of organizations', in M. Thompson and R. J. Ellis (Eds) (1997) *Culture Matters: Essays in honor of Aaron Wildavsky*, Boulder, CO: Westview Press, 59–78.

Coyle, D. and Ellis, R. (Eds) (1994) *Politics, Policy and Culture*, Boulder, CO: Westview Press.

Cyert, R. M. and March, J. G. (1963) *A Behavioral Theory of the Firm*, Englewood Cliffs, NJ: Prentice-Hall.

Czarniawska-Joerges, B. (1992) *Exploring Complex Organizations: A cultural perspective*, Newbury Park, CA: Sage.

Czarzasty, J. (2002) 'On the emerging organizational culture of a Finnish company's Polish subsidiary', *Human Resource Development International*, 5(3): 369–75.

Datta, D. K. (1991) 'Organizational fit and acquisition performance: Effects of post-acquisition integration', *Strategic Management Journal*, 12(4): 281–97.

Davis, S. M. (1984) *Managing Corporate Culture*, Cambridge, MA: Ballinger.

Deal, T. and Kennedy, A. (1982) *Corporate Cultures*, Reading, MA: Addison-Wesley.

DeJoy, D. (2005) 'Behavior change versus culture change: Divergent approaches to managing workplace safety', *Safety Science*, 43(2): 105–129.

De Luque, M. and Sommer, S. (2000) 'The impact of culture on feedback-seeking behavior: An integrated model and propositions', *Academy of Management Review*, 25(4): 829–849.

Denison, D. (1990) *Corporate culture and organizational effectiveness,* New York: Wiley.

Denison, D. R. and Spreitzer, G. M. (1991) 'Organizational culture and organizational development: A competing values approach', *Research in Organizational Change and Development*, 5: 1–21.

Denison, D. R. and Mishra, A. K. (1995) 'Toward a theory of organizational culture and effectiveness', *Organization Science*, 6(2): 204–223.

Deshpande, R. and Farley, J. (1999) 'Executive insights: Corporate culture and competitive orientation: Comparing Indian and Japanese firms', *Journal of International Marketing*, 7(4): 111–27.

Deshpande, R. and Webster, F. (1989) 'Organizational culture and marketing: Defining the research agenda', *Journal of Marketing*, 53(January): 3–15.

Deshpande, R., Farley, J. U. and Webster, F. E. (1993), 'Corporate culture, customer orientation, and innovativeness in Japanese firms: A quadrad analysis', *Journal of Marketing*, 57(1): 23–37.

DiBella, A. J. (1993) 'The role of assumptions in implementing management practices across cultural boundaries', *Journal of Applied Behavioral Science*, 29(3): 311–27.

Diener, E., Oishi, S. and Lucas, R.E. (2003) 'Personality, culture, and subjective well-being: Emotional and cognitive evaluations of life', *Annual Review of Psychology*, 54: 403–25.

Doney, P. M., Cannon, J. P. and Mullen, M. R. (1998) 'Understanding the influence of national culture on the development of trust', *Academy of Management Review*, 23: 601–20.

Douglas, M. (1970) *Natural Symbols*, London: Barrie and Rockliffe.

——(1978) 'Cultural bias', Occasional paper, London: *Royal Anthropological Institute*, 35. http://www.psych.lse.ac.uk/complexity/workshops/MaryDouglas.pdf

——(Ed.) (1982) *Essays in the Sociology of Perceptions*, London: Routledge and Kegan Paul.

——(1986) *How Institutions Think*, London: Routledge and Kegan Paul.

——(1996) *Thought Styles: Critical essays on good taste*, London: Sage.

——(2005) 'Grid and group, new developments' prepared following the *Workshop on Complexity and Cultural Theory in Honour of Michael Thompson*, London School of Economics.

Douglas, M. and Wildavsky, A. (1983) *Risk and Culture: An essay on the selection of technological and environmental dangers*, Berkeley and Los Angeles: University of California Press.

Driskill, L. P. (1997) Guest Editor, Introduction. Special issue on international communication, 'How can we address issues in international business and technical communication?', *The Journal of Business and Technical Communication*, 11: 253–60.

Durkheim, E. (1893) *The Division of Labour in Society*, trans. W. D. Hall (1984), Basingstoke: MacMillan.

——(1965) *The Elementary Forms of Religious Life*, trans. J. W. Swain, New York, NY: Collier.

——1984 [1893] *The Division of Labour in Society*. Tr. Hall, W. D. Basingstoke: MacMillan.

Earley, P. C. (1986) 'Trust, perceived importance of praise and criticism, and work performance: An examination of feedback in the United States and England', *Journal of Management*, 12: 457–73.

——(1989) 'Social loafing and collectivism: A comparison of the United States and the People's Republic of China', *Administrative Science Quarterly*, 34(4): 565–81.

——(1993) 'East meets West meets Mideast: Further explorations of collectivistic and individualistic work groups', *Academy of Management Journal*, 36: 319–348.

Ekeh, P. (1974) *Social Exchange Theory: The two traditions*, London: Heinemann.

Elisseeff, V. (2000) *The Silk Roads: Highways of culture and commerce*, Oxford/New York: UNESCO Publishing/Berghahn Books.

Erez, M. and Earley, C. (1993) *Culture, Self-Identity and Work*, New York, NY: Oxford University Press.

Ergeneli A, Gohar, R. and Temirbekova, Z. (2007) 'Transformational leadership: Its relationship to cultural value dimensions' *International Journal of Intercultural Relations*, 31(1): 703–24.

Emden, Z., Yaprak, A. and Cavusgil, S. T. (2005) 'Learning from experience: Antecedents and performance implications in the context of international alliances', *Journal of Business Research*, 58(7): 883–92.

Etzioni, A. (1975) *A Comparative Analysis of Complex Organizations* (Revised Edition), New York, NY: Free Press.

Featherstone, M. (1990) 'Global culture: Nationalism, globalization, and modernity', *A Theory, Culture and Society special issue*, London and Newbury Park, CA: Sage.

——(1995) *Undoing Culture: Globalization, postmodernism and identity*, London and Thousand Oaks, CA: Sage.

Fedor, K. and Werther, W. (1996). 'The fourth dimension: Creating culturally responsive international alliances', *Organizational Dynamics*, 25(2): 39–54.

Feldman, M. (1991) 'The meaning of ambiguity: Learning from stories and metaphors', in P. Frost, L. Moore, M. Louis, C. Lundberg and J. Martin (Eds), *Reframing Organizational Culture*, 145–56, Newbury Park, CA: Sage.

Festinger, L. (1957) *A Theory of Cognitive Dissonance*, Palo Alto, CA: Stanford University Press.

Filby, I. and Wilmott, H. (1986) 'Ideology, myth and humour: An ethnography of a public relations department in a State Bureaucracy', *Unpublished Paper.* Management Centre, Aston University.

Fiol, C. (1991) 'Managing culture as a competitive resource: An identity-based view of sustainable competitive advantage', *Journal of Management*, 17(1): 191–211.

Frake, C. (1977) 'Plying frames can be dangerous: Some reflections on methodology in cognitive anthropology', *Quarterly Newsletter of the Institute for Comparative Human Development*, 1(3): 1–7, New York: Rockefeller University.

Frosdick, S. (1995a) 'Organizational structure, culture and attitudes to risk in the British stadia safety industry', *Journal of Contingencies and Crisis Management*, 3(1): 43–57.

——(1995b) 'Safety cultures in British stadia and sporting venues: Understanding cross-organizational collaboration for managing public safety in British sports grounds', *Disaster Prevention and Management*, 4(4): 13–25.

——(2006) *Risk and Cultural Theory: A management consultancy approach*, Paragon Publishing: Rothersthorpe, UK.

Frost, P., Moore, L., Louis, M., Lundberg, C. and Martin, J. (Eds) (1991) *Reframing Organizational Culture*, Newbury Park, CA: Sage.

Fu, P. P., Kennedy, J., Tata, J., Yukl, G., Bond, M. H. *et al.* (2004) 'The impact of societal cultural values and individual social beliefs on the perceived effectiveness of managerial influence strategies: A meso approach', *Journal of International Business Studies*, 35: 284–305.

Fukuyama, F. (1995) *Trust: Social virtues and the creation of prosperity*, New York, NY: Free Press.

Geertz, C. (1973) 'Thick descriptions: Towards an interpretive theory of culture', in *The Interpretation of Culture*, New York: Basic Books.

——(1980) *Negara: The theater state in nineteenth-century Bali*, New York, NY: Basic Books.

Gelfand, M. J. and Cai, D. A. (2004) 'Cultural structuring of the social context in negotiation', in M. J. Gelfand and J. M. Brett (Eds) *The Handbook of Negotiation and Culture*, 238–57, Palo Alto, CA: Stanford University Press.

Gelfand, M. J. and Christakopoulou, S. (1999) 'Culture and negotiator cognition: Judgment accuracy and negotiation processes in individualistic and collectivistic cultures', *Organizational Behavior and Human Decision Processes*, 79(3): 248–69.

Gelfand, M. J. and Dyer, N. (2000) 'A cultural perspective on negotiation: Progress', pitfalls, and prospects', *Applied Psychology*, 49: 62–99.

Gelfand, M. J. and Realo, A. (1999) 'Individualism-collectivism and accountability in intergroup negotiations', *Journal of Applied Psychology*, 84: 721–36.

Gelfand, M., Nishii, L. and Raver, J. (2006) 'On the nature and importance of cultural tightness–looseness', *Journal of Applied Psychology*, 91(6): Nov 2006, 1225–1244.

Gelfand, M. J., Erez, M., and Aycan, Z. (2007) 'Cross-Cultural organizational behavior', *Annual Review of Psychology*, 58: 479–514.

Gelfand, M. J., Higgins, M., Nishii, L. H., Raver, J. L., Dominguez, A., *et al.* (2002) 'Culture and egocentric biases of fairness in conflict and negotiation', *Journal of Applied Psychology*, 87: 833–45.

Gelfand, M. J., Lun, J., Lyons, S. and Shteynberg, G. (2011) 'Descriptive norms as carriers of culture in negotiation', *International Negotiation*, 16: 361–81.

Gellner, E. (1983) *Nations and Nationalism*, Oxford: Blackwell.

Gibson, C. B., Maznevski, M. and Kirkman, B. L. (2009) 'When does culture matter?' in R. S. Bhagat and R. M. Steers (Eds) *Cambridge Handbook of Culture, Organizations, and Work*, 46–68, Cambridge, UK: Cambridge University Press.

Gierlach, E., Belsher, B. E. and Beutler, L. E. (2010) 'Cross-cultural differences in risk perceptions of disasters', *Risk Analysis*, 30 (10): 1539–1549.

Gilsenan, M. (1976) 'Lying, Honor and Contradiction', in B. Kapferer (Ed.) *Transaction and Meaning: Directions in the anthropology of exchange and symbolic behavior*, Philadelphia, PA: Institute for the Study of Human Issues.

Glendon, A. and Litherland, D. (2001) *Safety Science* 'Safety climate factors, group differences and safety behavior in road construction', 39(3): 157–188.

Glynn, M. A. and Raffaelli, R. (2010) 'Uncovering mechanisms of theory development in an academic field: lessons from leadership research', *Academy of Management Annals*, 4(1): 359–401.

Goffman, E. (1959) *The Presentation of Self in Everyday Life*, Garden City, NY: Doubleday.

Gong, W., Lee, Z. and Stump, R. (2007) 'Global internet and access: Cultural considerations', *Asia Pacific Journal of Marketing*, 19(1), 57–74.

Gray, B., Bougon, M. and Donneilon, A. (1985) 'Organizations as constructions and deconstructions of meaning', *Journal of Management*, 11(2), 83–98.

Gregory, B. T., Harris, S. G., Armenakis, A. A. and Shook, C. L. (2009) 'Organizational culture and effectiveness: A study of values, attitudes, and organizational outcomes', *Journal of Business Research*, 62: 613–9.

Grendstad, G. and Selle, P. (1997) 'Cultural theory, postmaterialism and environmental attitudes', in R. J. Ellis and M. Thompson (Eds) *Culture Matters: Essays in honor of Aaron Wildavsky*, Boulder, CO: Westview Press.

Gross, J. and Rayner, S. (1985) *Measuring Culture: A paradigm for the analysis of social organization*, New York, NY: Columbia Press.

Gupta, V. and Hanges, P. J. (2004) 'Regional and climate clustering of societal cultures', in R. J. House, P. J. Hanges, M. Javidan, P. W. Dorfman and V. Gupta (Eds) *Culture, Leadership and Organizations: The GLOBE study of 62 societies*, 178–218, Thousand Oaks, CA: Sage Publications.

Gutterman, A. (2010) 'Shalom Schwartz's dimensions of societal cultures', Available http://alangutterman.typepad.com/files/cms–schwartzs-cultural-dimensions-1.pdf (accessed on 16/04/2013).

Hall, E. T. (1960) 'The silent language in overseas business', *Harvard Business Review*, 38(3): 87–96.

——(1977) *Beyond Culture*, New York, NY: Doubleday.

——(1983) *The Dance of Life*, Garden City, NY: Anchor Press/Doubleday.

——(1985) *Hidden Differences: Studies in international communication*, Hamburg: Gruner and Jahr.

——(1987) *Hidden Differences: Doing business with the Japanese*, Garden City, NY: Anchor Press/Doubleday.

Hall, E. and Hall, M. (1990) *Understanding Cultural Differences*, Boston, MA., London: Intercultural Press.

Hambrick, D. C. and Brandon, G. L. (1988) 'Executive values', in D. C. Hambrick (Ed.) *The Executive Effect: Concepts and methods for studying top managers*, 3–34, Greenwich, CT: JAI Press.

Hambrick, D. C. and Cannella, A. (1993) 'Relative standing: A framework for understanding departures of acquired executives', *Academy of Management Journal*, 36(4): 733–62.

Handelman, D. (1976) 'Bureaucratic transactions: The development of official-client relationships in Israel', in B. Kapferer (Ed.), *Transaction and Meaning: Directions in the anthropology of exchange and symbolic behavior*, Philadelphia, PA: Institute for the Study of Human Issues.

Harbison, F. and Myers, C. (1959) *Management in the Industrial World: An international analysis*. New York, NY: McGraw-Hill.

Harris, M. (1968) *The Rise of Anthropological Theory*, New York, NY: Crowell.

Hartnell, C., Ou, A. and Kinicki, A. (2011) 'Organizational culture and organizational effectiveness: A meta-analytic investigation of the competing values framework's theoretical suppositions', *Journal of Applied Psychology*, 96(4): 677–94.

Harvey, F. (1997) 'National cultural differences in theory and practice: Evaluating Hofstede's national cultural framework', *Information Technology and People*, 10(2): 132–46.

Harzing, A. W. and Hofstede, G. (1996) 'Planned change in organizations: The influence of national culture', in S. B. Bacharach, P. A. Bamberger and M. Erez, *Research in the Sociology of Organizations: Cross-cultural analysis of organizations*, 14: 297–340 Greenwich, CT: JAI Press.

Haspelasgh, P. and Jemison, D. (1991) *Managing Acquisitions: Creating value through corporate renewal*, New York, NY: The Free Press.

Hassan, F., Shah, B., Ikramullah, M., Zaman, T. and Khan, H. (2011) 'The role of organization culture in predicting organizational effectiveness: A case from developing countries', *International Business and Management*, 3(2): 99–111.

Hatch, M. (1993) 'The dynamics of organization culture', *Academy of Management Review*, 18: 657–93.

Havold, J. (2007) 'National cultures and safety orientation: A study of seafarers working for Norwegian shipping companies', *Work and Stress: An International Journal of Work, Health and Organisations*, 21(2): 173–195.

Heine, S. J., Kitayama, S., Lehman, D. R., Takata, T., Ide, E., Leung, C. and Matsumoto, H. (2001) 'Divergent consequences of success and failure in Japan and North America: An investigation of self-improving motivations and malleable selves', *Journal of Personality and Social Psychology*, 81: 599–615.

Helmreich, R. L. and Merritt, A. C. (1998) *Culture at Work: National, organizational, and professional influences*, Aldershot, United Kingdom: Ashgate.

Hendon, D. W., Roy, M. H. and Ahmed, Z. U. (2003) 'Negotiation concession patterns: A multicountry, multiperiod study', *American Business Review*, 21: 75–81.

Hendry, J. (1999) 'Cultural theory and contemporary management organization', *Human Relations*, 52(5): 557–77.

Herbig, P. and Dunphy, S. (1998) 'Culture and innovation', *Cross Cultural Management: An international journal*, 5(4): 13–21.

Herodotus, Marincola, J. M. and de Selincourt, A. (2003) *The Histories*, London: Penguin Classics.

Herskovits, M. (1955) *Cultural Anthropology*, New York, NY: Alfred A. Knopf.

Hirsch, P. M. and Andrews, J. A. Y. (1983) 'Ambushes, shootouts, and knights of the roundtable: The language of corporate takeovers', in L. R. Pondy, P. J. Frost, G. Morgan and T. C. Dandridge (Eds) *Organizational Symbolism/Monographs in Organizational Behavior and Industrial Relations*, vol. 1:145–55, Greenwich, CT: JAI Press.

Hirschman, A. (1970) *Exit, Voice and Loyalty: Responses to decline in firms, organizations and states* Cambridge, MA: Harvard University Press.

Hoecklin, L. (1993) 'Managing cultural differences for competitive advantage', *The Economist Intelligence Unit*, Special Report No. 656.

Hofstede, G. (1980 [1984]). *Culture's Consequences: International differences in work-related values*, London: Sage.

Hofstede, G. (1986) 'The usefulness of the "organizational culture" concept', *Journal of Management Studies*, 23(3): 253–58.

——(1991) *Cultures and Organizations: Software of the mind*, London: McGraw-Hill.

——(1994) 'Management scientists are human', *Management Science*, 20(Jan): 4–13.

——(2001) *Culture's Consequences: Comparing values, behaviors, institutions, and organizations across nations*, 2nd edn, Thousand Oaks, CA: Sage.

——(2005) *Cultures and Organizations: Software of the mind*, London: McGraw-Hill.

Hofstede, G. and Bond, M. (1988) 'The Confucius connection: From cultural roots to economic growth', *Organizational Dynamics*, 16(4): 4–21.

Hofstede, G., Neuijen, B., Ohayv, D. and Sanders, G. (1990) 'Measuring organizational cultures: A qualitative and quantitative study across twenty cases', *Administrative Science Quarterly*, 35: 286–316.

Hofstetter, P. (1998) *Perspectives in Life Cycle Impact Assessment: A structured approach to combine models of the technosphere, ecosphere, and valuesphere*, Boston, MA: Kluwer Academic Publishers.

Holden, N. (1999) '*International Cross-Cultural Management Communication: The need for a more robust concept in the age of globalized learning corporation*', Paper presented at the ENCoDE conference, ESADE, Barcelona.

Holland, J. (1985) *Making Vocational Choices* (2nd edn) Odessa, FL.: Psychological Assessment Resources, Inc.

Hong, Y., Morris, M. W., Chiu, C. and Benet-Martinez, V. (2000) 'Multicultural minds: A dynamic constructivist approach to culture and cognition', *American Psychologist*, 55: 709–20.

House, J. H. and M. Javidan (2004) 'Overview of Globe', in R. J. House, P. J. Hanges, M. Javidan, P. W. Dorfman and V. Gupta (Eds) *Culture, Leadership, and Organizations: The GLOBE study of 62 societies*, 9–28, Thousand Oaks, CA: Sage.

House, R. J., Quigley, N. R. and Sully de Luque, M. F. (2010) 'Insights from Project GLOBE: Extending global advertising research through a contemporary framework', *International Journal of Advertising*, 29(1): 111–39.

House, R. J., Hanges, P. J., Javidan, M., Dorfman, P. W. and Gupta, V. (2004) *Culture, Leadership and Organizations: The GLOBE study of 62 societies*, Thousand Oaks, CA: Sage.

House, R. J., Hanges, P. J., Ruiz-Quintanilla, S., Dorfman, P. W., Javidan, M., Dickson, M. W., Gupta, V., and 159 co-authors (1999) 'Cultural influences on leadership and organizations: Project GLOBE', in W. Mobley, J. Gessner, and V. Arnold (Eds) *Advances in Global Leadership*, Stamford, CN: JAI Press.

House, R., Javidan, M., Hanges, P. and Dorfman, P. (2002) 'Understanding cultures and implicit leadership theories across the globe: An introduction to Project GLOBE' *Journal of World Business*, 37(1): 3–10.

Huang, X. and van de Vliert, E. (2004) 'Job-level and national culture as joint roots of job satisfaction', *Applied Psychology: An international review*, 53: 329–48.

Hui, C. H. and Yee, C. (1999) 'The impact of psychological collectivism and work-group atmosphere on Chinese employees' job satisfaction', *Applied Psychology*, 48: 175–85.

Ilgen, D. R., Fisher, C. D. and Taylor, M. S. (1979) 'Consequences of individual feedback on behavior in organizations', *Journal of Applied Psychology*, 64: 349–71.

Inglehart, R. and Baker, W. E. (2000) 'Modernization, cultural change, and the persistence of traditional values', *American Sociological Review*, 65: 19–51.

Iyengar, S. S. and Lepper, M. R. (1999) 'Rethinking the value of choice: A cultural perspective on intrinsic motivation', *Journal of Personality and Social Psychology*, 76: 349–66.

Javidan, M. and House, R. J. (2001) 'Cultural acumen for the global manager: Lessons from Project GLOBE', *Organizational Dynamics*, 29: 289–305.

Johnston, W. B. (1991) 'Global workforce 2000: The new world labor market', *Harvard Business Review*, 69(2): 115–27.

Jupp, V. (2006) *The SAGE Dictionary of Social Research Methods*, London: Sage Publications.

Kailani, M. and Kumar, R. (2011) 'Investigating uncertainty avoidance and perceived risk for impacting internet buying: A study in three national cultures', *International Journal of Business and Management*, 6(5): 76–92.

Kanungo, R. N. and Mendonca, M. (1996) *Ethical Dimensions of Leadership*, Thousand Oaks, CA: Sage Publications.

Kapferer, B. (1972) *Strategy and Transaction on an African Factory: African workers and Indian management in a Zambian town*, Manchester: Manchester University Press.

——(1976) 'Introduction' by Bruce Kapferer in *Transaction and Meaning: Directions in the anthropology of exchange and symbolic behaviour*, Philadelphia, PA: ISHI.

Kelley, L., MacNab, B. and Worthley, R. (2006) 'Crossvergence and cultural tendencies: A longitudinal test of the Hong Kong, Taiwan and United States banking sectors', *Journal of International Management*, 12(1): 67–84.

Kilmann, R., Saxton, M., Serpa, R. and Associates. (1985) *Gaining Control of the Corporate Culture, San Francisco*, CA: Jossey-Bass.

Kim, H. S. and Drolet, A. (2003) 'Choice and self-expression: A cultural analysis of variety-seeking', *Journal of Personality and Social Psychology*, 85(2): 373–82.

King, R. C. and Bu, N. (2005) 'Perceptions of the mutual obligations between employees and employers: A comparative study of new generation IT professionals in China and the United States', *International Journal of Human Resource Management*, 16: 46–64.

Kirkman, B., Lowe, K. and Gibson, B. (2006) 'A quarter century of culture's consequences: a review of empirical research incorporating Hofstede's cultural values framework', *Journal of International Business Studies*, 37: 285–320.

Kitayama, S. (2002) 'Culture and basic psychological theory–toward a system view of culture: comment on Oyserman *et al.* (2002)', *Psychological Bulletin*, 128: 89–96.

Kitayama, S., Markus, H. R., Matsumoto, H. and Norasakkunkit, V. (1997) 'Individual and collective processes in the construction of the self: Self-enhancement in the United States and self-criticism in Japan', *Journal of Personality and Social Psychology*, 72(6): 1245–67.

Kitching, J. (1967) 'Why do mergers miscarry?', *Harvard Business Review*, 45(6): 84–101.

Klein, K. and Kozlowski, S. (2000) 'From micro to meso: Critical steps in conceptualizing and conducting multilevel research', *Organization Research Methods*, 3(3): 211–36.

Kluger, A. N. and DeNisi, A. (1996) 'The effects of feedback interventions on performance: A historical review, meta-analysis, and a preliminary feedback intervention theory', *Psychological Bulletin*, 119: 254–84.

Koopman, P., Den Hartog, D., Konrad, E., Akerblom, S., Audia, G. *et al.* (1999) 'National culture and leadership profiles in Europe: Some results from the GLOBE study', *European Journal of Work and Organizational Psychology*, 8(4): 503–20.

Kotter J. P. and Heskett, J. L. (1992) *Corporate Culture and Performance*, New York, NY: Free Press.

Kozinets, R. (2006) 'Click to connect: Netnography and tribal advertising'. *Journal of Advertising Research*, September issue: 279–288.

Kreiser, P., Marino, L. Dickson, P. and Weaver, M. (2010) 'Cultural influences on entrepreneurial orientation: The impact of national culture on risk taking and proactiveness in SMEs', *Entrepreneurship Theory and Practice*, 34(5): 959–983.

Kroeber, A. and Kluckhohn, C. (1952) 'Culture: A critical review of concepts and definitions', in *Papers of the Peabody Museum of American Archeology and Ethnology*, Harvard University, Cambridge, MA, 47(1): 1–223.

Kurman, J., Yoshihara-Tanaka, C. and Elkoshi, T. (2003) 'Is self-enhancement negatively related to constructive self-criticism? Self-enhancement and self-criticism in Israel and in Japan', *Cross-Cultural Psychology*, 34: 24–37.

Leach, E. (1954) *Political Systems of Highland Burma*, London: G. Bell and Sons.

——(1961) *Pul Eliya: A village in Ceylon*, London: G. Bell and Sons.

Leung, K., Bond, M., Reimel de Carrasquel, S., Munoz, C., Hernandez, M., Murakami, F., Yamaguchi, S., Bierbrauer, G. and Singelis, T. (2002) 'Social axioms: The search for universal dimensions of general beliefs about how the world functions', *Journal of Cross-Cultural Psychology*, 3: 286–302.

Leung, K. and Bond, M. (2004) 'Social axioms: A model of social beliefs in multicultural perspective', in M. P. Zanna (Ed.) *Advances in Experimental Social Psychology*, San Diego, CA: Elsevier Academic Press.

Leung, K., Bhagat, R., Buchan, N., Erez, M. and Gibson, C. (2005) 'Culture and international business: Recent advances and their implications for future research', *Journal of International Business Studies*, 36(4): 357–78.

Levinson, N. and Asahi, M. (1995) 'Cross-national alliances and inter-organizational learning', *Organizational Dynamics*, Autumn, 24(2): 50–64.

Levitt, T. (1983) 'The globalization of markets', *Harvard Business Review*, 61(3): 92–102.

Li, J. (2002) 'A cultural model of learning-Chinese "heart and mind for wanting to learn"', *Journal of Cross-Cultural Psychology*, 33: 248–69.

Li, J., Lam, K. and Qian, G. (2001) 'Does culture affect behavior and performance of firms: The case of joint ventures in China', *Journal of International Business Studies*, 32(1): 115–31.

Liberman, V. (2011) 'What about the rest of us?: Beyond CEO pay', *The Conference Board Review*, Summer: 40–44.

Linstead, S. (1991) '*The Text of Culture: Implications of post-modern thought for the analysis of culture in organizations*', Paper presented at the European Group for Organizational Studies conference, Vienna.

Liu, C., Borg, I. and Spector, P. E. (2004) 'Measurement equivalence of the German Job Satisfaction Survey used in a multinational organization: Implications of Schwartz's culture model', *Journal of Applied Psychology*, 89: 1070–82.

Lockhart, C. (1997) 'Political culture and political change', in R. J. Ellis and M. Thompson (Eds) *Culture Matters: Essays in honor of Aaron Wildavsky*, Oxford: Westview Press.

Louis, M. (1980) '*A Cultural Perspective on Organizations: The need for and consequences of viewing organizations as culture-bearing milieux*', Paper presented at the National Academy of Management Meetings, Detroit, MI.

——(1981) 'A cultural perspective on organizations: The need for and consequences of viewing organizations as culture-bearing milieux', *Human Systems Management*, 2: 246–258.

Lowe, J. (1996) Book Review of 'The seven cultures of capitalism: Values systems for creating wealth in the United States, Britain, Japan, Germany, France, Sweden and the Netherlands', by Fons Trompenaars and Charles Hampden-Turner (1993) London: Doubleday. Book Review published in *International Journal of Human Resource Management*, 7(1): 273–76.

Lubatkin, M., Calori, R., Very, P. and Veiga, J. F. (1998) 'Managing mergers across borders: A two-nation exploration of a nationally bound administrative heritage', *Organization Science*, 9(6): 670–84.

McDermott, C. M. and Stock, G. N. (1999) 'Organizational culture and advanced manufacturing technology implementation', *Journal of Operations Management*, 17: 521–33.

McSweeney, B. (2002) 'Hofstede's model of national cultural differences and their consequences: A triumph of faith – a failure of analysis', *Human Relations*, 55(1): 89–18.

——(2009) 'Dynamic diversity: Variety and variation within countries', *Organization Studies*, 30(9): 933–57.

Ma, Z., Anderson, T., Wang, X., Wang, Y., Jaeger, A. and Saunders, D. (2002) 'Individual perception, bargaining behavior, and negotiation outcomes: a comparison across two countries', *International Journal of Cross-Cultural Management*, 2: 171–84.

Maine, H. S. (1861) *Ancient Law*, London: John Murray.

Mamadouh, V. (1999) 'Grid-Group cultural theory: An introduction', *GeoJournal*, 47: 395–409.

——(1999) 'National political cultures in the European Union', in M. Thompson, G. Grendstad and P. Selle (Eds) (1999) *Cultural Theory as Political Science*, London, New York: Routledge/ECPR Studies in European Political Science.

Mars, G. (1972) 'An anthropological study of longshoremen and of industrial relations in the port of St. John's, Newfoundland, Canada', *PhD Thesis*, University of London.

——(1982) *Cheats at Work: An anthropology of workplace crime*, London: Allen & Unwin.

——(2001) '*Corporate Cultures and the Use of Space: An approach from cultural theory*', Paper presented at the SCOS International Conference on Spacing and Timing, Palermo, Italy, November 1–3, 2001.

——(2005) 'Locating causes of accidents in the social organization of building workers and some wider implications: An approach from cultural theory', *International Journal of Nuclear Knowledge Management*, 1(3): 255–69.

March, J. and Simon, H. (1958) *Organizations*, New York, NY: Wiley.

Martin, J. (1992) *Cultures in organizations*, New York: Oxford University Press.

——(2002) *Organizational Culture: Mapping the terrain*, London, New Delhi: Sage Publications.

——(2004) 'Organizational culture', research paper no. 1847, Stanford University, in N. Nicholson, P. Audia and M. Pillutla (Eds) *The Blackwell Encyclopedic Dictionary of Organizational Behavior*, 2nd edn, Oxford: Basil Blackwell, Ltd.

Martin, J. and Siehl, C. (1983) 'Organizational culture and counterculture: An uneasy symbiosis', *Organizational Dynamics*, 12(2): 52–64.

Martin, J. and Meyerson, D. (1988) 'Organizational culture and the denial, channeling and acknowledgment of ambiguity', in L. Pondy, R. Boland, Jr. and H. Thomas (Eds) *Managing Ambiguity and Change*, 93–125, New York, NY: John Wiley.

Marx, K. (1977[1859]) *A Contribution to the Critique of Political Economy*, Moscow: Progress Publishers.

Masuda, Jeffrey and Garvin, T.. (2006) 'Place, culture and the social amplification of risk', *Risk Analysis*, 26(2): 437–454.

Mathews, G. (2000) *Global Culture/Individual Identity: Searching for home in the cultural supermarket*, London: Routledge.

Matsumoto, T. (2004) 'Learning to "do time" in Japan: A study of US interns in Japanese organizations', *International Journal of Cross-Cultural Management*, 4: 19–37.

Marriott, M. (1976) 'Hindu transactions: Diversity without dualism', in B. Kepferer (Ed.) *Transaction and Meaning: Directions in the anthropology of exchange and symbolic behaviour*, Philadelphia, PA: ISHI Publications.

Mead, G. (1934) *Mind, Self and Society*, Chicago, IL: University of Chicago Press.

Merritt, A. (2000) 'Culture in the cockpit. Do Hofstede's dimensions replicate?' *Journal of Cross Cultural Psychology*, 31: 283–301.

Meschi, P. (1997) 'Longevity and cultural differences of international joint ventures: Toward time–based cultural management', *Human Relations*, 50(2): 221–28.

Meyerson, D. (1991) 'Acknowledging and uncovering ambiguities in cultures', in P. Frost, L. Moore, M. Louis, C. Lundberg, and J. Martin (Eds) *Reframing Organizational Culture*, 254–70, Newbury Park, CA: Sage.

Meyerson, D. and Martin, J. (1987) 'Cultural change: An integration of three different views', *Journal of Management Studies*, 24: 623–47.

Milton, K. (1996) *Environmentalism and Cultural Theory*, London: Routledge.

Mitroff, I. and Kilmann, R. (1976) 'On organizational stories: An approach to the designs and analysis of organizations through myths and stories', in R. Kilmann,

L. R Pondy. and D. P. Slevin (Eds) *The Management of Organization Design*, New York, NY: Elsevier-North Holland.

Money, B. and J. Crotts. (2003) 'The effect of uncertainty avoidance on information search, planning, and purchases of international travel vacations', *Tourism Management*, 24(1): 191–202.

Morey, N. C. and Luthans, F. (1985) 'Refining the displacement of culture and the use of scenes and themes in organizational studies', *Academy of Management Review*, 10: 219–29.

Morgan, G. (1986) *Images of Organization*, Beverly Hills, CA: Sage.

Morris, M. and Gelfand, M. (2004) 'Cultural differences and cognitive dynamics: Expanding the cognitive perspective on negotiation', in M. Gelfand and J. Brett (Eds) (2004) *The Handbook of Negotiation and Culture*, Stanford, CA: Stanford University Press.

Morris, M. W. and Fu, H. (2001) 'How does culture influence conflict resolution? A dynamic constructivist analysis', *Social Cognition*, 19: 324–49.

Morris, M. W., Leung, K., Ames, D. and Lickel, B. (1999) 'Views from inside and outside: Integrating emic and etic insights about culture and justice judgments', *Acad. Manage. Rev*, 24: 781–96.

Morrison E. W., Chen Y. and Salgado S. R. (2004) 'Cultural differences in newcomer feedback seeking: A comparison of the United States and Hong Kong', *Appl. Psychol*, 53: 1–22

Nahavandi, A. and Malekzadeh, A. (1998) *Organizational Behavior: The person-organization fit*, Upper Saddle River, New Jersey: Prentice Hall.

Nowicka, E. (2000) *World of Humans – World of Culture*, Warsaw, PWN.

Ofori-Dankwa, J. and Ricks, D. (2000) 'Research emphases on cultural differences and/or similarities: Are we asking the right questions?', *Journal of International Management*, 6: 172–86.

Ogbonna, E. and Harris, L. (2002) 'Organizational culture: A ten year, two-phase study of change in the UK food retailing sector', *Journal of Management Studies*, 39 (5): 673–706.

Ohmae, K. (1985) *Triad Power: The coming shape of global competition*, New York, NY: The Free Press.

Olk, P. and Earley, P. C. (1996) 'Rediscovering the individual in the formation of international joint ventures', *Research in the Sociology of Organizations*, Special issue on cross-cultural management, 14: 223–61.

O'Reilly, A. (1991) 'The emergence of the global consumer', *Directors and Boards*, 15(2): 9–13.

O'Reilly, C. A. I., Chatman, J. and Caldwell, D. F. (1991) 'People and organizational culture: A profile comparison approach to assessing person-organization fit', *Academy of Management Journal*, 34: 487–516.

Osland, J. and Bird, A. (2000) 'Beyond sophisticated stereotyping: cultural sensemaking in context', *Academy of Management Executive*, 14(1): 65–77.

Ostroff, C. (1993) 'Rater perceptions, satisfaction and performance ratings', *Journal of Occupational and Organizational Psychology*, 66(4): 345–56.

Ouchi, W. (1980) 'Markets, bureaucracies and clans', *Administrative Science Quarterly*, 25(1): 129–41.

Oyserman, D., Coon, H. M. and Kemmelmeier, M. (2002) 'Rethinking individualism and collectivism: Evaluation of theoretical assumptions and meta-analyses', *Psychological Bulletin*, 128: 3–72.

Parkhe, A. (1998) 'Building trust in international alliances', *Journal of World Business*, 33(4): 417–37.

Patel, T. (2005) 'Using dynamic cultural theory to explain viability of international strategic alliances: A focus on Indo-French alliances', *PhD Thesis*. Open University.

——(2007a) 'Using cultural theory to explain the viability of international strategic alliances: A focus on Indo-French alliances', *Management Decisions*, 45(10): 1532–59.

——(2007b) *Stereotypes of Intercultural Management*, Delft, Holland: Eburon.

Patel, T. and Patel, C. (2008) 'Learning cultures for sustained innovation success', *Innovation: The European Journal of Social Science Research*, 21(3): 233–51.

Patel, T. and Rayner, S. (2012a) 'Towards a transactional approach to culture: Illustrating the application of Douglasian Cultural Framework in a variety of management settings', *European Management Review*, 9: 121–38.

——(2012b) 'A transactional culture analysis of corporate sustainability reporting practices: Six examples from India', *Business and Society*, DOI: 10.1177/0007650312445132.

Patel, T. and Schaefer, A. (2009) 'Making sense of the diversity of ethical decision making in business: An illustration of the Indian context', *Journal of Business Ethics*, 90(2): 157–70.

Pelto, P. (1968) 'The differences between "tight" and "loose" societies,' *Trans-action*, 5(5): 37–40.

Peters, T. and Waterman, R. (1982) *In Search of Excellence: Lessons from America's best–run companies*, New York, NY: Harper and Row.

Pettigrew, A. (1979) 'On studying organizational cultures', *Administrative Science Quarterly*, 24: 570–81.

Pfeffer, J. (1981) 'Management as symbolic action: The creation and maintenance of organizational paradigms', in L. L. Cummings and B. M. Staw (Eds) *Research in Organizational Behavior*, vol. 4, Greenwich, CT: JAI Press.

Piccolo, R. F., Judge, T. A., Takahashi, K., Watanabe, N. and Locke, E. A. (2005) 'Core self-evaluations in Japan: relative effects on job satisfaction, life satisfaction, and happiness', *Journal of Organizational Behavior*, 26: 965–84.

Price, M. and Thompson, M. (1996) 'The complex life: Human land uses in mountain ecosystems', *Global Ecology and Biogeography Letters*, 6: 77–90.

Poster, M. (1988) 'Introduction', in M. Poster (Ed.) *Jean Baudrillard: Selected writings*, Stanford, CA: Stanford University Press.

Putnam, R. (2000) *Bowling Alone: The collapse and revival of American community*, New York, NY: Simon and Schuster.

Quinn, R. E. and Rohrbaugh, J. (1983) 'A spatial model of effectiveness criteria: Toward a competing values approach to organizational analysis', *Management Science*, 29(3): 363–77.

Quinn, R. E. and Kimberly, J. R. (1984) 'Paradox, planning, and perseverance: Guidelines for managerial practice', in J. R. Kimberly and R. E. Quinn (Eds) *Managing Organizational Transitions*, 295–313, Homewood, IL: Dow Jones-Irwin.

Ralston, D. A., Gustafson, D. J., Cheung, F. M. and Terpstra, R. H. (1993) 'Differences in managerial values: A study of U.S., Hong Kong and PRC managers', *Journal of International Business Studies*, 24(2): 249–75.

Ralston, D., Terpstra-Tong, J., Terpstra, R., Wang, X. and Egri, C. (2006) 'Today's state-owned enterprises of China: Are they dying dinosaurs or dynamic dynamos?', *Strategic Management Journal*, 27(9): 825–843.

Rayner, S. (1982) 'The perceptions of time and space in egalitarian sects: A millenarian cosmology', in M. Douglas (Ed.) *Essays in the Sociology of Perception*, London: Routledge and Kegan Paul.

——(1986) 'Management of radiation hazards in hospitals: Plural rationalities in a single institution', *Social Studies of Science*, 16: 573–91.

——(1991) 'A cultural perspective on the structure and implementation of global environmental agreements', *Evaluation Review*, 15(1): 75–102.

——(1992) 'Cultural theory and risk analysis', in S. Krimsky and D. Golding (Eds) *Social Theories of Risk*, Westport, Connecticut: Praeger.

——(1995) 'A conceptual map of human values', in A. Katama (Ed.) *Equity and Social Considerations Related to Climate Change*, Nairobi: ICIPE Science Press.

Rayner, S. and Malone, E. 1999 'Security, governance and the environment', in Lowi, M. R. and Shaw, B. R. (Eds) *Environment and Security: Discourse and practices*, Basingstoke. Macmillan.

Renn, O. (1992). 'Concepts of risk: A clarification'. in S. Krimsky, and D. Golding, (Eds) *Social Theories of Risk*, Westport, Connecticut: Praeger.

——(2003) 'Acrylamide: Lessons for risk management and communication', *Journal of Health Communication: International Perspectives*, 8(5): 435–441.

Roberts, K. and Boyacigiller, N. (1984) 'Cross-national organizational research: The grasp of the blind men', in B. Staw and L. Cummings (Eds) *Research in Organizational Behavior*, 6: 423–75, Greenwich, CT: JAI.

Robertson, M. and Swan, J. (2003) 'Control-what control? Culture and ambiguity within a knowledge intensive firm', *Journal of Management Studies*, 40: 831–58.

Rodriguez (2005) 'Emergence of a third culture: Shared leadership in international strategic alliances', *International Marketing Review*, 22(1): 67–95.

Rokeach, M. (1973) *The Nature of Human Values*, New York, NY: Free Press.

Sagie, A., Elizur, D. and Yamauchi, H. (1996) 'The structure and strength of achievement motivation: A cross-cultural comparison', *Journal of Organizational Behavior*, 7: 431–44.

Saïd, E. (1979) *Orientalism*, New York, NY: Vintage.

Sales, A. and Mirvis, P. (1984) 'When cultures collide: Issues of acquisition', in J. Kimberly and R. Quinn (Eds) *Managing Organizational Transition*, 107–33, Homewood, IL: Irwin.

Sarup, M. (1996) *Identity, Culture and the Postmodern World*, Edinburgh: Edinburgh University Press.

Sathe, V. (1985) *Culture and Related Corporate Realities*, Homewood, IL: Irwin.

Schein, E. (1985) *Organizational Culture and Leadership: A dynamic view*, San Francisco, CA: Jossey-Bass.

——(1991) 'What is culture?', in P. Frost, L. Moore, M. Louis, C. Lundberg and J. Martin (Eds) *Reframing Organizational Culture*, 243–53, Newbury Park, CA: Sage.

Schein, E. H. (1992) *Organizational Culture and Leadership*, San Francisco, CA: Jossey-Bass.

Scherer, C. and Cho, H. (2003) 'A social network contagion theory of risk perception', *Risk Analysis*, 23(2): 261–267.

Schneider, B. and Rentsch, J. (1988), 'Managing climates and cultures: A futures perspective', in J. Hage (Ed.) *Futures of Organizations*, Lexington, MA: Lexington Books.

Schneider, B., Goldstein, H. W. and Smith, D. B. (1995) 'The ASA Framework: An update', *Personnel Psychology*, Winter, 48(4): 747–73.

Schneider, S. (1988) 'National vs. corporate cultures: Implications for human resource Management', *Human Resource Management*, 27(2) In: Redding, op. cit., pp. 231–46.

Schoenberg, R., Denuelle, N. and Norbern, D. (1995) 'National conflicts within European alliances', *European Business Journal*, 7(1): 8–16.

Schultz, M. and Hatch, M. J. (1996) 'Living with multiple paradigms: The case of paradigm interplay in organizational culture studies', *Academy of Management Review*, 21(2): 529–57.

Schwartz, H. and Davis, S. (1981) 'Matching corporate culture and business strategy', *Organizational Dynamics*, Summer: 30–48.

Schwarz, M. and Thompson, M. (1990) *Divided We Stand: Redefining politics, technology and social choice*, London: Harvester Wheatsheaf.

Schwartz, S. H. (1992) 'Universals in the content and structure of values: Theoretical advances and empirical tests in two countries', in L. Berkowitz (Ed.) *Advances in Experimental Social Psychology*, 1–65, San Diego, CA: Academic Press.

——(1994) 'Are there universal aspects in the content and structure of values?' *Journal of Social Issues*, 50, 19–45.

——(1996) 'Value priorities and behavior: Applying a theory of integrated value systems', in C. Seligman, J. M. Olson and M. P. Zanna (Eds) *The Psychology of Values: The Ontario Symposium*, vol. 8, 1–24, Hillsdale, NJ: Erlbaum.

——(2004) 'Mapping and interpreting cultural differences around the world', in H. Vinken, J. Soeters and P. Ester (Eds) *Comparing Cultures, Dimensions of Culture in a Comparative Perspective*, Leiden, The Netherlands: Brill.

——(2005a) 'Basic human values: Their content and structure across countries', in A. Tamayo and J. B. Porto (Eds) *Valores e Comportamento nas Organizações* [Values and behavior in organizations], 21–55, Petrópolis, Brazil: Vozes.

——(2005b) 'Robustness and fruitfulness of a theory of universals in individual human values', in A. Tamayo and J. B. Porto (Eds), *Valores e Comportamento nas Organizações* [Values and behavior in organizations], 56–95, Petrópolis, Brazil: Vozes.

——(2006) 'Basic human values: theory, measurement and applications', *Revue Francaise de Sociologie*, 47(4): n.s.

Schwartz, S. H. and Bardi, A. (1997) 'Influences of adaptation to communist rule on value priorities in Eastern Europe', *Political Psychology*, 18: 385–410.

Shane, S. (1991) *A Cultural Approach to Marketing in Japan*, Yarmouth, ME: Intercultural Press.

——(1992) 'Why do some societies invent more than others?', *Journal of Business Venturing*, 7: 29–46.

Sharp, L. (1952) 'Steel axes for stone-age Australians', in E. H. Spicer (Ed.) *Human Problems in Technological Change*, New York, NY: Russell Sage Foundation.

Shenkar, O. and Zeira, Y. (1992) 'Role conflict and role ambiguity of chief executive officers in international joint ventures', *Journal of International Business Studies*, 23 (1): 55–75.

Shepstone, C. and Currie, L. (2008) 'Transforming the academic library: Creating an organizational culture that fosters staff success', *The Journal of Academic Librarianship*, 34(4): 358–68.

Shrivastava, P. (1986) 'Post-merger integration', *Journal of Business Strategy*, 7(1) 65–76.

Shweder, R. and LeVine, R. (1984) *Culture Theory: Essays on mind, self, and emotion*, London: Cambridge University Press.

Siehl, C. and Martin, J. (1981) '*Learning Organizational Culture*', Working paper, Stanford University Graduate School of Business.

Simon, H. (1978) 'Rationality as process and as product of thought'. *The American Economic Review* vol. 68, No. 2, Papers and Proceedings of the Ninetieth Annual Meeting of the American Economic Association (May, 1978), 1–16. Published by: American Economic Association.

Singh, J. (1990) 'Managing culture and work-related values in India', *Organization Studies*, 11(1): 75–101.

Sjöberg, L. (1998) 'Why do people demand risk reduction?', in S. Lydersen, G. Hansen, and H. Sandtorv (Eds) *ESREL–98: Safety and reliability*, 751–58, Trondheim: A. A. Balkema.

Skinner, B. F. (1981) 'Selection by consequences', *Science*, 213: 501–4.

Skvoretz, W. Jr. and Conviser, R. (1974) 'Interests and alliances: A reformulation of Barth's model of social organization', *Man* (n.s.), 9(1): 53–67.

Smircich, L. (1983) 'Concepts of culture and organizational analysis', *Administrative Science Quarterly*, 28(3): 339–58.

Smircich, L. and Morgan, G. (1983) 'Leadership: The management of meaning', *Journal of Applied Behavioral Science*, 18: 257–73.

Soares, M., Farhangmehr, M. and Shoham, A. (2007) 'Hofstede's dimensions of culture in international marketing studies', *Journal of Business Research*, 60(3): 277–84.

Spector, P. E., Cooper, C. L., Sanchez, J. I., O'Driscoll, M., Sparks, K. *et al.* (2002) 'Locus of control and well-being at work: How generalizable are Western findings?', *Academy of Management Journal*, 45: 453–66.

Spekman, R. and Lynn, A. (2000) *Alliance Competence: Maximizing the value of our partnerships*, New York, NY: John Wiley & Sons, Inc.

Spradley, J. (1979) *The Ethnographic Interview*, Belmont, CA: Wadsworth Group/ Thomson Learning.

Stahl, G. K., Miller, E. L. and Tung, R. L. (2002) 'Toward the boundaryless career: A closer look at the expatriate career concept and the perceived implications of an international assignment', *Journal of World Business*, 37(3): 216–27.

Steensma, K., Marino, L., Weaver, M. and Dickson, P. (2000) 'The influence of national culture on the formation of technology alliances by entrepreneurial firms', *Academy of Management Journal*, 43(5): 951–973.

Stone, D. (1962) *The Talamancan Tribes of Costa Rica*, Cambridge, MA: Peabody Museum.

Sully de Luque, M. and Sommer, S. (2000) 'The impact of culture on feedback seeking behavior: an integrated model and propositions', *Academy of Management Review*, 25(4): 829–49.

Tambiah, S. (2002) *Edmund Leach: An anthropological life*, Cambridge: University of Cambridge Press.

Tang, L. and Koveos, P. E. (2008) 'A framework to update Hofstede's cultural value indices: economic dynamics and institutional stability', *Journal of International Business Studies*, 39: 1045–63.

Tanghe, J., Wisse, B. and Van der Flier, H. (2010). 'The role of group member affect in the relationship between trust and cooperation', *British Journal of Management*, 21: 359–74.

Tansey, J. (2004) 'Risk as politics, culture as power', *Journal of Risk Research*, 7(1): 17–32.

Taylor, M. (1982) *Community, Anarchy and Liberty*, Cambridge: Cambridge University Press.

Taras, V., Kirkman, B. and Steel, P. (2010) 'Examining the impact of culture's consequences: A three-decade, multilevel, meta-analytic review of Hofstede's cultural value dimensions', *Journal of Applied Psychology*, 95(3): 405–39.

Tayeb, M. (1994) 'Organization and national culture: Methodology considered', *Organization Studies*, 15(3): 429–47.

——(2001) 'Conducting research across cultures: Overcoming drawbacks and obstacles', *International Journal of Cross Cultural Management*, 1(1), 91–108.

Tellis, G., Prabhu, J. and Chandy, R. (2009) 'Radical innovation across nations: The preeminence of corporate culture', *Journal of Marketing*, 73(1): 3–23.

Tharaldsen, J. E. and Knut, H. 2009 'Culture and behavioral perspectives on safety – Towards a balanced approach', *Journal of Risk Research*, 12(3–4): 375–388.

Thomas, A. and Mueller, S. (2000)' A case for comparative entrepreneurship: Assessing the relevance of culture', *Journal of International Business Studies*, 31 (2): 287–301.

Thompson, M. (1984) 'Among the energy tribes: A cultural framework for the analysis and design of energy policy'. *Policy Sciences*, 17: 321–339.

——(1992) 'The dynamics of cultural theory and implications for the enterprise culture', in S. Hargreaves Heap and A. Ross, (Eds) (1992) *Understanding the Enterprise Culture: Themes in the Work of Mary Douglas*, Edinburgh: Edinburgh University Press.

——(1996) *Inherent Relationality: An anti-dualistic approach to institutions*, report no. 9608, Bergen, Norway: LOS Centre Publication.

——(1997a) 'Rewriting the precepts of policy analysis', in M. Thompson and R. J. Ellis (Eds) (1997) *Culture Matters: Essays in honor of Aaron Wildavsky*, Boulder, CO: Westview Press.

——(1997b) 'Cultural theory and technology assessment' in F. Fischer and M. Hajer (Eds) (1997) *Living with Nature: Environmental discourse and cultural politics*, Oxford: Oxford University Press.

——(1997c) 'Cultural theory and integrated assessment', *Environmental Modelling and Assessment*, 2: 139–50.

——(2003) 'Man and nature as a single but complex system', *Social and Economic Dimensions of Global Environmental Change*, 5: 384–393. (Ed) Peter Timmerman in *Encyclopedia of Global Environmental Change*.

Thompson, M. and Wildavsky, A. (1986) 'A cultural theory of information bias in organizations'. *Journal of Management Studies*, 23(3): 273–286.

Thompson, M., Rayner, S. and Ney, S. (2000) 'Risk and governance Part II: Policy in a complex and plurally perceived world', in G. Mars and D. Weir (Eds) *Risk Management Volume I (International Library of Management)*. Aldershot: Ashgate, 517542. [Reprint of 1998 paper in *Government and Opposition*.]

Thompson, M. and Ellis, R. J. (Eds) (1997) *Culture Matters: Essays in honor of Aaron Wildavsky*, Boulder, CO: Westview Press.

Thompson, M., Ellis, R. and Wildavsky, A. (1990) *Cultural Theory*, Boulder, CO: Westview Press.

Thompson, M., Grendstad, G. and Selle, P. (eds) (1999) *Cultural Theory as Political Science*, London: Routledge/ECPR Studies in European Political Science.

Thompson, M., Verweij, M. and Ellis, R. (2005) 'Why and how culture matters', in R. E. Goodin and C. Tilly (Eds) *The Oxford Handbook of Contextual Political Analysis*, Oxford: Oxford University Press.

Tichy, N. (1982) 'Managing change strategically: The technical, political and cultural keys', *Organizational Dynamics*, 11(2): 59–80.

Tinsley, C. and Brodt, S. (2004) 'Conflict management in Asia: A dynamic framework and future directions', in K. Leung and S. White (Eds) *Handbook of Asian Management*, 439–58, New York, NY: Kluwer Academic Publishers.

Tinsley, C. H. and Pillutla, M. M. (1998) 'Negotiating in the United States and Hong Kong', *Journal of International Business Studies*, 29: 711–28.

Toennies, F. (1887) *Gemeinschaft und Gesellschaft*, Leipzig: Fues's Verlag, 2nd ed. 1912, 8th edition, Leipzig: Buske, 1935 (reprint 2005, Darmstadt: Wissenschaftliche Buchgesellschaft).

Tompkins, D., Galbraith, D. and Tompkins, P. (2010) 'Universalism, particularism and cultural self-awareness: A comparison of American and Turkish university students', *Journal of International Business and Cultural Studies*, 3 (May issue).

Tong, S. (2009) 'Varieties of universalism', *European Journal of Social Theory*, 12(4): 449–63.

Tönnies, F. (1887) *Gemeinschaft und Gesellschaft*. Wissenschaftlich Darmstadt.

Tosi, H. L. and Greckhamer, T. (2004) 'Culture and CEO compensation', *Organization Science*, 15: 657–70.

Triandis, H. C. (1972) *The Analysis of Subjective Culture*, New York, NY: Wiley.

——(1989) 'The self and social behavior in differing cultural contexts', *Pscyhological Review*, 96(3): 506–520.

——(1994) *Culture and Social Behavior*, New York, NY: McGraw-Hill.

Trice, H. M. and Beyer, J. M. (1984) 'Studying organizational cultures through rites and ceremonials,' *Academy of Management Review*, 9: 653–69.

Trompenaars, F. and Hampden-Turner, C. (1993) *The Seven Cultures of Capitalism: Values systems for creating wealth in the United States, Britain, Japan, Germany, France, Sweden and the Netherlands*, 417, London: Doubleday.

——(1997) *Riding the Waves of Culture: Understanding diversity in global business*, New York, NY: McGraw-Hill.

Tsui, A., Nifadkar, S. S. and Yi Ou, A. (2007) 'Cross-national, cross-cultural organizational behavior research: advances, gaps, and recommendations', *Journal of Management*, 33(3): 426–78.

Tung, R. (1998) 'American expatriates abroad: From neophytes to cosmopolitans', *Journal of World Business*, 33(2): 125–44.

——(2008) 'The cross-cultural research imperative: The need to balance cross-national and intra-national diversity', *Journal of International Business Studies*, 39: 41–46.

Ubius, U. and Alas, R. (2009) 'Organizational culture types as predictors of corporate social responsibility', *Engineering Economics*, 1(61): 90–99.

Usunier, J. (1998) *International and Cross-Cultural Management Research* London: Sage Publications.

Vaara, E. (2002) 'On the discursive construction of success/failure in narratives of post-merger integration', *Organization Studies*, 23(2): 213–50.

Van de Vliert, E., Shi, K., Sanders, K., Wang, Y. and Huang, X. (2004) 'Chinese and Dutch interpretations of supervisory feedback', *Journal of Cross-Cultural Psychology*, 35: 417–35.

Van Maanen, J. (Ed.) (1979) *Qualitative Methodology*, Beverly Hills, CA: Sage.

——(1991) 'The smile factory: Work at Disneyland', in P. Frost, L. Moore, M. Louis, C. Lundberg and J. Martin (Eds) *Reframing Organizational Culture*, 58–76, Newbury Park, CA: Sage.

Van Maanen, J. and Barley, S. R. (1984) 'Occupational communities: Culture and control in organizations', in L. L. Cummings and B. M. Staw (Eds) *Research in Organizational Behavior*, 6, Greenwich, CT: JAI Press.

Van Velsen, J. (1964) *The Politics of Kinship*, Manchester: Manchester University Press.

Veiga, J., Lubatkin, M., Calori, R. and Very, P. (2000) 'Measuring organizational culture clashes: A two-nation post-hoc analysis of a cultural compatibility index', *Human Relations*, 53(4): 539–57.

Verweij, M. and Thompson, M. (2006) *Clumsy Solutions for a Complex World: Governance, politics and plural perceptions* Basingstoke/New York: Palgrave Macmillan.

Very, P., Calori, R., and Lubatkin, M. (1993) 'An investigation of national and organizational cultural influences in recent European mergers', in P. Shrivastava, A. Huff, and J. Dutton (Eds) *Advances in Strategic Management*, 9: 323–46, Greenwich, CT: JAI Press.

Wade-Benzoni, K. A., Brett, J. M., Tenbrunsel, A. E., Okumura, T., Moore, D. A. and Bazerman, M. H. (2002) 'Cognitions and behavior in asymmetric social dilemmas: A comparison of two cultures', *Journal of Applied Psychology*, 87: 87–95.

Wallerstein, I. (1990) 'Culture as the ideological battleground of the modern world system', *Theory, Culture and Society*, 7: 31–55.

Warden, C. and Chen, J. (2009) 'Chinese negotiators' subjective variations in intercultural negotiations', *Journal of Business Ethics*, 88: 529–37.

Weber, M. (1905) *The Protestant Ethic and the Spirit of Capitalism*, New York, NY: Scribner.

——(1930) *The Protestant Ethic and the Spirit of Capitalism*, London: Allen and Unwin.

Weber, Y., Shenkar, O. and Raveh, A. (1996) 'National and corporate cultural fit in mergers/acquisitions: an exploratory study', *Management Science*, 42(8): 1215–27.

Weick, K. (1979) *The Social Psychology of Organizing*, Reading, MA: Addison-Wesley.

——(1985) 'The significance of corporate culture', in P. J. Frost *et al.* (Eds) *Organizational Culture*, Beverly Hills, CA: Sage.

——(1991) 'The vulnerable system: An analysis of the Tenerife air disaster', in P. Frost, L. Moore, M. Louis, C. Lundberg and J. Martin (Eds) *Reframing Organizational Culture*, 117–30, Newbury Park, CA: Sage.

Weick, K. and Quinn, R. (1999) 'Organizational change and development', *Annual Review of Psychology*, 50: 361–86.

Westley, F. R. and Jaeger, A. M. (1985) '*An Examination of Organizational Culture: How is it linked to performance*', Paper, McGill University Faculty of Management, Montreal.

Wildavsky, A. (1987) 'Cultural theory of responsibility', in J. E. Lane (Ed.) (1987) *Bureaucracy and Public Choice*, London: Sage.

Wilkins, A. and Martin, J. (1980) '*Organizational Legends*', Working paper, Stanford University Graduate School of Business.

Wilkins, A. L. and Ouchi, W. G. (1983) 'Efficient culture: Exploring the relationship between culture and organizational performance', *Administrative Science Quarterly*, 28: 468–81.

Williamson, O. (1975) *Markets and Hierarchies: Analysis and antitrust implications*, New York, NY: Free Press.

Willmott, H. (1993) 'Strength is ignorance; slavery is freedom: Managing culture in modern organizations', *Journal of Management Studies*, 30: 515–52.

Woodcock, P. and Geringer, J. P. (1991) 'An exploratory study of agency costs related to the control structure of multi-partner international joint ventures', *Academy of Management Best Paper Proceedings*, 115–18.

Wynne, B. and Otway, H. J. (1982) 'Information technology: power and managers', in N. Bjorn-Anderson, *et al.* (Eds) *Information Society: For richer for poorer*, Amsterdam: North–Holland.

Yamaguchi, S., Gelfand, M., Ohashi M. M. and Zemba, Y. (2005) 'The cultural psychology of control: Illusions of personal versus collective control in the United States and Japan', *Journal of Cross-Cultural Psychology*, 36: 750–61

Yardley, I. J. L. and Neal, D. J. (2007) 'Understanding the leadership and culture dynamic within a military context: Applying theory to an operational and business context', *Defence Studies*, 7(1): 21–41.

Yeh, R. and Lawrence, J. (1995) 'Individualism and Confucian dynamism: A note on Hofstede's cultural root to economic growth', *Journal of International Business Studies*, 26(3): 655–69.

Young, E. (1991) 'On the naming of the rose: Interests and multiple meanings as elements of organizational culture', in P. Frost, L. Moore, M. Louis, C. Lundberg and J. Martin (Eds) *Reframing Organizational Culture*, 90–103, Newbury Park, CA: Sage.

Zaheer, S. and Zaheer, A. (2006) 'Trust across borders', *Journal of International Business Studies*, 37: 21–29.

6, P. (2003) 'Institutional viability: A neo-Durkheimian theory', *Innovation: The European Journal of Social Science Research*, 16(4): 395–415.

——(2004) 'What's in a frame? Social organization, risk perception and the sociology of knowledge', *Journal of Risk Research*, 8(2): 91–118.

6, P. and Peck, E. (2004) 'New labour's modernization in the public sector: A neo-Durkheimian approach and the case of mental health services', *Public Administration*, 82(1): 83–108.

6, P. and Mars, G. (2008) 'Introduction', in P. 6 and G. Mars (Eds) *The Institutional Dynamics of Culture: The new Durkheimians*, vols 1–2, 1–20, Aldershot, UK: Ashgate.

Index